IMAGES
of America

SPRINGFIELD

A REFLECTION IN PHOTOGRAPHY

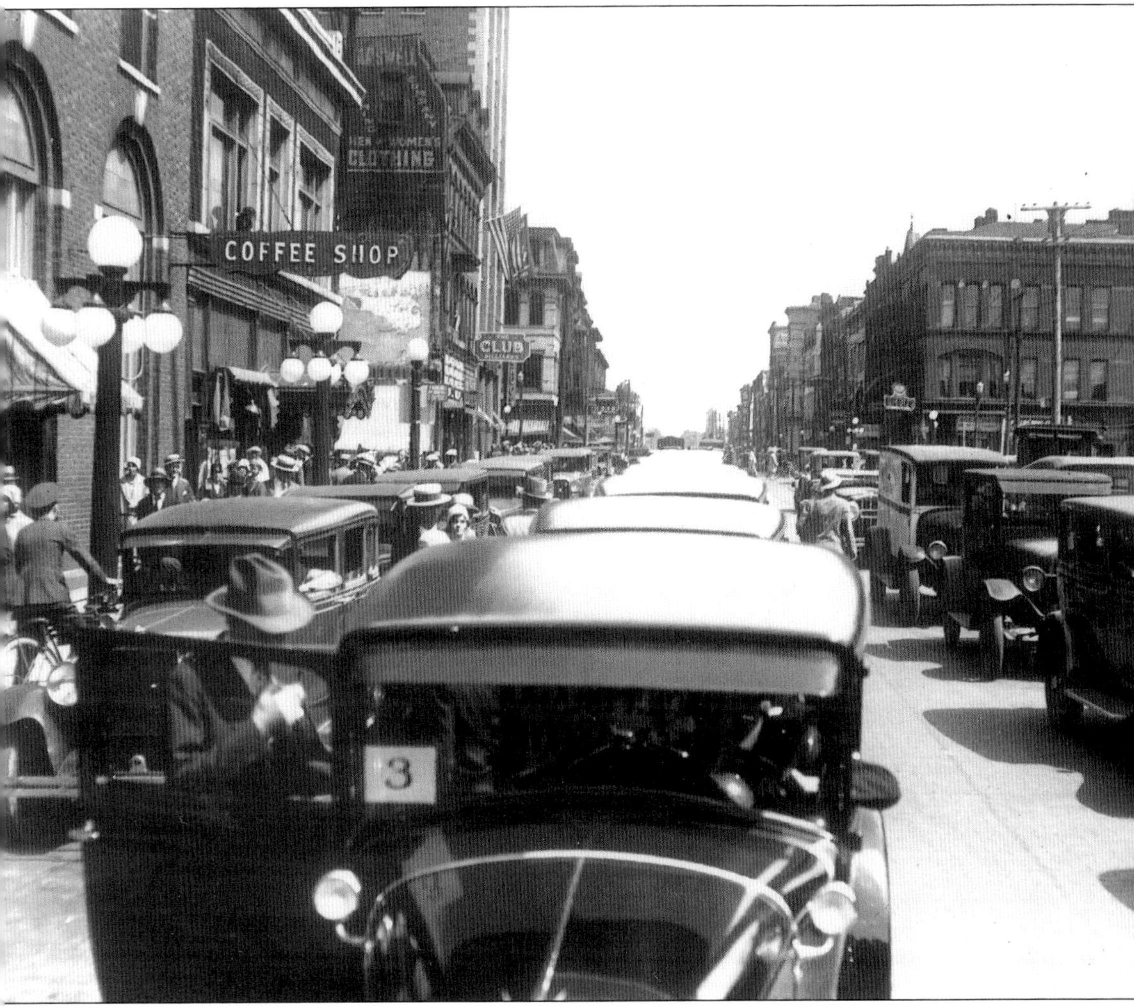

Looking north on Sixth Street at Capitol, c. 1932.

IMAGES
of America

SPRINGFIELD

A REFLECTION IN PHOTOGRAPHY

Edward J. Russo, Curtis R. Mann,
and Melinda L. Garvert

ARCADIA
PUBLISHING

ISBN 978-0-7385-2013-1

Published by Arcadia Publishing
Charleston, South Carolina

Printed in the United States of America

Library of Congress Catalog Card Number: 2002108575

For all general information contact Arcadia Publishing at:
Telephone 843-853-2070
Fax 843-853-0044
E-mail sales@arcadiapublishing.com
For customer service and orders:
Toll-Free 1-888-313-2665

Visit us on the Internet at www.arcadiapublishing.com

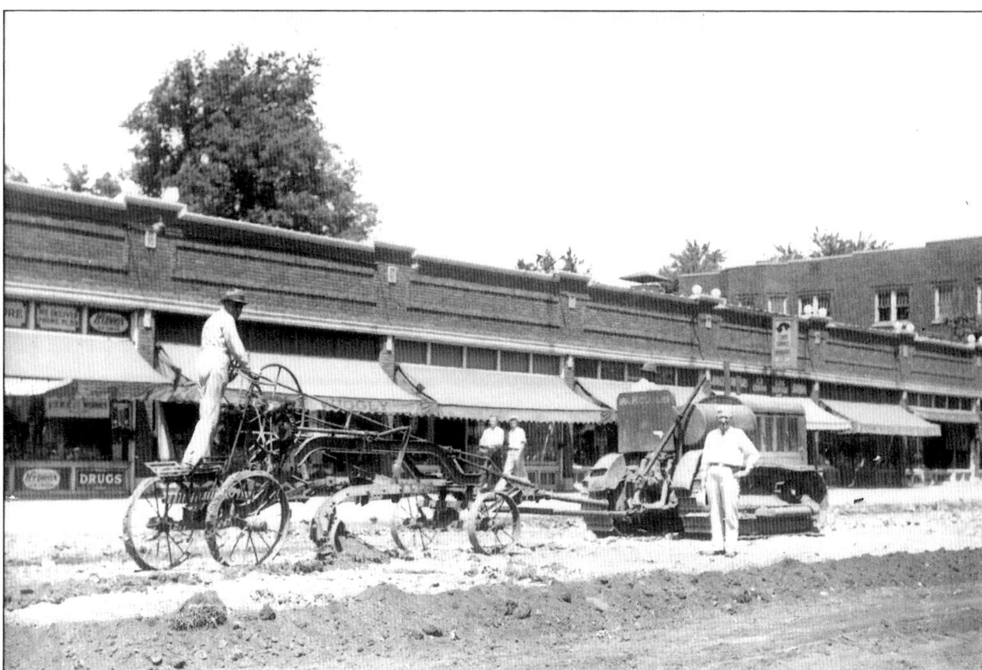

Street grading on South Grand Avenue between Fifth and Sixth Streets in the 1930s.

Contents

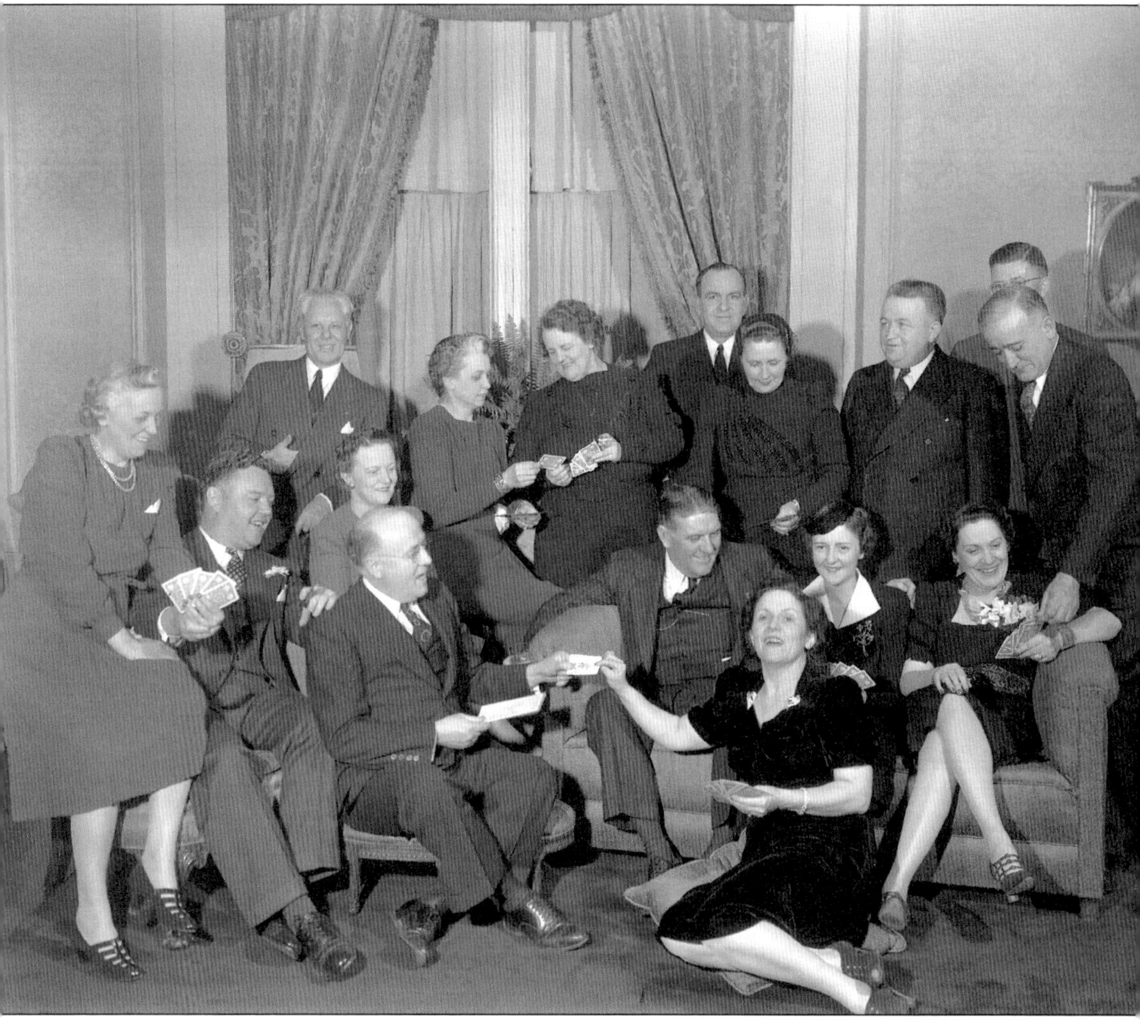
New Year's Eve Party at Illinois Governor's Mansion, December 31, 1940.

INTRODUCTION

Photographs play a vital role in documenting the history of a community. Early pioneers of local photography, later professional photographers, and all along amateur family photographers, with their diverse talent, subject matter, and point-of-view, help tell the story of a place.

The city of Springfield, Illinois has a rich and diversified history. Though many books have been written about the community, each new one reveals another dimension. Over the past decade, the authors have produced a number of pictorial works about the city. Using the photographic resources of the Sangamon Valley Collection located in the Lincoln Library, they have told the stories of Springfield's businesses, entertainment and recreation, churches, schools, neighborhoods, and government among many other topics. With over 30,000 images to choose from in the Collection presently and more being acquired on a regular basis, the previous works came no where near exhausting this supply of images. At the same time there were numerous photographs that were selected out for lack of room or for another view chosen in its place. This collection of previously unselected photographs formed a natural collection that became the book you are holding in your hands.

The focus of the book is on providing a brief glimpse of all the various aspects of Springfield, from business and transportation to social life and community service. Chapter divisions are only a convenience for organizing rather than segregating photographs. *Springfield, A Reflection in Photographs* is just that. As in a scrapbook, photos are loosely organized. We find ourselves skipping randomly from one to another—lingering over those that catch our attention. Some photos are compelling for their sheer drama or humor. The Ide Engine Works engulfed in flames or a tiny, twin-engine plane silhouetted against the immensity of clouds and sky contrast with local ladies run ragged hosting a choral convention and playfully posing with their aching feet, and are further contrasted with Liberace fundraising with the local Lions club members.

Others capture us in their very ordinariness, an ordinariness that yet transcends the commonplace—the teen talking by the hour on the telephone (leashed to the immobile instrument in pre-cell days), and white-aproned employees at the corner market lined up proudly in front of their place of work. And old photos can serve to remind of all that has changed in our daily lives—of the gritty, tedious and uncomfortable things once part of so much work. The neatly-dressed occupants toiling away in a department store's alterations department through sweltering, pre-air-conditioned summers or workers laboriously excavating a skyscraper's basement using horses and wagons, are object lessons in the dramatic changes of the last few generations. There are scenes of women on the assembly line—in the early 1900s and the 1950s and at the end-of-shift exodus from the factory.

The underside of life is here too. A devastating race riot of 1908 is limned best not in the scenes of property destruction but in the patient, sorrowful bearing of displaced black families standing alongside railroad tracks. The infamous "Levee" district, with its bars, brothels, and rampant vice, legendary throughout central Illinois, and subject of a book of 1910, *Hell at Midnight in Springfield, Or a Burning History of the Sin and Shame of the Capital City of Illinois*, is seen by day. Its streets of modest brick storefronts look more sad than wicked, but are nonetheless a reminder of when "fashionably dressed men and women" ordered drinks and, "out in the public street laughed and shamelessly quaffed the beverages of hell…the load of rich and dissipated merrymakers, stopping and ordering drinks from the lowest shambles."

Chapters are arranged around Springfield at work, at play, our public life, and getting about in public and private transportation and on foot. Transportation grew from the horse and buggy to the railroad and finally the automobile, which has done so much to change the development of this city. Springfield's social life ranges from sports and recreation to public banquets and movie-going, and a thousand other events. Community service comprises all those areas in which people give something of themselves to the public—charitable activities certainly, fundraising and caring for the less fortunate. But there is also the community service of people like firemen and police officers. The images refuse to be bound neatly by such categories. What you will find here are people who have paused for a moment for the camera's eye in the midst of their lives. That moment, transfixed permanently by the camera, is available for us to see, and to ponder. These frozen, unchanging scenes and faces are somehow the most visceral reminders that change is the paramount thing in all our lives. We invite you to tour Springfield as it is reflected in these images and believe you will find a place you know well, but have never seen.

The authors would like to thank all the photographers, know and unknown, whose images appear in here and the generosity of donors who first placed them in a public repository. To those individuals we gratefully dedicate this book.

Edward J. Russo
Curtis R. Mann
Melinda L. Garvert

One

SPRINGFIELD AT WORK

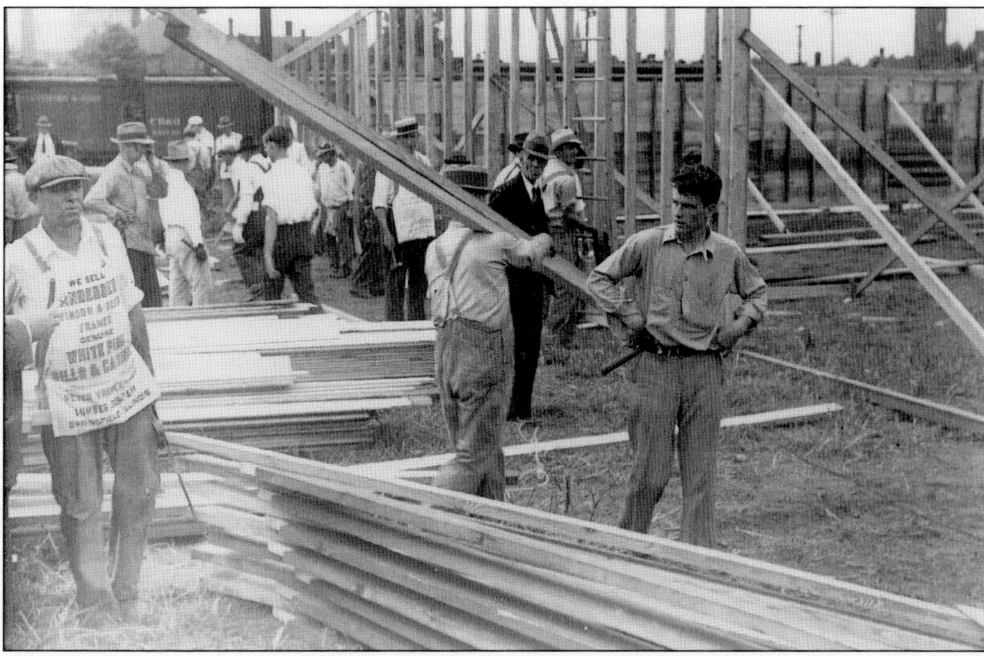

Laboring men and women built Springfield—literally, in many cases. The town increased in size rapidly in the late 19th through the early 20th century, going from a population of 17,000 in 1870 to over 50,000 in 1910. Housing for the expanding population required an army of carpenters, contractors, lumber dealers, architects, and mill work suppliers. But it was the growth of the building and loan associations that allowed working men and women to own their homes. The growth in real estate values followed and early 20th century businessmen including Mayor John Schnepp marveled that he had direct knowledge of "many increases of more than 500 percent in business property values in less than 20 years. And local U.S. Congressman James M. Graham concurred, "The advancement of value of Springfield real estate. . .has been extraordinary. . . ." Builders in this 1920s scene erect a temporary tabernacle near the State Capitol.

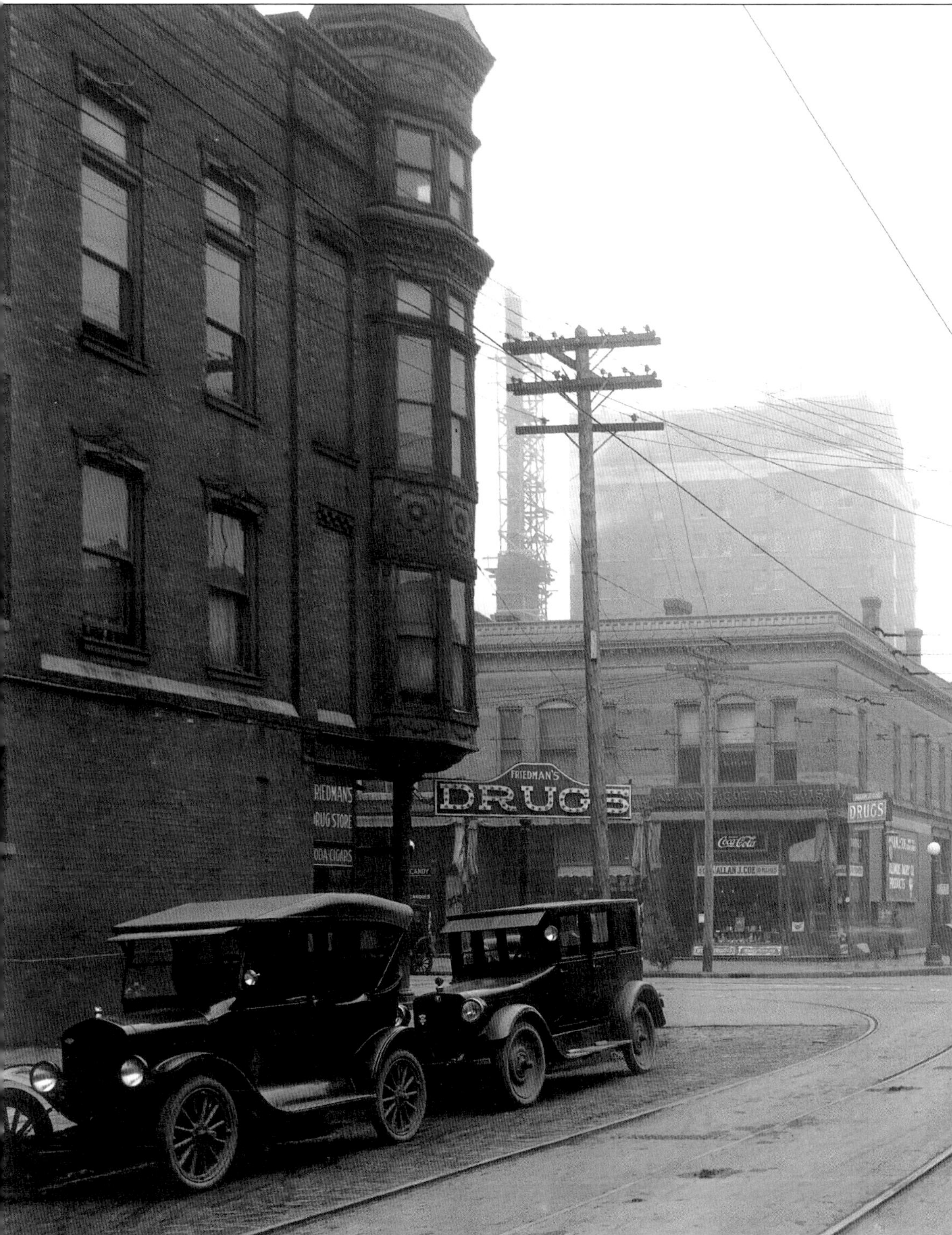

There is not a parking place to be had in this scene along Jefferson Street looking west at Fifth Street about 1926. In the 1820s Jefferson Street was Springfield's first business district, but

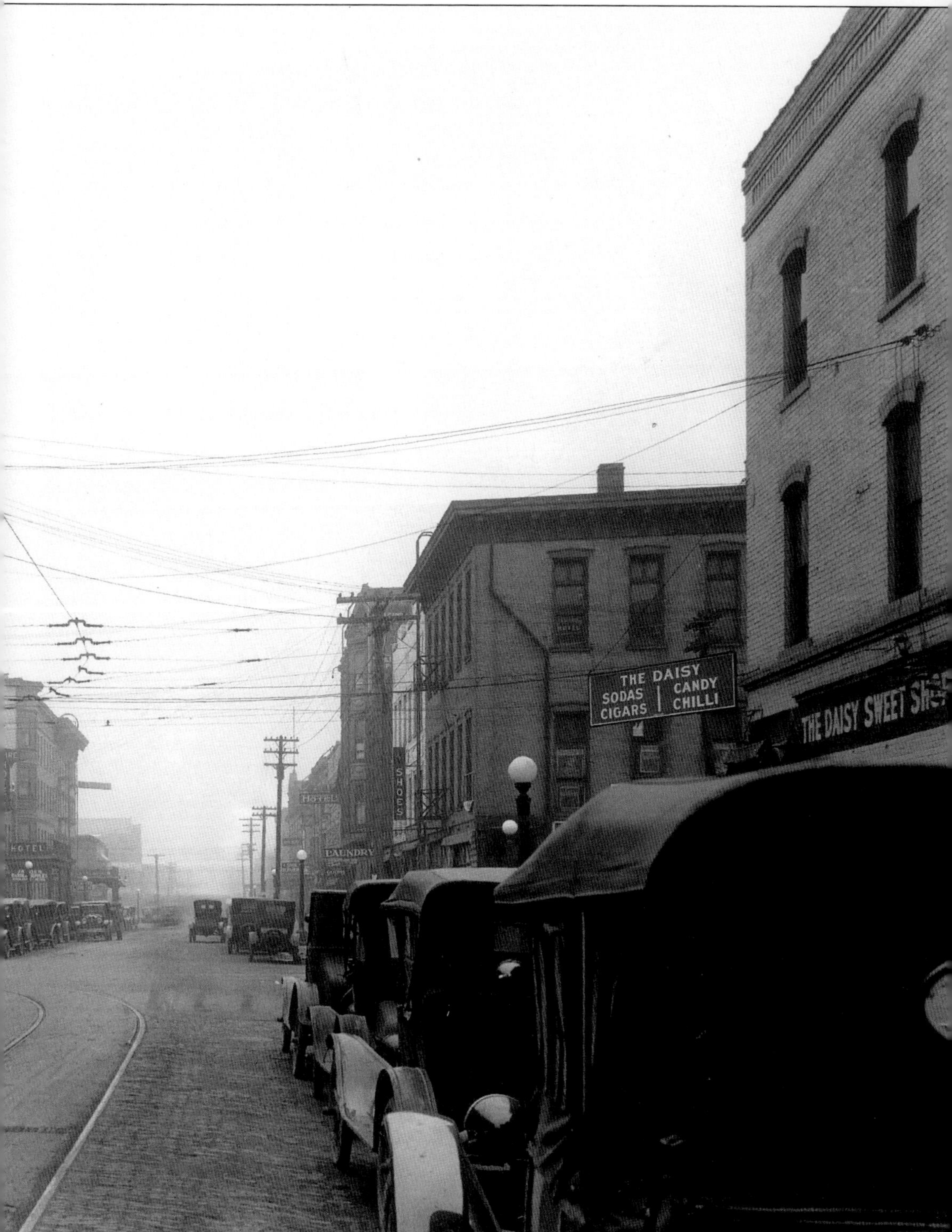

moved by 1840 to the public square. Still, business spilled beyond the square into this adjacent area. The opulent Orpheum Theater replaced the turreted building at the left in 1927.

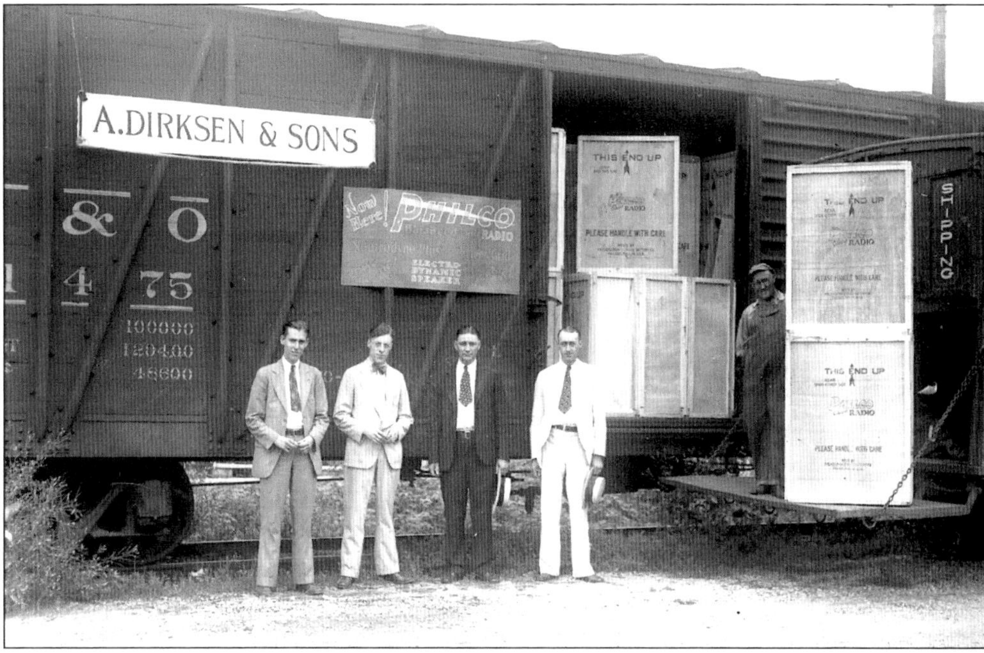

Before the days of semi-tractor trailer trucks, large, bulky items traveled by the railroads. In 1929 A. Dirksen and Sons furniture store ran this photo in an advertisement to announce their new shipment of Philco radios.

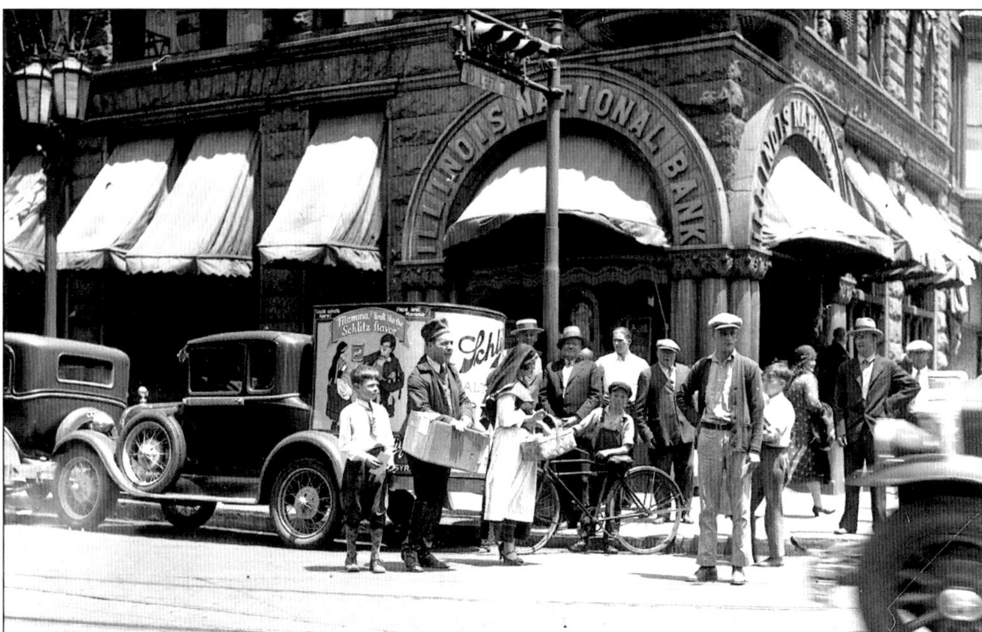

It was 1933 and prohibition was over. These Schlitz promoters, dressed to look like their counterparts pictured in the advertising sign on the car, are out on the corner of Fifth and Washington Streets to let the public know they are back in business with the 'wholesome' drink—beer.

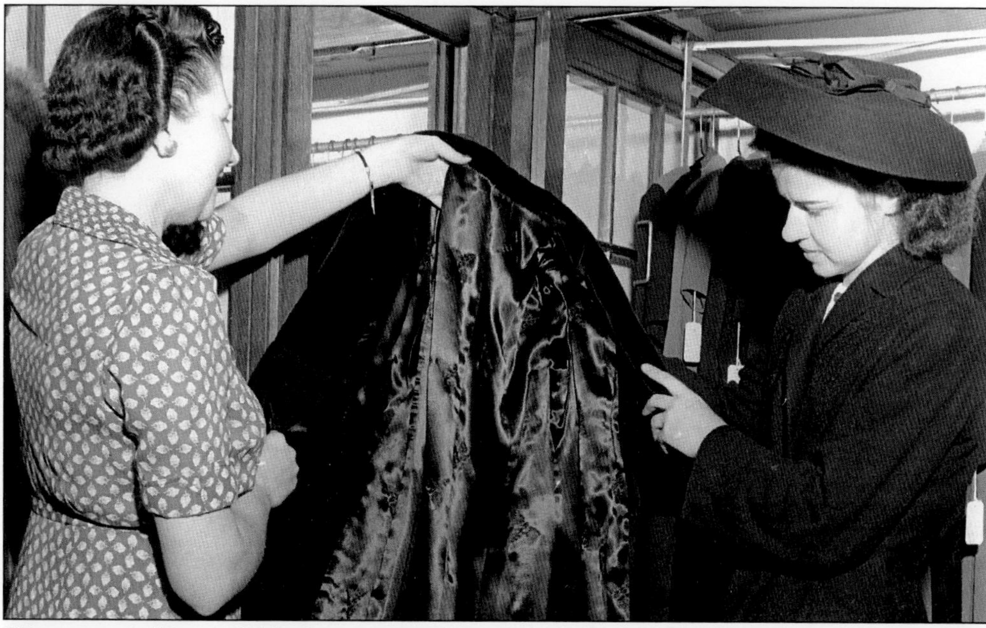

When many of Springfield's department stores were locally owned, each business would send its buyers to New York or other clothing centers to personally choose the styles offered here. This discriminating Springfield shopper expected and checked for generous seams, secure buttons, and an exacting fit.

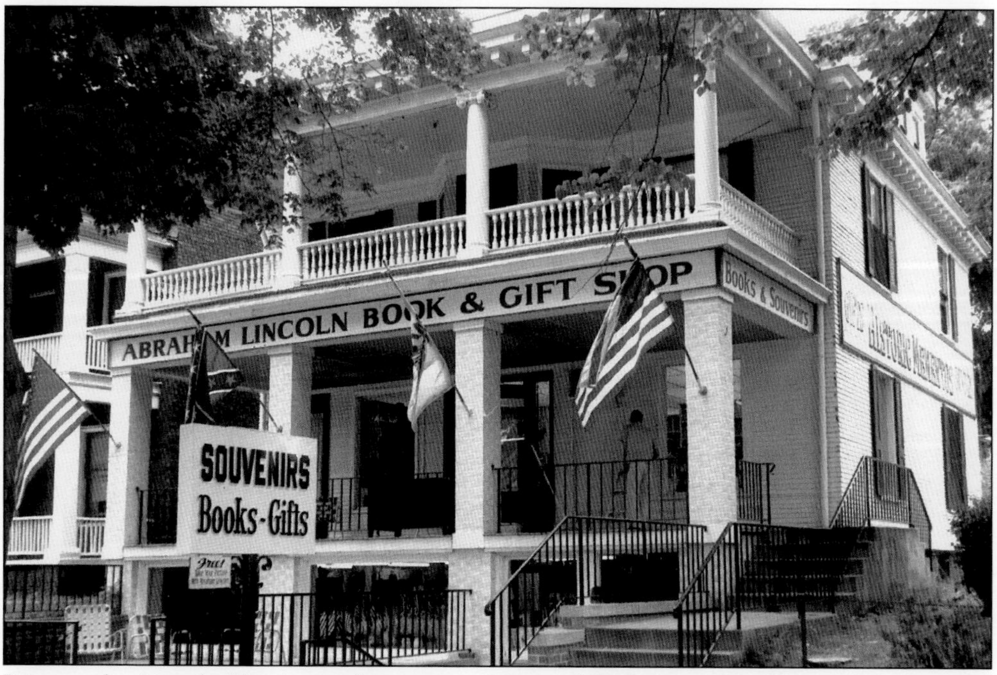

Prior to the Lincoln Home area becoming a National Park, souvenir shops and commercial museums were located right next door to the home, and directly across the street. This was one of the more attractive shops. Abraham Lincoln has meant jobs and income for many tourist-related businesses.

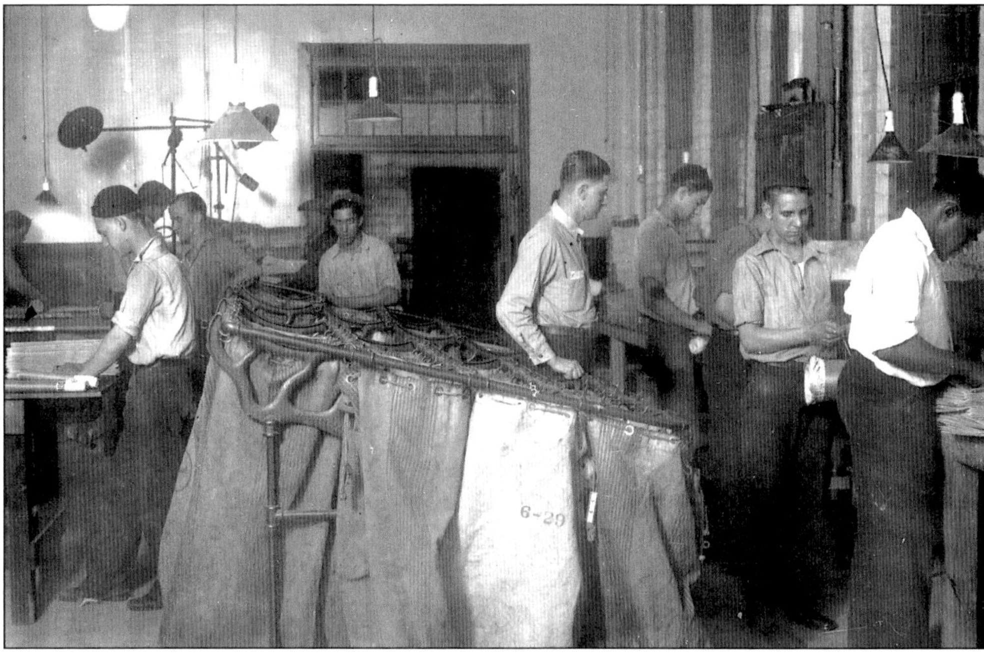

Lots of us enjoy reading our newspapers and look forward to each new issue. These employees of the Illinois State Journal were responsible for preparing the paper to be mailed to rural readers in the early 1930s.

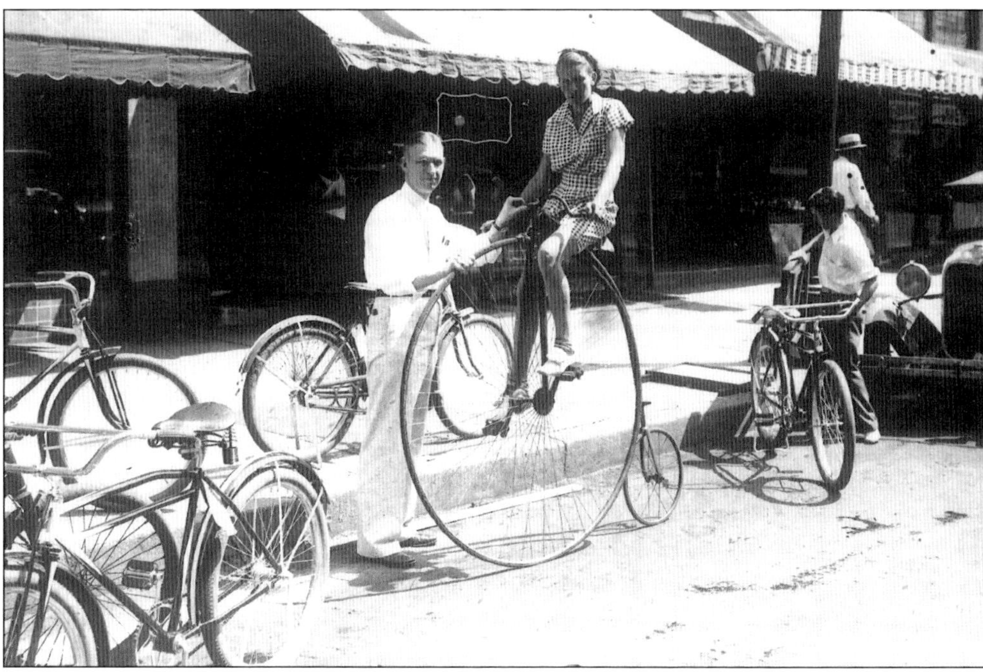

Giving an old-fashioned bicycle a test ride perhaps convinced this young lady in 1933 that one of the newer models offered at the Sears, Roebuck and Company store might offer a smoother ride. Sears, Roebuck and Company was located at 621–623 East Adams Street in downtown Springfield.

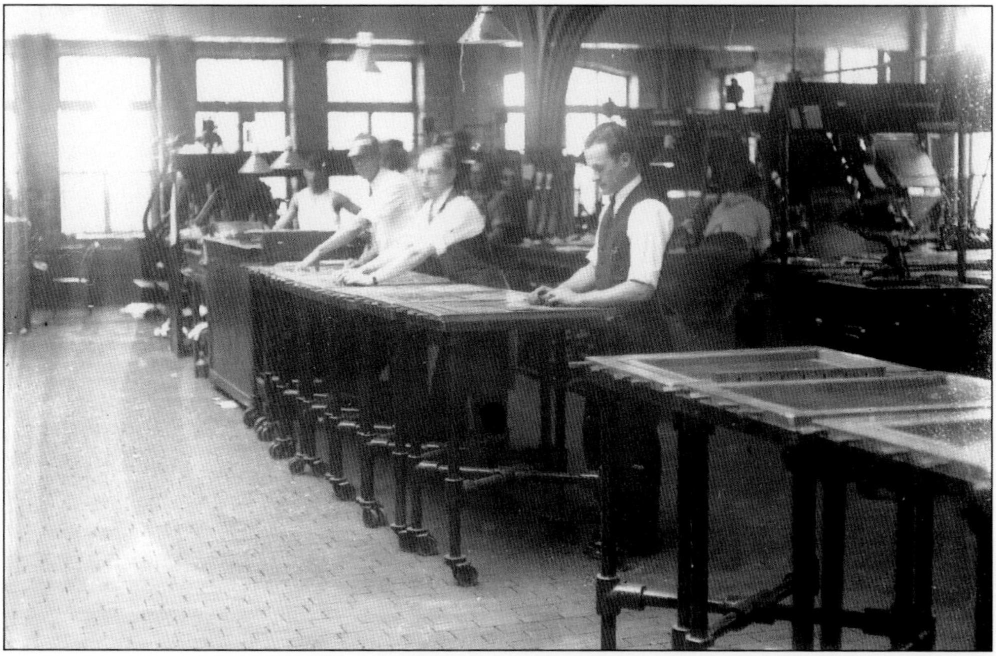

The composing room at the Illinois State Journal covered the entire third floor of the old Journal Building at 313 South Sixth Street. The journeyman printers seen here in the 1930s worked in the composing room, getting one of the paper's two daily editions ready.

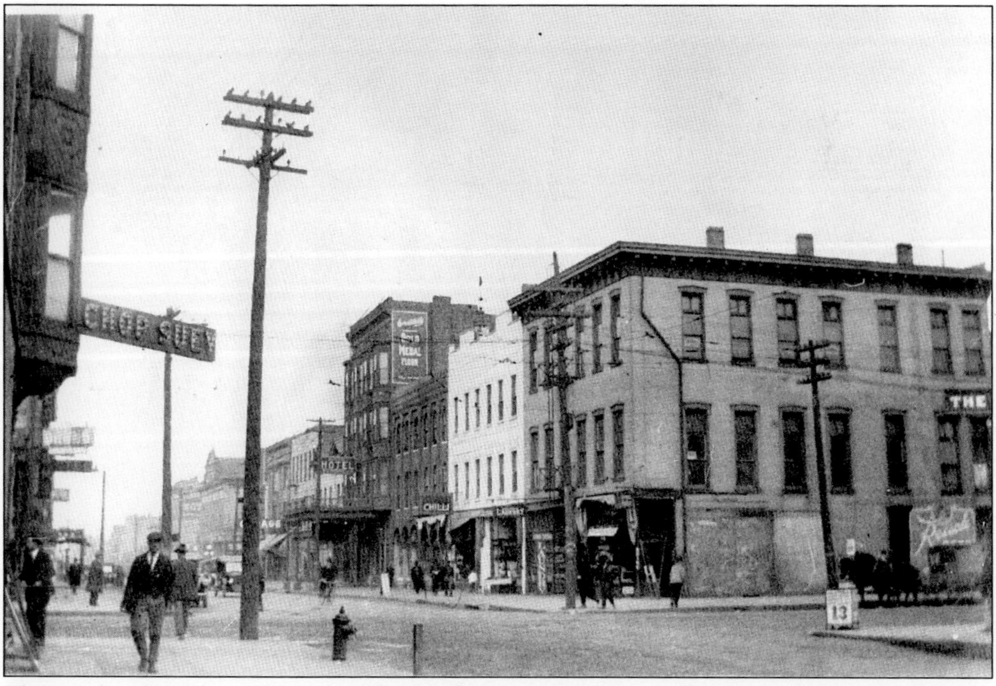

The north side of the 400 block of East Jefferson Street was a collection of restaurants, hotels, shoe stores, and a Chinese laundry, one of four in the city at time this photograph was taken in 1919. This business district was slightly lower rent than the nearby public square.

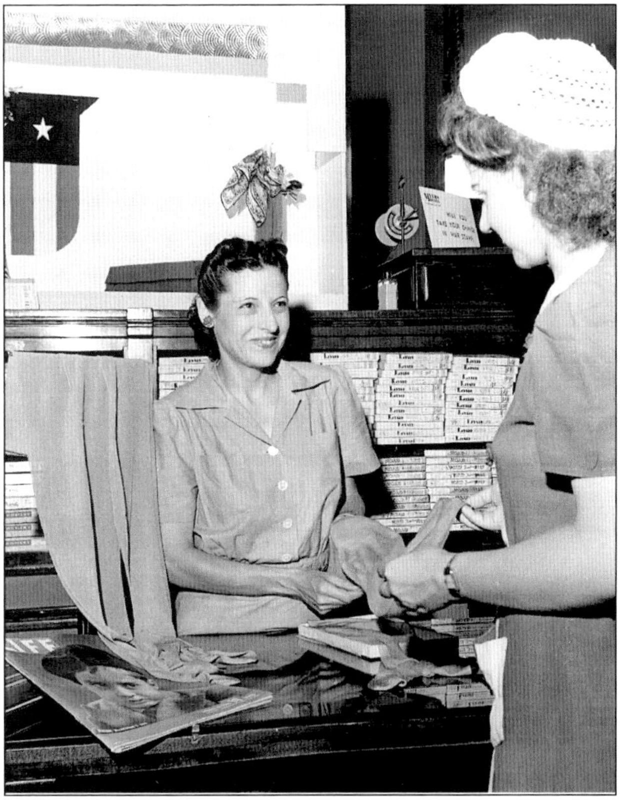

In the days before self-service became the norm, shopping nearly always meant lots of direct contact with store personnel. From ladies hosiery to garden hoses, store clerks were expected to know their inventory, give helpful advice, make special orders and always smile. In the 19th century clerks often arrived about 6:00 a.m. and, except for lunch and dinner breaks, usually stayed until late evening. Conditions had improved mightily by the 1940s, when these Springfield shoppers crowded local stores.

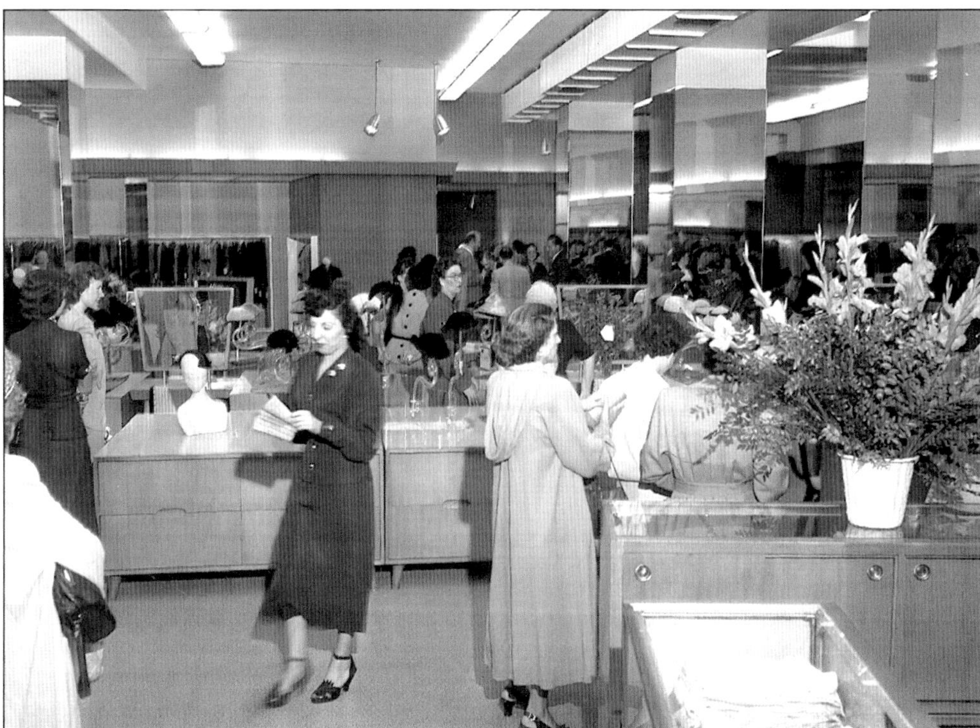

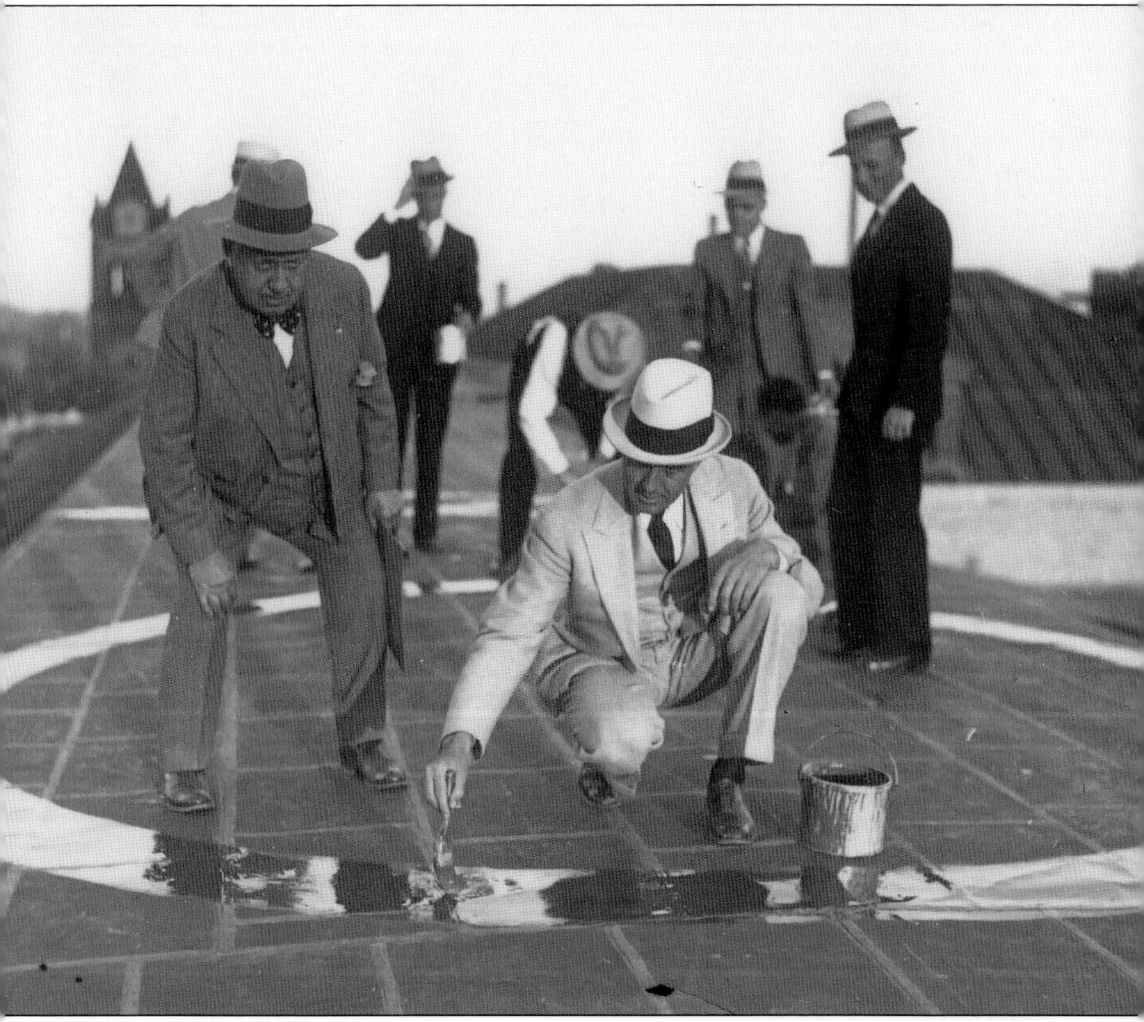

Members of the local American Business Club repaint an air traffic sign on top of the Federal Building at 6th and Monroe streets in 1930. Postmaster William Conkling, squatting at left, was an avid promoter of air service. He was responsible for bringing airmail to the city piloted by a then-unknown young pilot—Charles Lindbergh. After his famous 1927 transatlantic flight, Lindbergh returned to Springfield to a hero's welcome. In this first year of the Great Depression, Conkling and other city businessmen envisioned airplanes replacing railroads as the chief form of travel. Springfield would be a transportation hub with connections to all parts of the globe. Things did not turn out exactly that way, but residents of the day had high hopes.

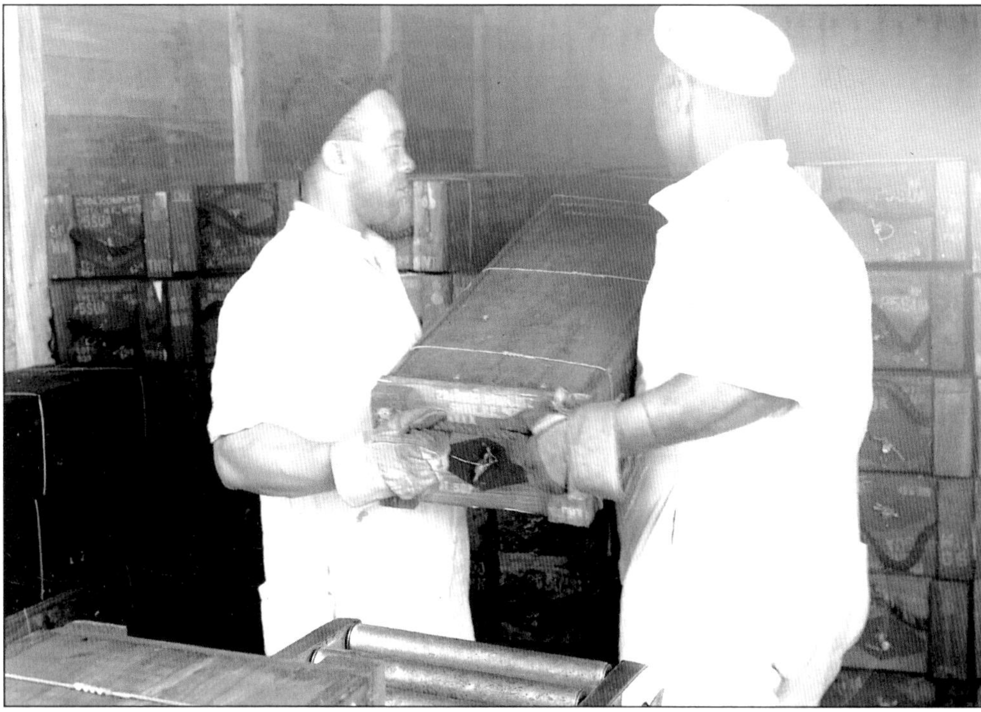

After the U.S. entered World War II, ordnance plants were built at Illiopolis to manufacture munitions. Many Springfieldians found work at the factories, and eleven train cars were brought in from New York for use on the Illinois Terminal tracks to transport workers to and from Springfield.

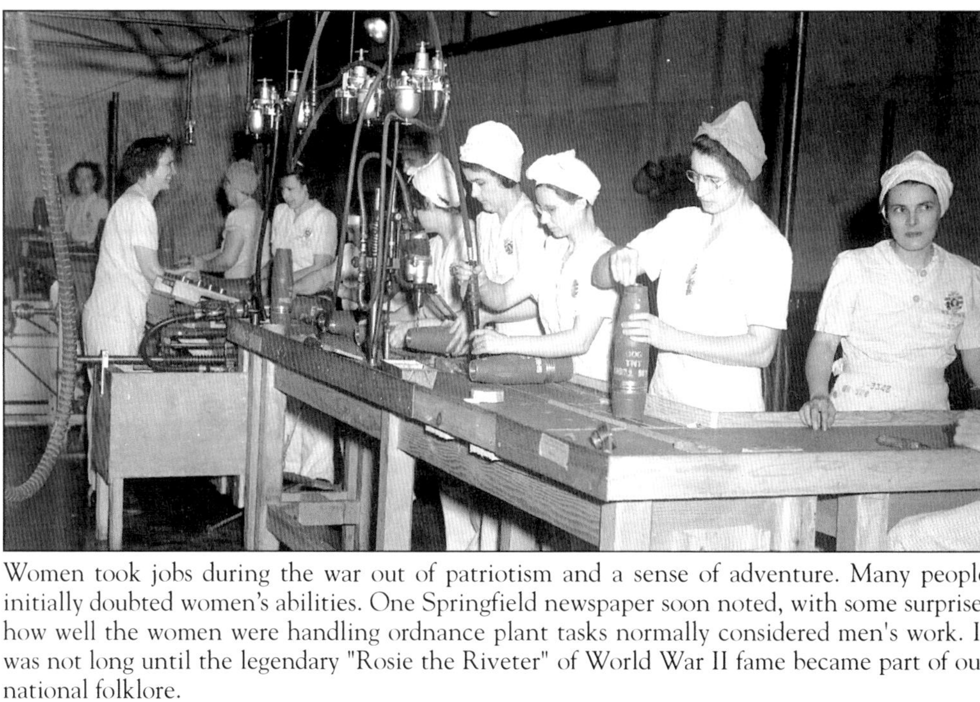

Women took jobs during the war out of patriotism and a sense of adventure. Many people initially doubted women's abilities. One Springfield newspaper soon noted, with some surprise, how well the women were handling ordnance plant tasks normally considered men's work. It was not long until the legendary "Rosie the Riveter" of World War II fame became part of our national folklore.

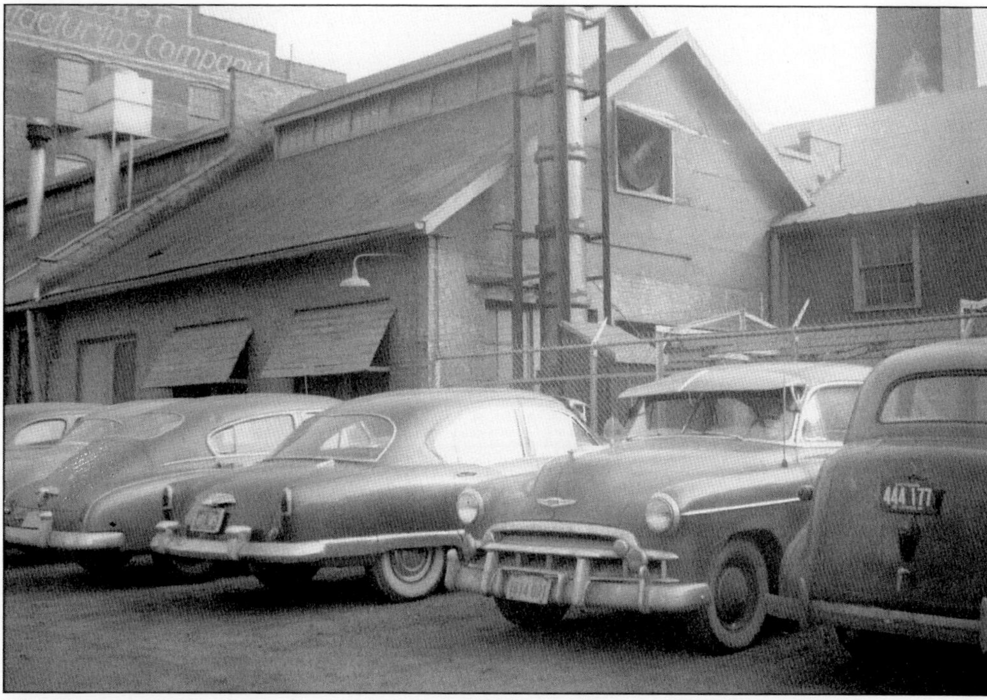

The Hummer Manufacturing Co., once a familiar sight on the corner of Ninth and South Grand, had a long history, beginning as the Post Implement Company in 1851, a maker of plows. Plow manufacturing changed to cream separators, water supply systems and poultry equipment, and then to precision parts for airplanes during World War II, and eventually to lawn mowers and pumps for Montgomery Ward. Hummer closed in the 1950s.

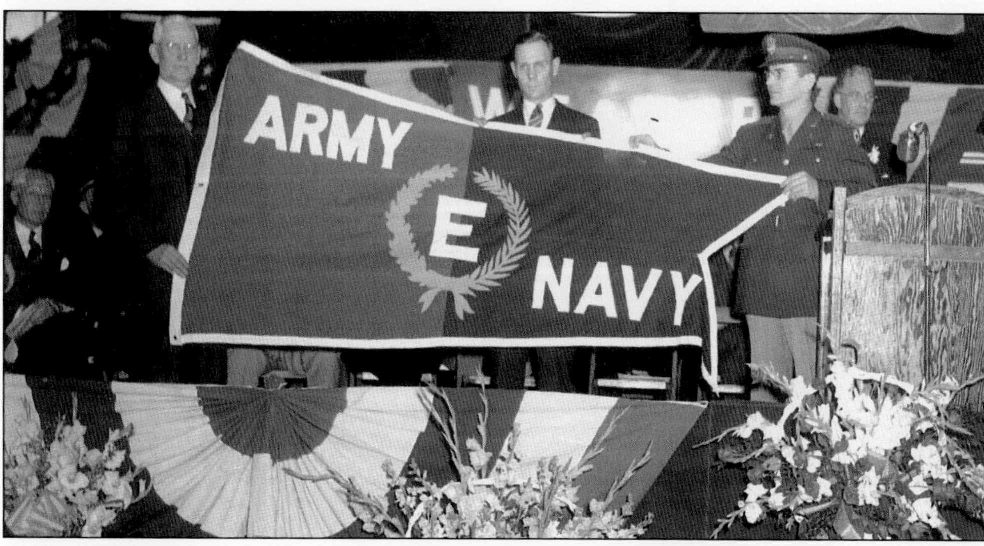

During World War II, Springfield proudly claimed the honor of being one of the few American cities to have as many as five of its manufacturers and their employees receive the prestigious Army-Navy E Awards—Allis Chalmers, Baker's Mfg., Pillsbury Mills, Sangamo Electric, and Weaver Mfg. The award was for excellence in providing quality as well as needed quantities of war supplies.

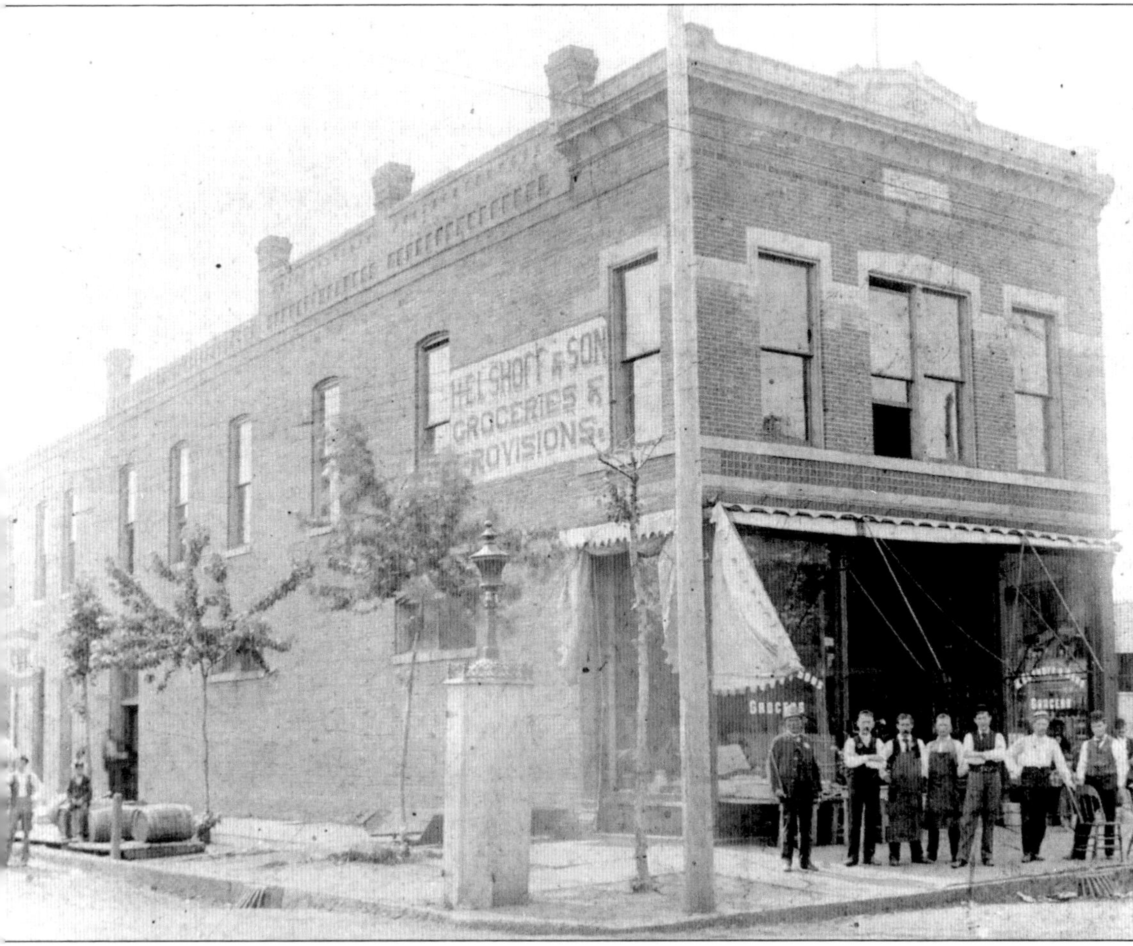

The corner grocery was a familiar sight in many older Springfield neighborhoods. Dozens of these establishments were located throughout the city. Henry Elshoff erected this building at the corner of Eleventh and Cook Streets in 1888 for use as a grocery and saloon. Henry and his son, Frank, started their grocery business in 1877. Four other sons eventually joined the store, which then became H. Elshoff and Sons. This 1890 photograph shows the Elshoffs outside their new store building. After Henry's death in 1900, the business name changed to Elshoff Brothers. Anton Elshoff bought the business from his brothers about 1905, and ran it until 1917 at that location, before moving to nearby South Eighth Street. This building later served as a billiards hall, lunch counter, and tavern until its demolition in 1987.

The insurance industry's growth in Springfield was bolstered in 1881 with the organization of Franklin Life Insurance. This company grew to become a major employer in the city by the mid-20th century, when sculptor James Earle Fraser created a statue of the company's namesake, Benjamin Franklin. The statue was dedicated on September 8, 1949.

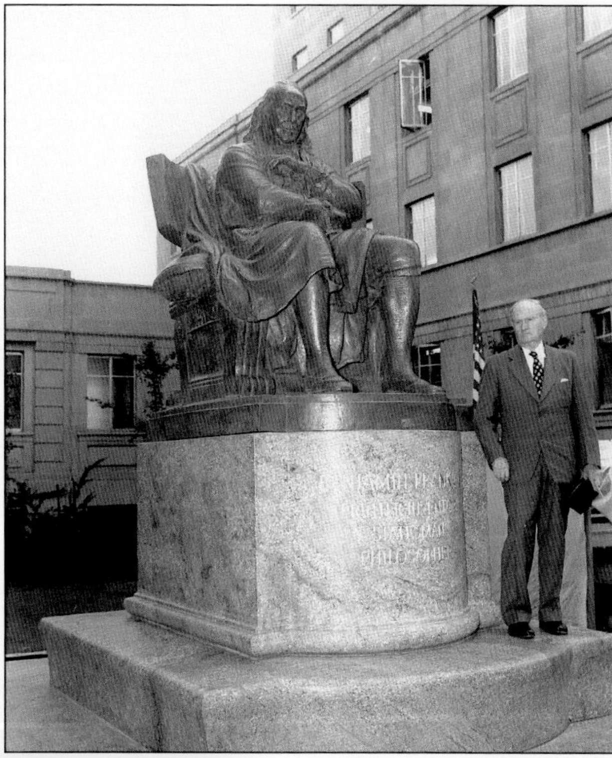

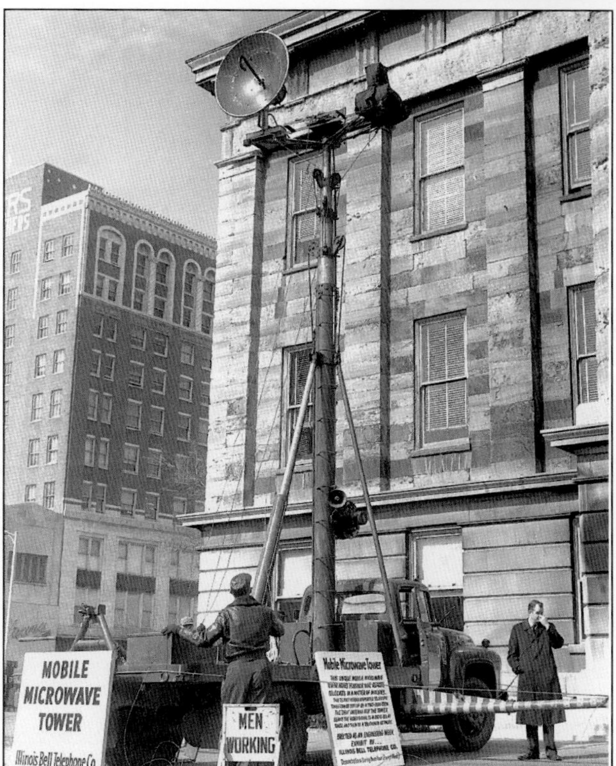

Illinois Bell Telephone was created in late 1920 when the Central Union Telephone Company of Springfield was acquired by the Chicago Telephone Company and renamed Illinois Bell. The company, ever at the forefront of technology, exhibited this mobile microwave tower at the Old State Capitol in the 1950s. The tower made it possible for live remote telecasts to be broadcast in a matter of minutes.

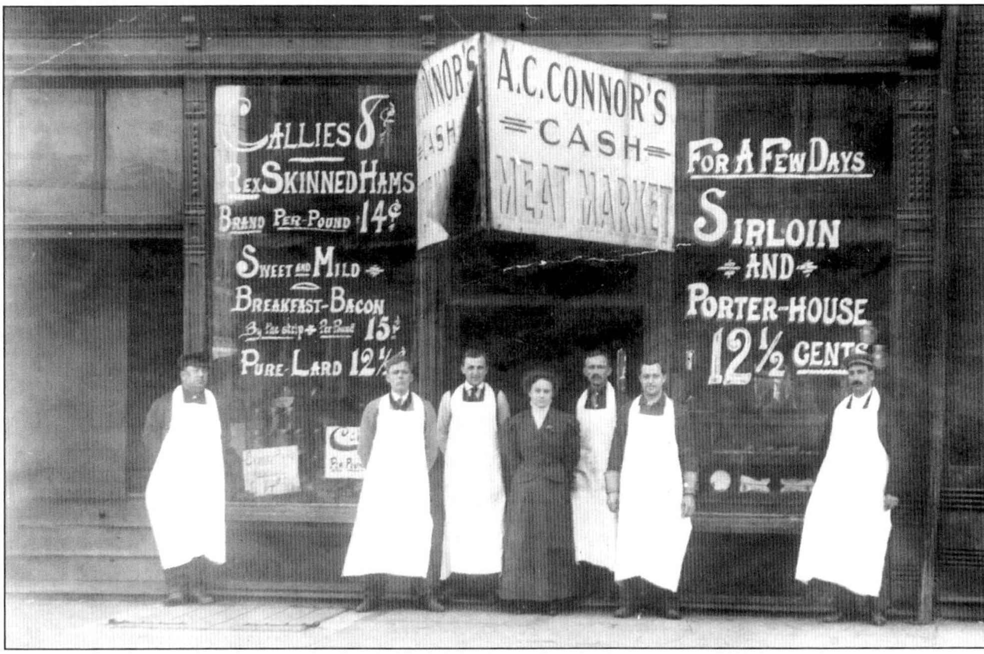

The era of the neighborhood grocery has long-since passed. Before the coming of the supermarket after World War II, Springfield housewives usually shopped at two or three places. Meat customers patronized places like Connor's (above), shown about 1912. Staples like flour, sugar and canned goods came from grocers like Oliver's (below), typical of the several dozen small markets in the city at any given time. Though the prices look good to us today, remember that a laborer might then earn only $5 a week.

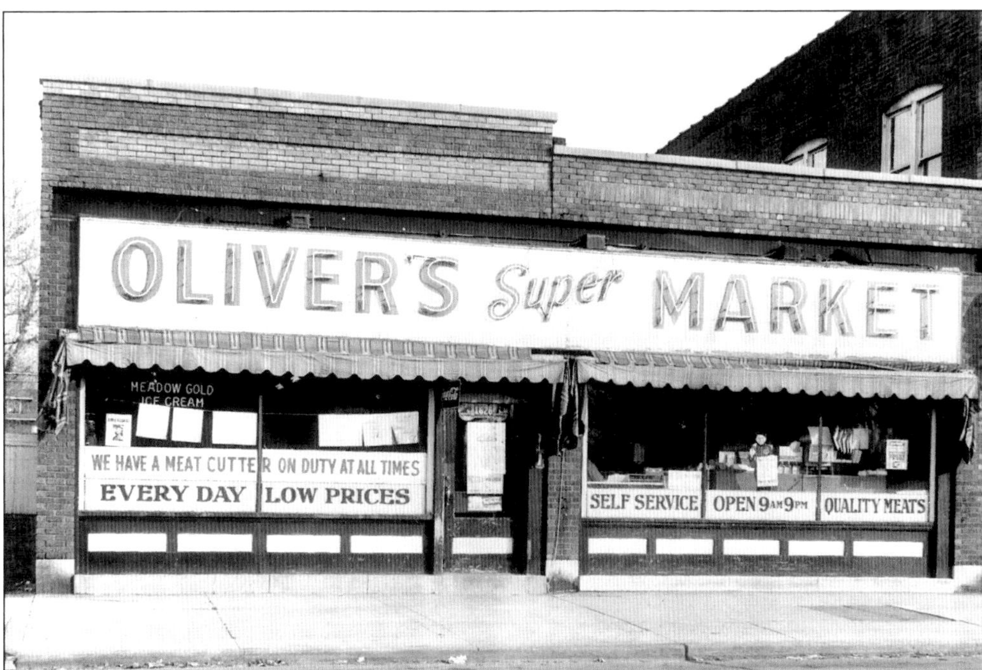

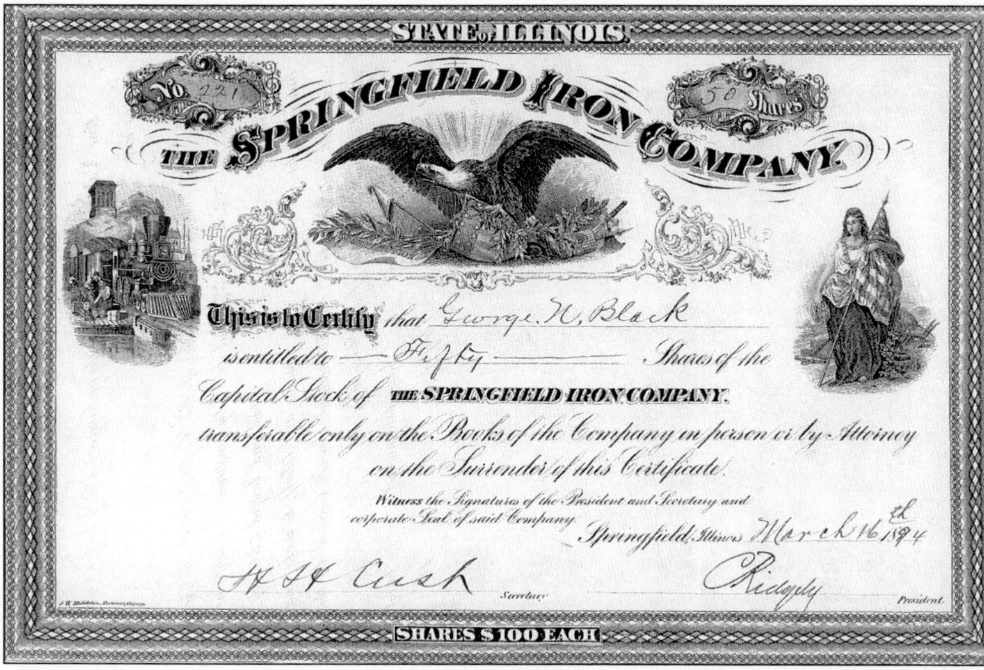
STATE OF ILLINOIS.

No. 221

50 Shares

THE SPRINGFIELD IRON COMPANY.

This is to Certify that George N. Black is entitled to — Fifty — Shares of the Capital Stock of THE SPRINGFIELD IRON COMPANY, transferable only on the Books of the Company in person or by Attorney on the Surrender of this Certificate.

Witness the Signatures of the President and Secretary and corporate Seal of said Company. Springfield, Illinois March 16th 1894

H H Cush Secretary

C Ridgely President.

SHARES $100 EACH.

Springfield entered its own industrial age in the years after the Civil War. Rich veins of coal discovered here were used to power new manufacturing plants. One of the largest was the Springfield Iron Company's rolling mills, which made rails for train tracks. Despite being sold to a larger steel firm, the company closed about 1902.

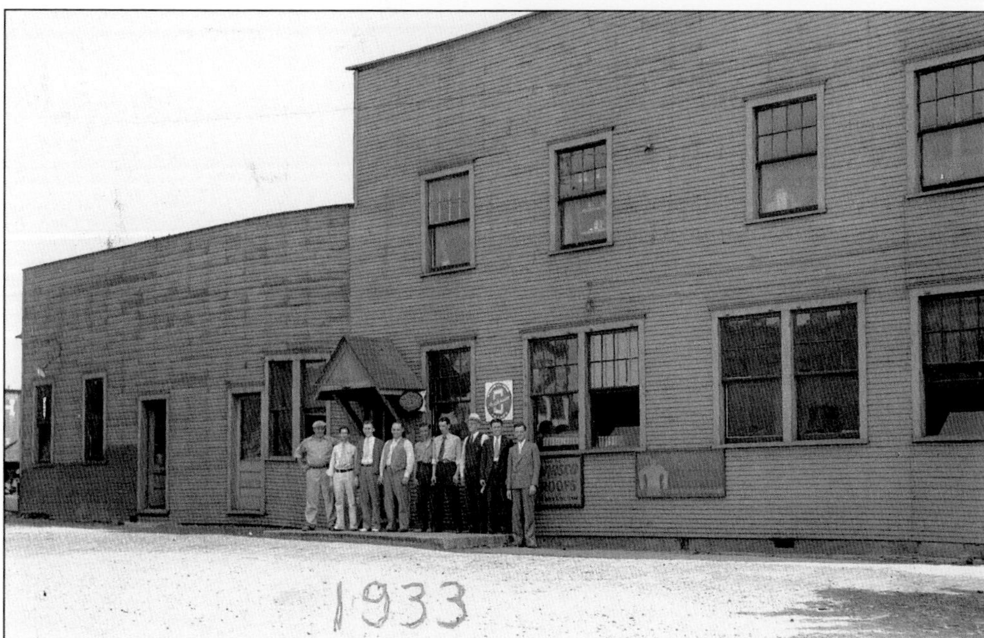

Springfield grew rapidly in the first part of the 20th century, and a half dozen lumberyards supplied the material for new homes, businesses, schools, churches, and office buildings. One of these, the J.R. Fitzpatrick Lumber Company on South 9th Street, is shown in a 1933 photo.

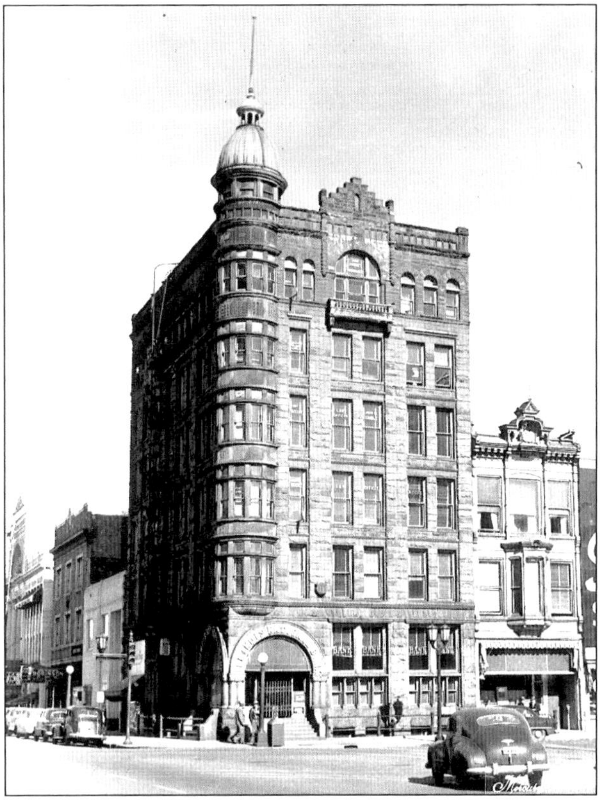

The banking business has long been a part of Springfield's public square. In 1893, when the Illinois National Bank built the red stone "skyscraper," shown here, they anticipated a growing demand for downtown office space. Naysayers wondered if anyone would want to work that high up, but offices were quickly leased.

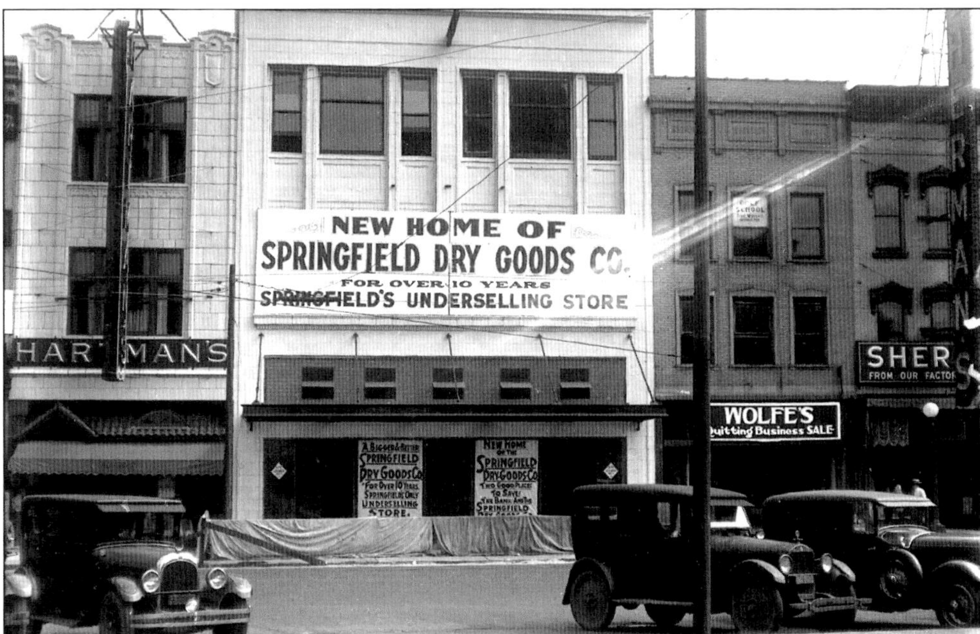

Dry goods stores with their fabrics, towels, ribbons, buttons, and bows were once a dominant business on the square. In 1929 the popular Springfield Dry Goods relocated from the east side of the public square to this new building on the north side.

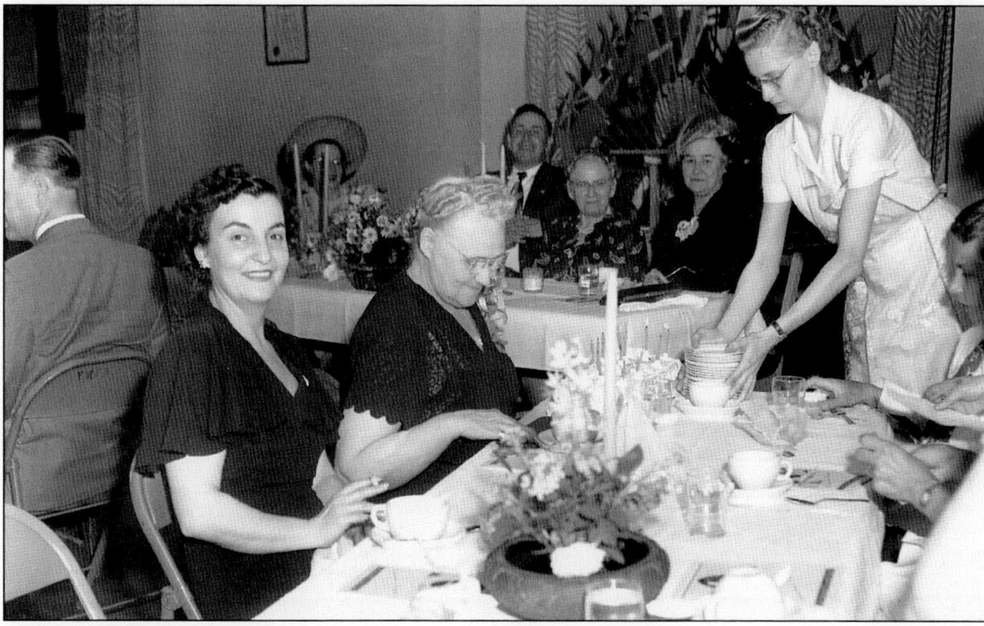

Dozens of public "banquets" are held annually in Springfield by civic groups to celebrate their progress and fete their membership. This one from about 1950 shows Mrs. Fran Satterlee and Mrs. Maude Lanham (center) enjoying after dinner coffee. Springfield hotels and restaurants eagerly sought clubs and organizations' business.

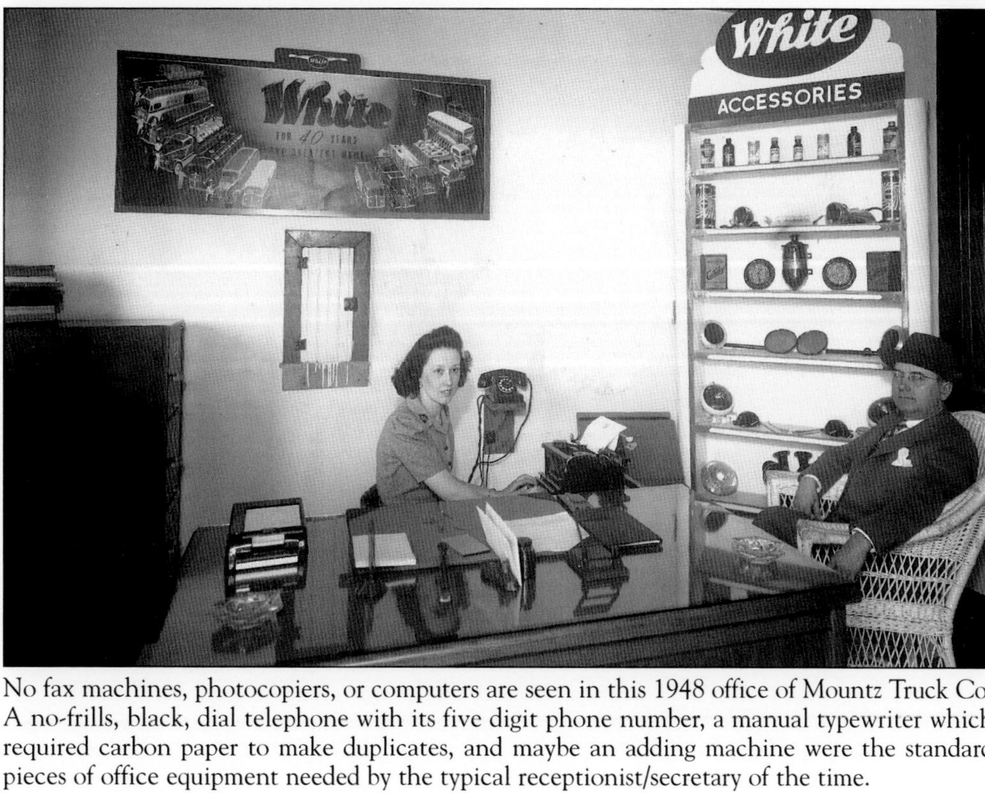

No fax machines, photocopiers, or computers are seen in this 1948 office of Mountz Truck Co. A no-frills, black, dial telephone with its five digit phone number, a manual typewriter which required carbon paper to make duplicates, and maybe an adding machine were the standard pieces of office equipment needed by the typical receptionist/secretary of the time.

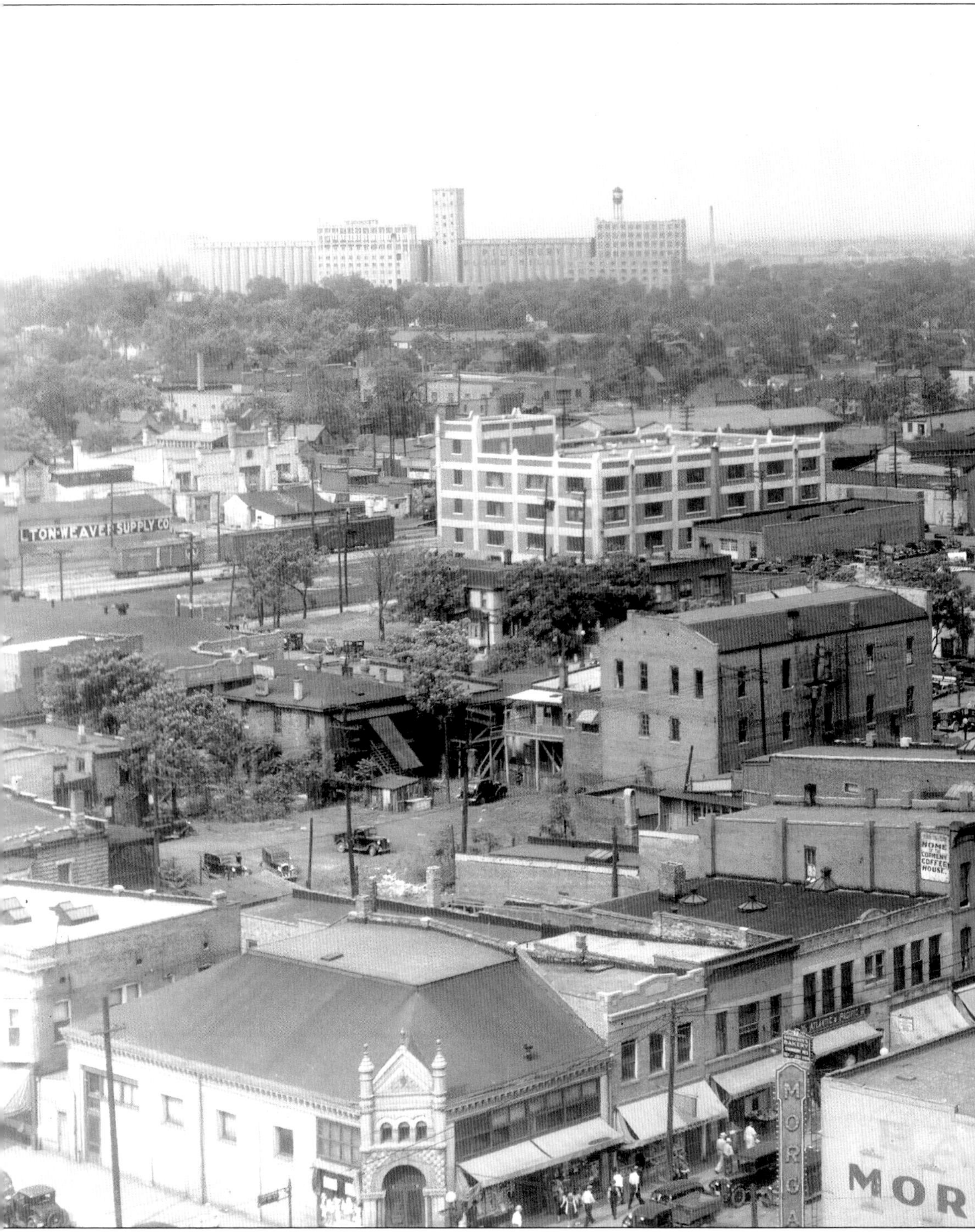

The northeast section of the downtown business sector was once notorious for its collection of saloons, brothels, gambling dens, and boarding houses. Known as the Levee, this area extended from Sixth Street to Tenth Street, Washington Street to Madison Street. The Levee district was bought up and completely demolished in the 1960s and 1970s during a wave of

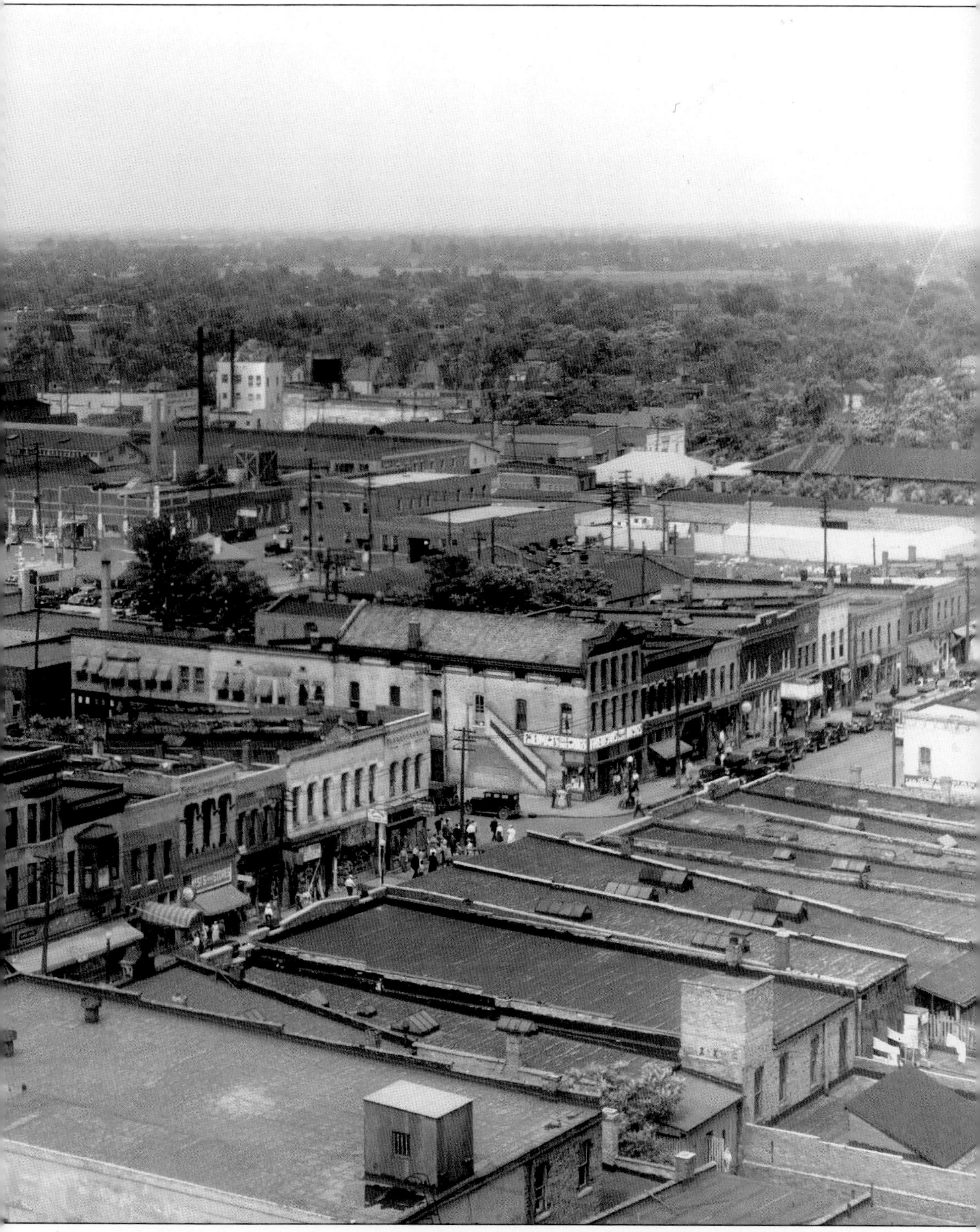

urban renewal. Horace Mann Insurance Company built its imposing office building on a two-block parcel, and the Prairie Capital Convention Center and parking garage were constructed directly across the street.

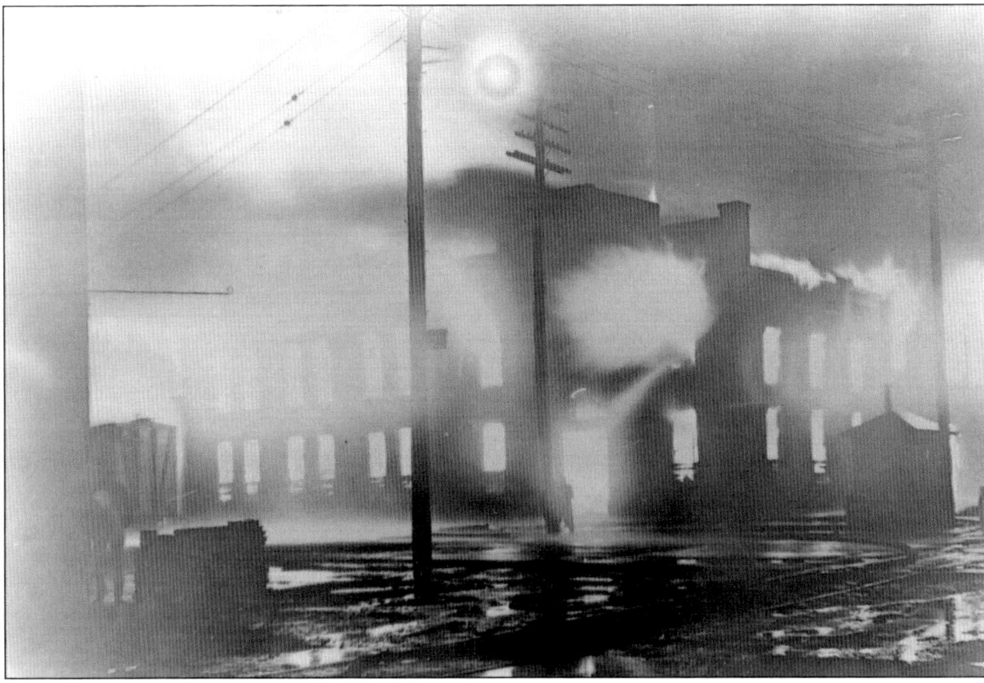

The Albert L. Ide & Sons Engine works factory once occupied a block and a half of ground at the northwest corner of Fifth and Madison Streets. Ide's manufactured the Ideal Engine, which was used primarily in the generation of electric power. In 1924 the plant was destroyed in a fire.

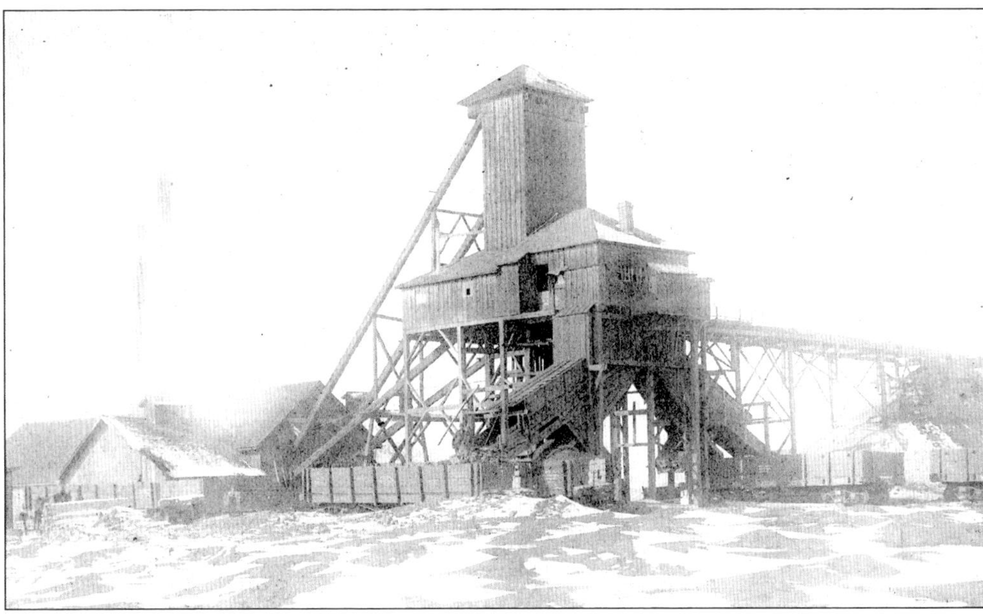

Coal mining began in earnest in Springfield in 1867. Numerous mines were soon opened around the city, providing coal for the city's growing manufacturing base and jobs for hundreds of miners. Coal was also shipped out to markets across the country. Mining was responsible for attracting a large number of immigrants increasing city and area population. Starne's coal mine, pictured here, was located in the northeast part of the city.

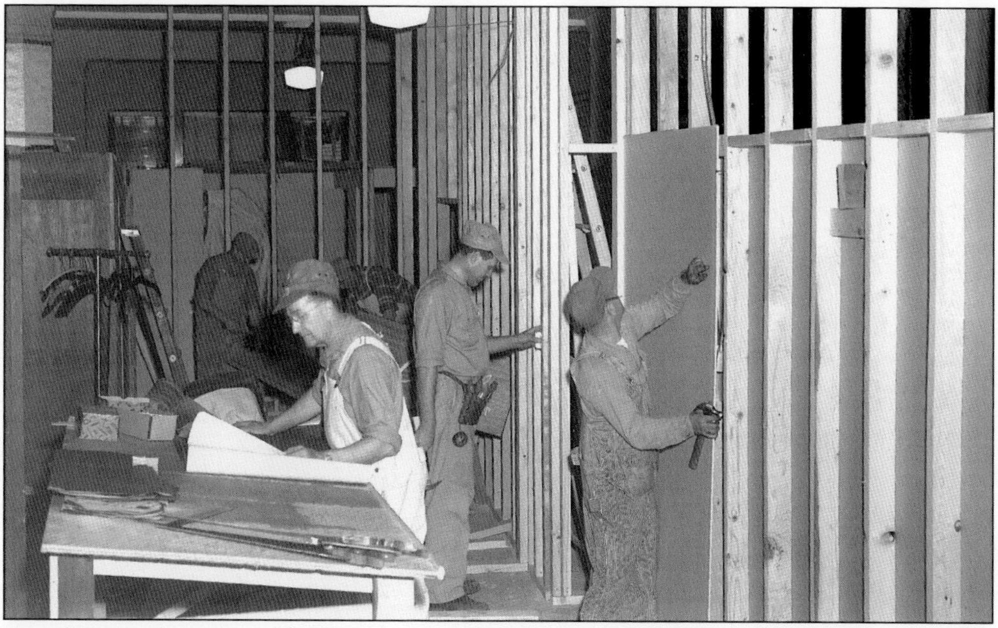

From large-scale projects like the construction of state capitols to small remodeling jobs like the one shown here in the Myers Brothers Department store, the city has seen continual construction and demolition, providing plenty of work for all types of building contractors and related trades.

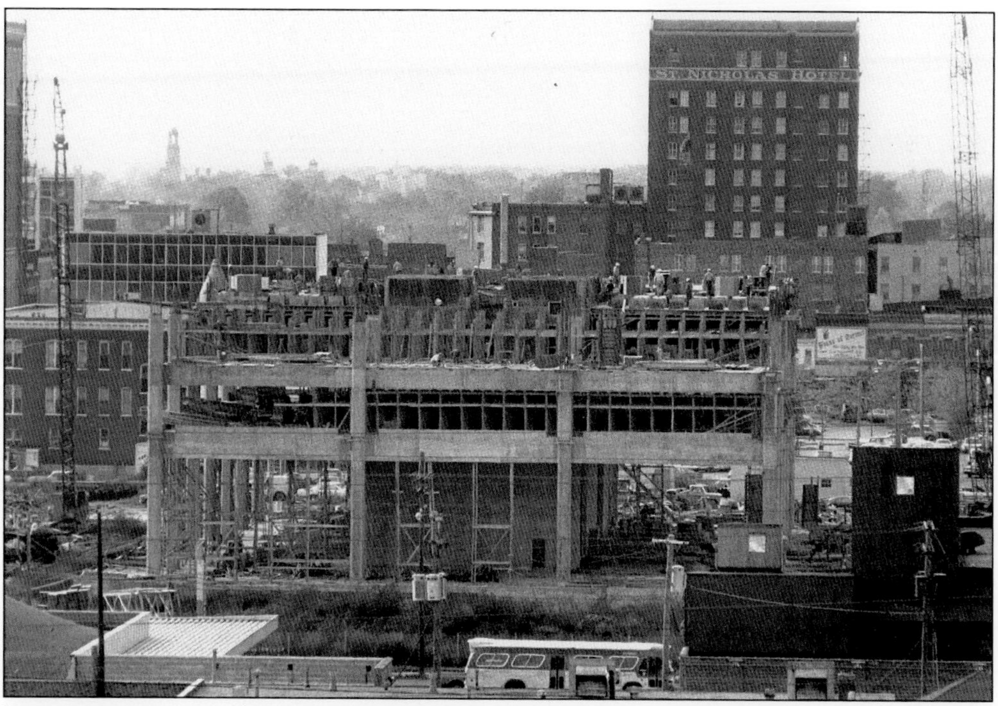

Large concrete and glass structures like the Horace Mann office building have gradually changed the landscape of the central business district. Once dominated by three and four-story brick storefronts, the downtown is now a mixture of architectural styles.

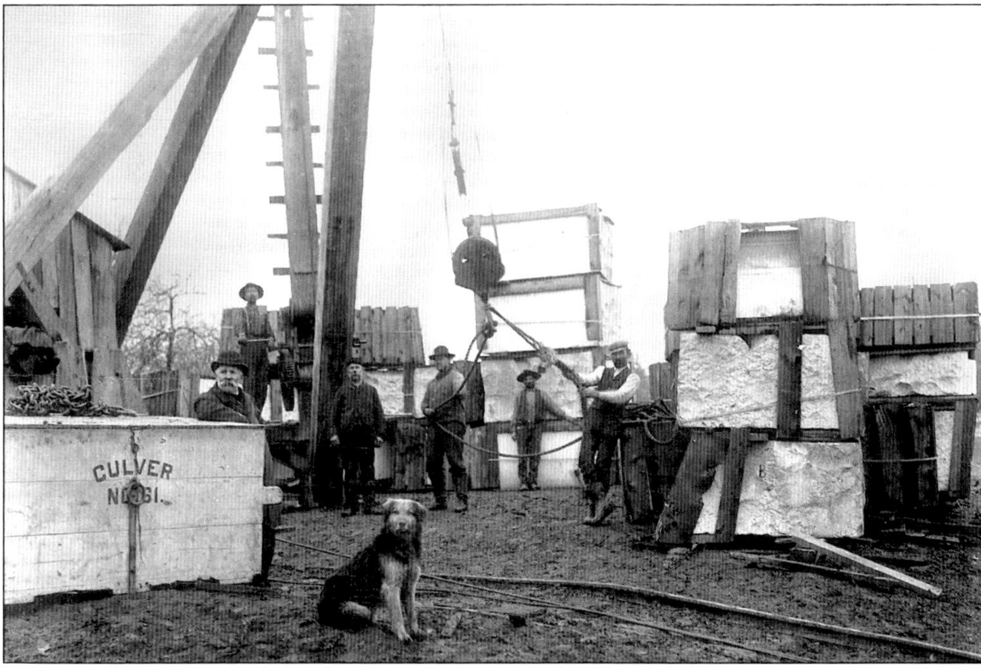

Col. James S. Culver's construction company received the lion's share of projects built of stone in the late 19th and early 20th centuries. From bridges to "skyscrapers," residences to battle field monuments, crews were kept constantly busy. Culver died in 1911 and his business closed shortly afterward.

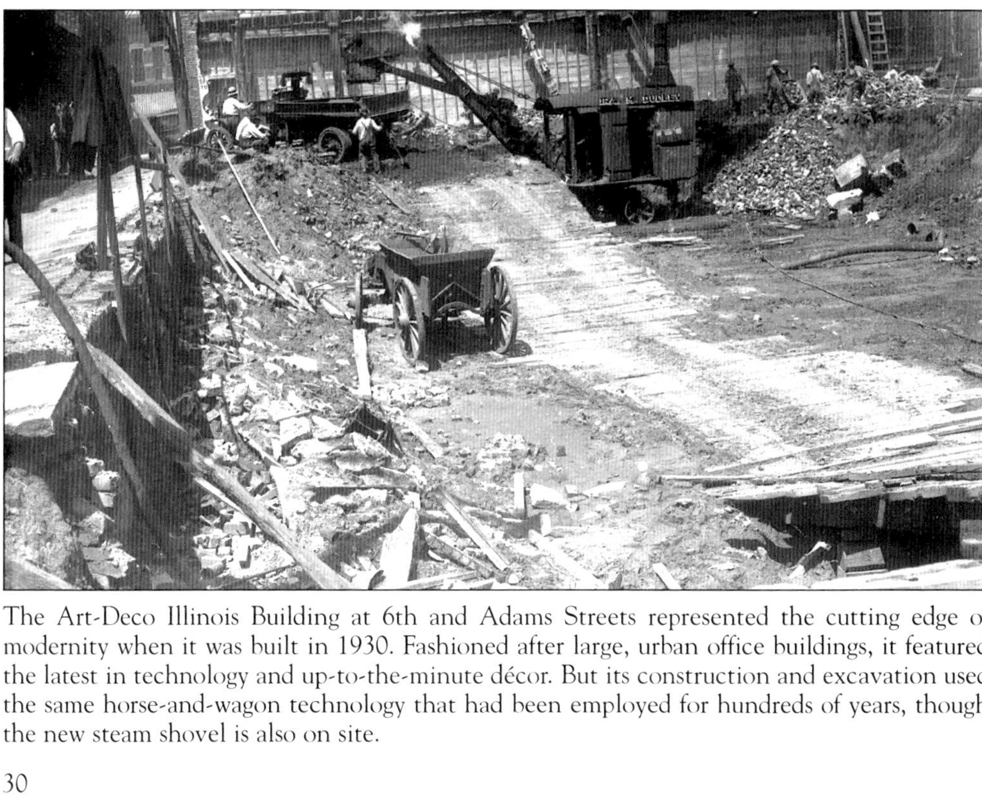

The Art-Deco Illinois Building at 6th and Adams Streets represented the cutting edge of modernity when it was built in 1930. Fashioned after large, urban office buildings, it featured the latest in technology and up-to-the-minute décor. But its construction and excavation used the same horse-and-wagon technology that had been employed for hundreds of years, though the new steam shovel is also on site.

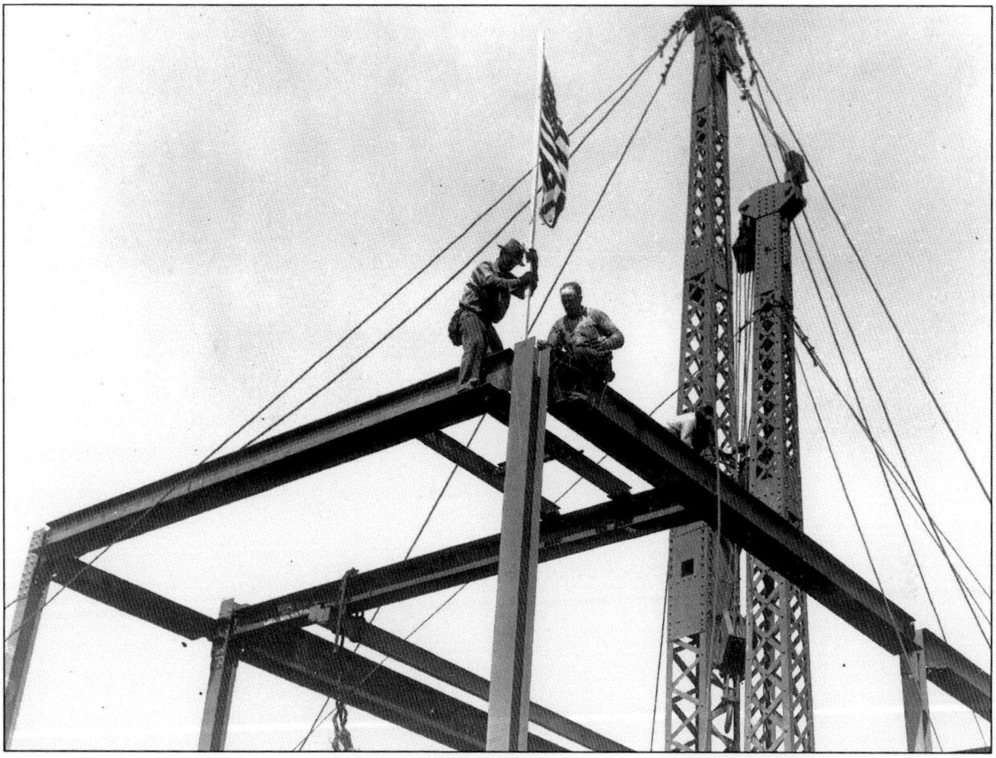

Steel frame construction became the very symbol of power in aggressive, modern cities as girder upon girder rose rapidly. Here a construction crew's members display an American flag on a newly-framed building downtown, about 1932.

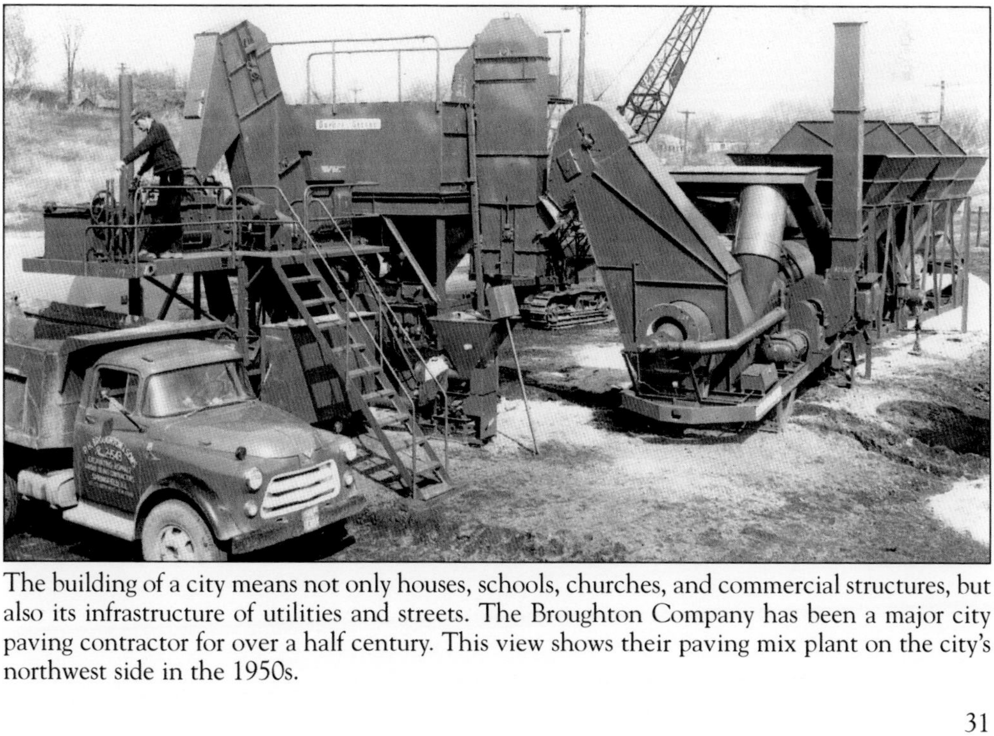

The building of a city means not only houses, schools, churches, and commercial structures, but also its infrastructure of utilities and streets. The Broughton Company has been a major city paving contractor for over a half century. This view shows their paving mix plant on the city's northwest side in the 1950s.

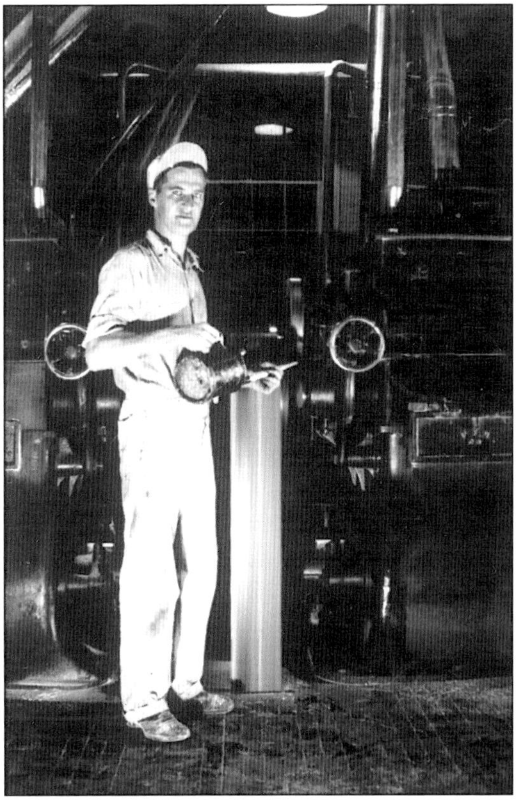

The opening of Pillsbury Mills in Springfield in 1930 brought opportunities for some 380 employees at the time of the Great Depression. Initially the plant produced eight types of flour, requiring a variety of workers for everything from keeping machinery oiled (at left) to baking in the test kitchens (below). At its peak employment in the late 1940s, over 1600 workers produced not only flour but also the first boxed cake and piecrust mixes.

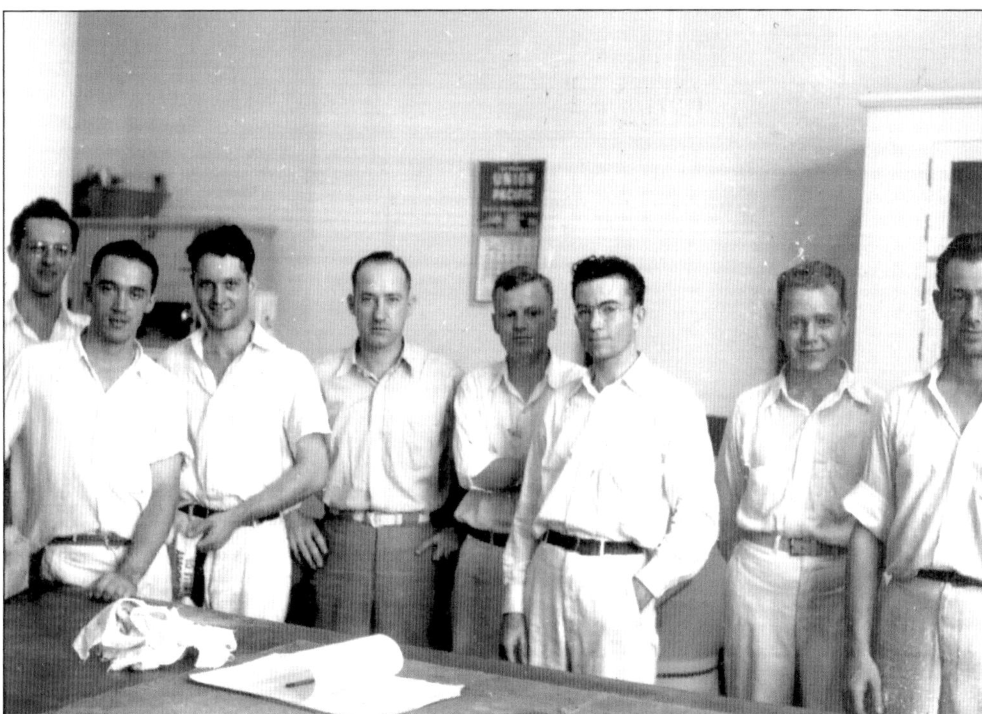

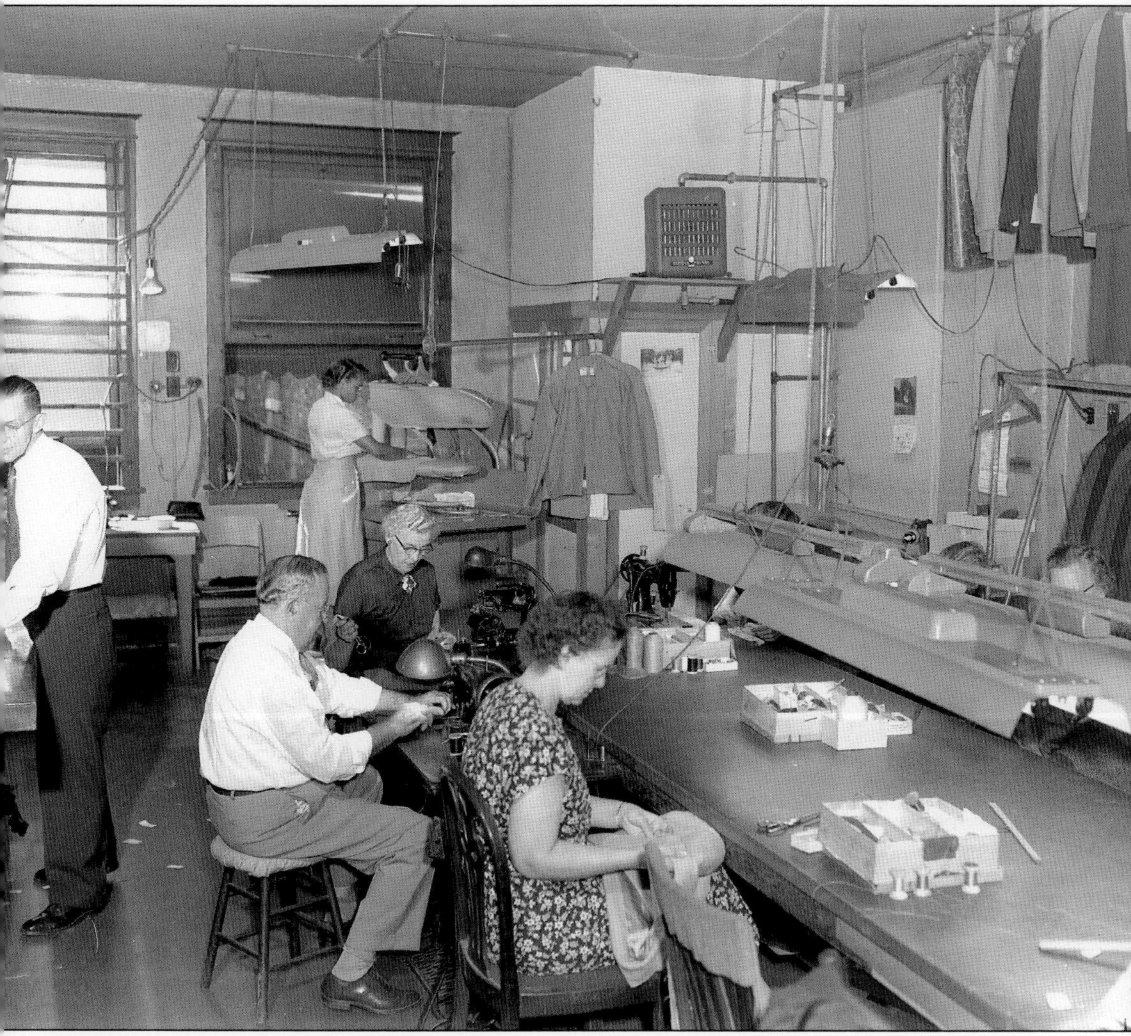

Department store workrooms contrasted greatly with the smart public display spaces, as illustrated in this 1950s scene. This tailoring department has electrical wires dangling to most every piece of equipment. There is the presser, the fluorescent and task lights, the sewing machines, and a lone fan. Spoiled by air-conditioning today, we wonder how five people endured working in this stifling room in the summer. There are no blue jeans and T-shirts seen here. The manner of dress indicates these employees took pride in their jobs and dressed to work with the public when called upon, despite most of their time being spent behind the scenes.

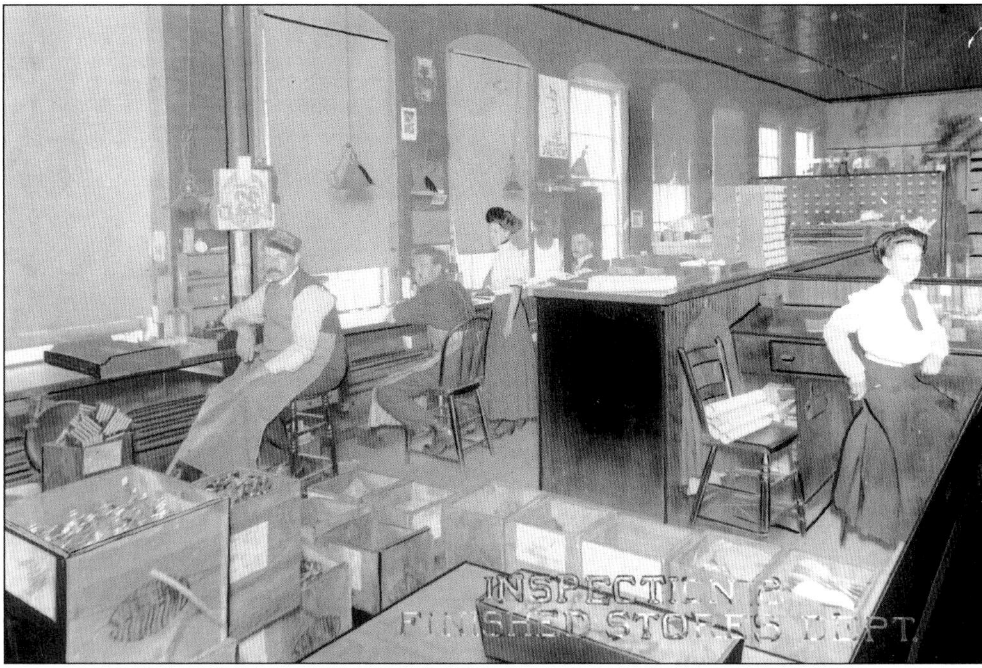

By 1910 nearly one fourth of all Springfield females over the age of ten were employed outside the home. The majority of these women found work in domestic and personal service, followed by manufacturing and mechanical industries, and then professional and clerical services. The Illinois Watch Factory, with its 940 employees, was one of the larger employers of women in manufacturing. Other employers were the International Shoe Company and Sangamo Electric. The top photo shows Sangamo employees from about 1910, and the lower employees from the 1950s.

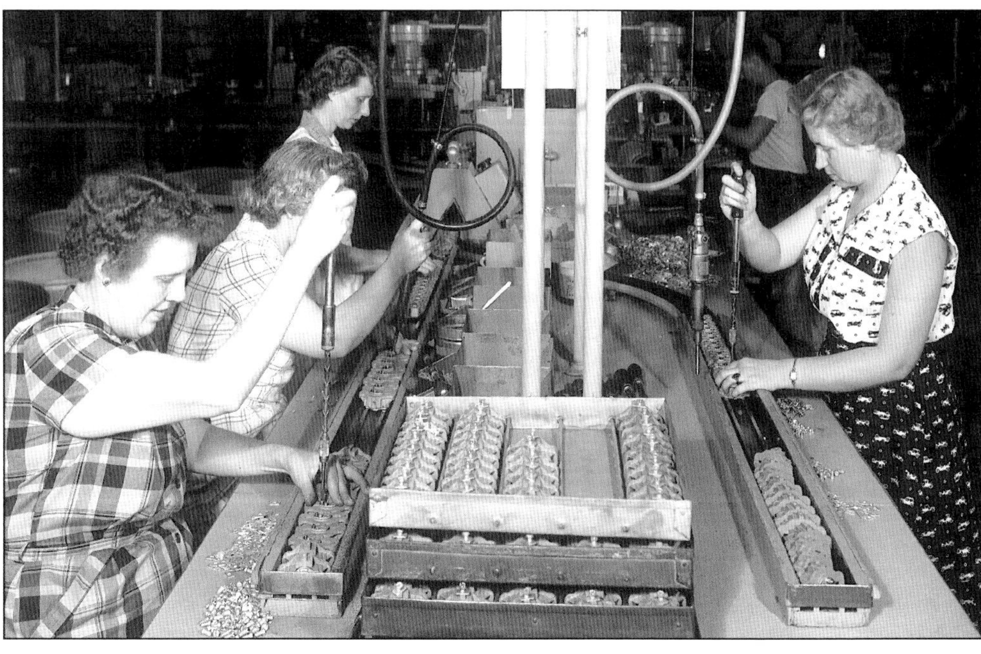

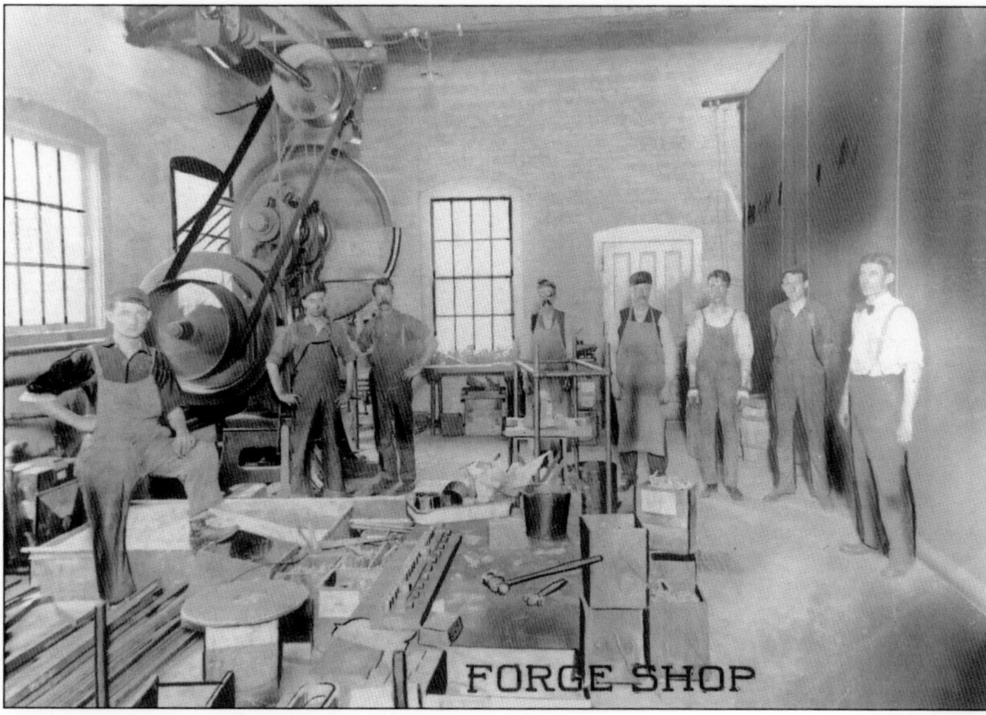

The making of meters at Sangamo Electric required heavy labor as well as meticulous handwork for the product that was marketed around the world. The company also dabbled for a time in refrigerators and radio sets.

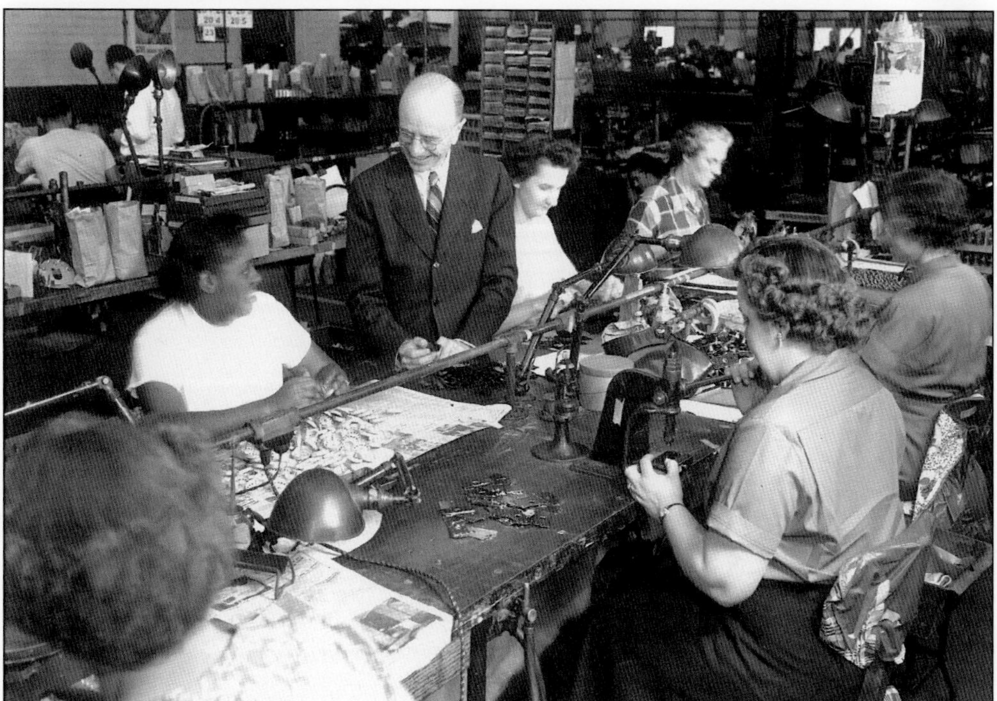

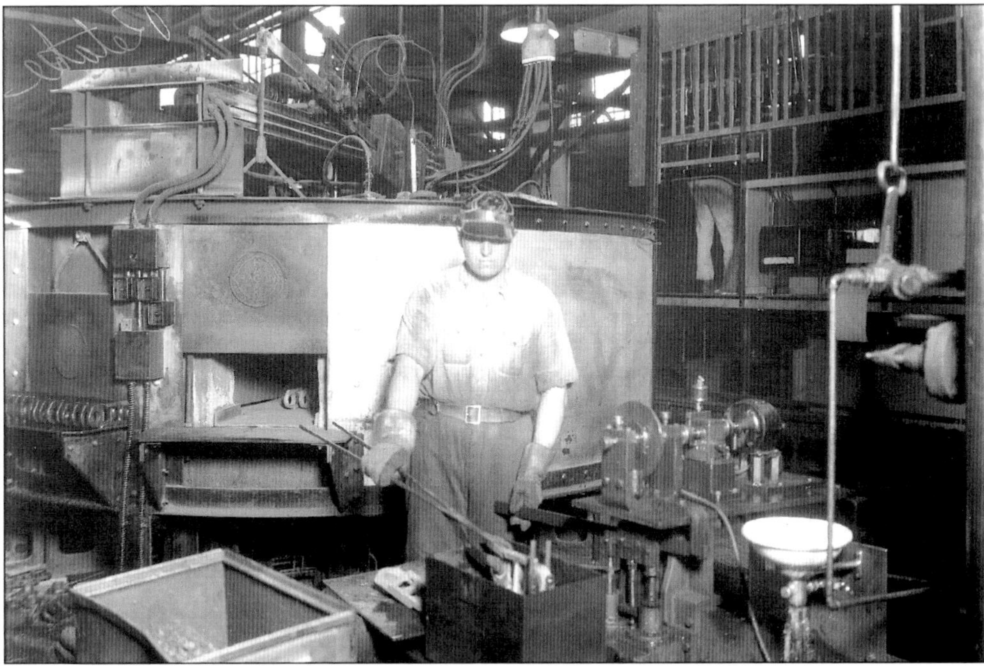

One of the city's largest industries was the Allis-Chalmers manufacturing company, maker of world-renowned earth-moving equipment. In the 1920s, the Monarch tractor company was located in the Harvard Park industrial business park on Springfield's southeast side. Allis Chalmers purchased their factory and eventually absorbed nearly the entire industrial park. Its closure in 1985 was a severe economic loss to the community. These two views from the 1930s give some idea of the extensive machinery and gigantic scale of the plant.

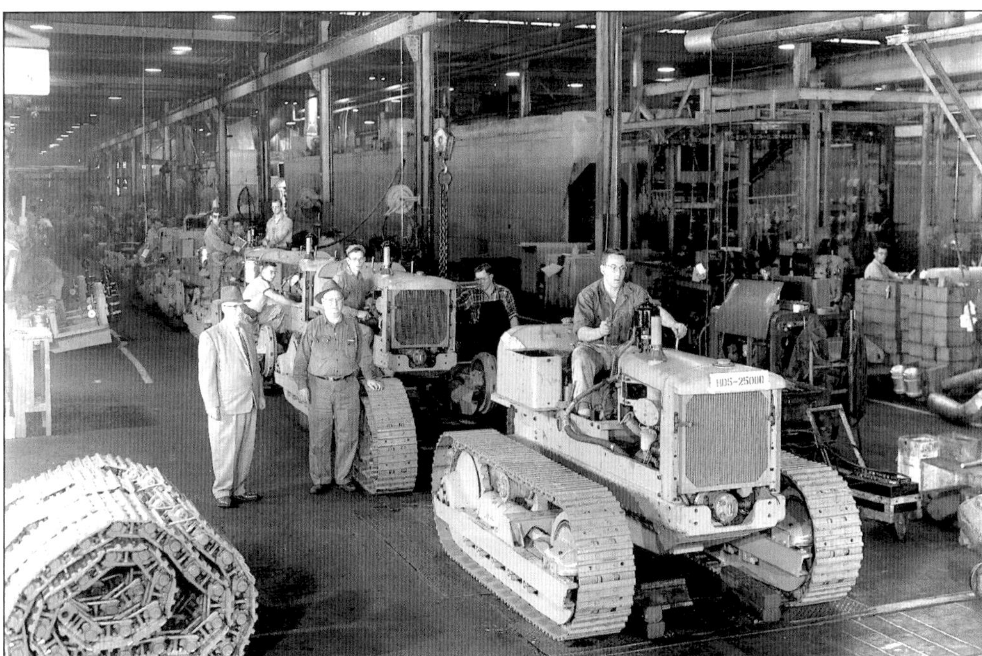

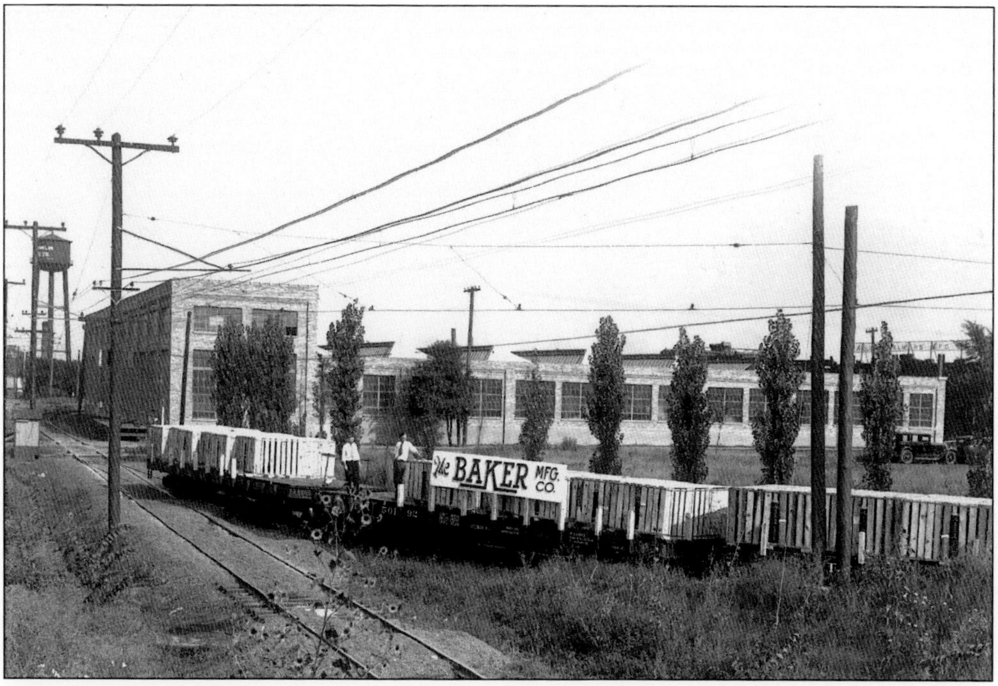

One of the first firms to locate in the Harvard Park industrial complex was the Baker Manufacturing Company, makers of earth-moving equipment, snowplows and accessories. Their products complimented the earth crawlers made by their neighbor Allis Chalmers. The plant, with its own railroad spur, is shown in the top photo. Product demonstration (bottom) took place on the grounds. Allis Chalmers absorbed Baker in the 1950s.

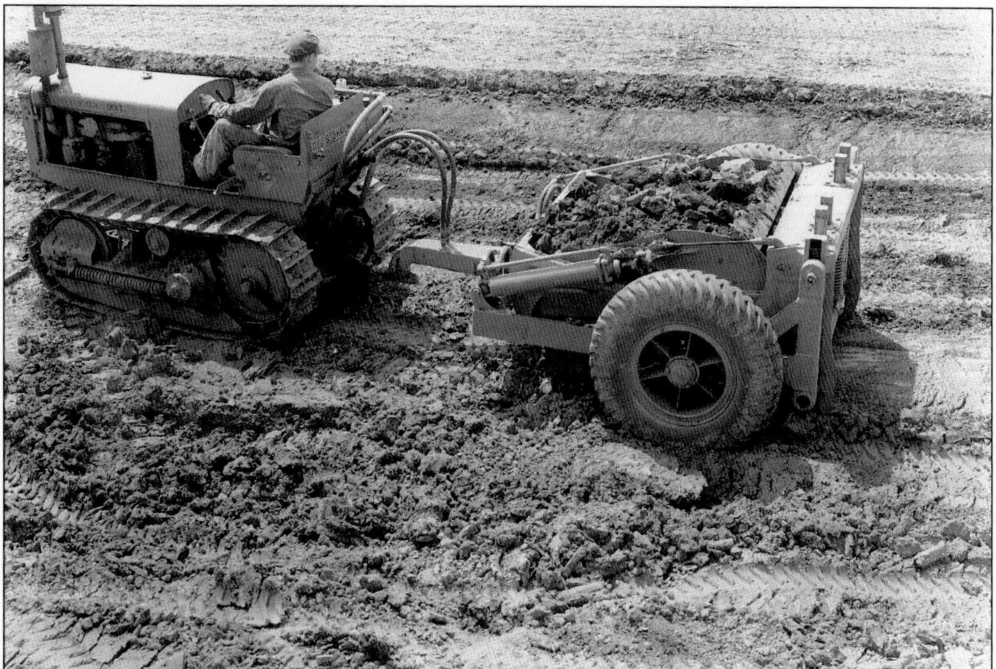

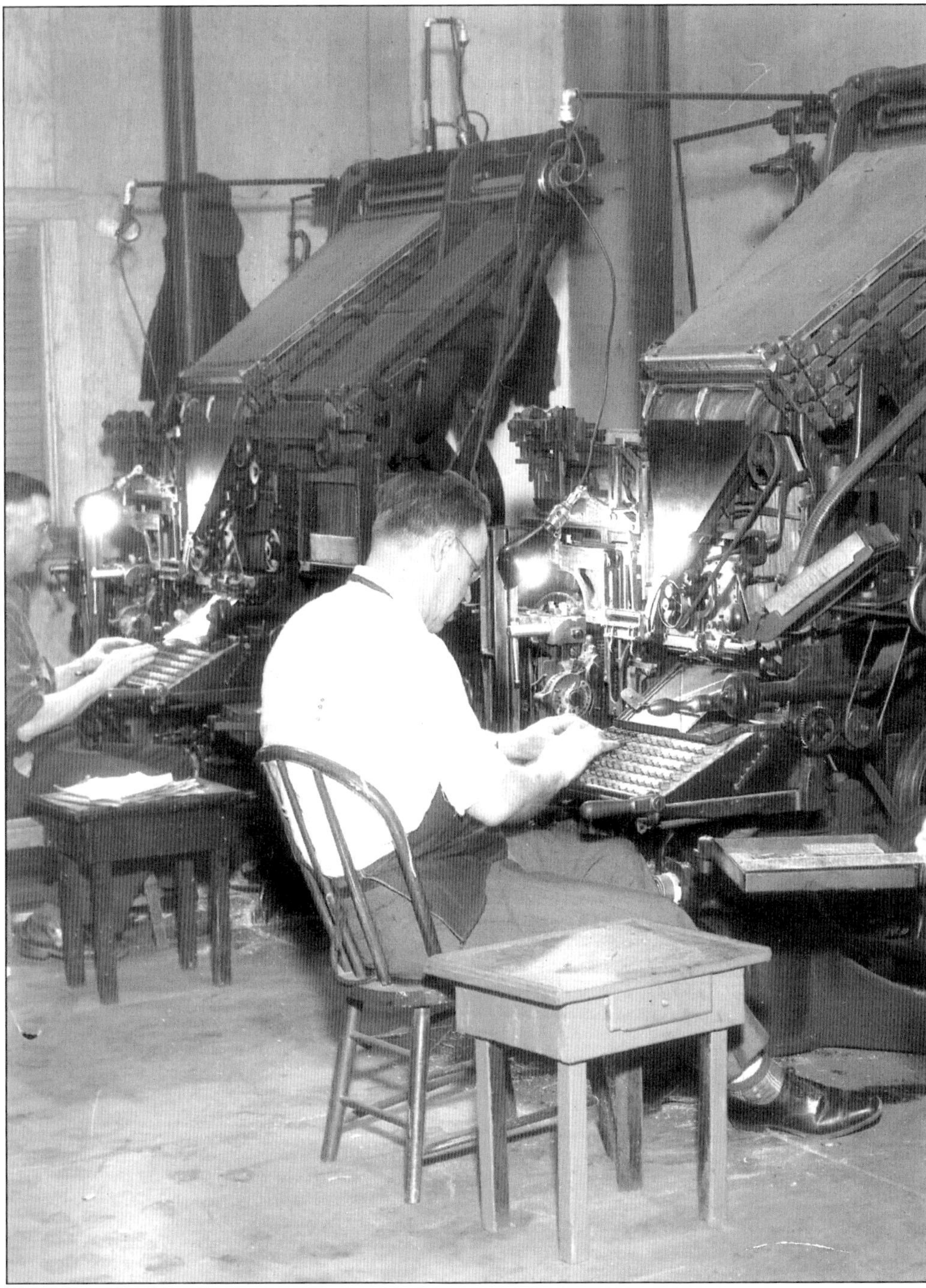

Sitting on a wooden, bow-back chair and typing in the latest news story on the linotype for the *Springfield Citizen's Tribune* was not, in 1943, the most physically comfortable job. The linotype machine revolutionized printing by allowing a whole line to be type set at once. Molten metal was forced against brass letter molds, creating a single slug to be placed in the printer's block, rather than setting one letter at a time. A fair amount of heat was generated but it was certainly a time saver.

Two

SPRINGFIELD ON WHEELS

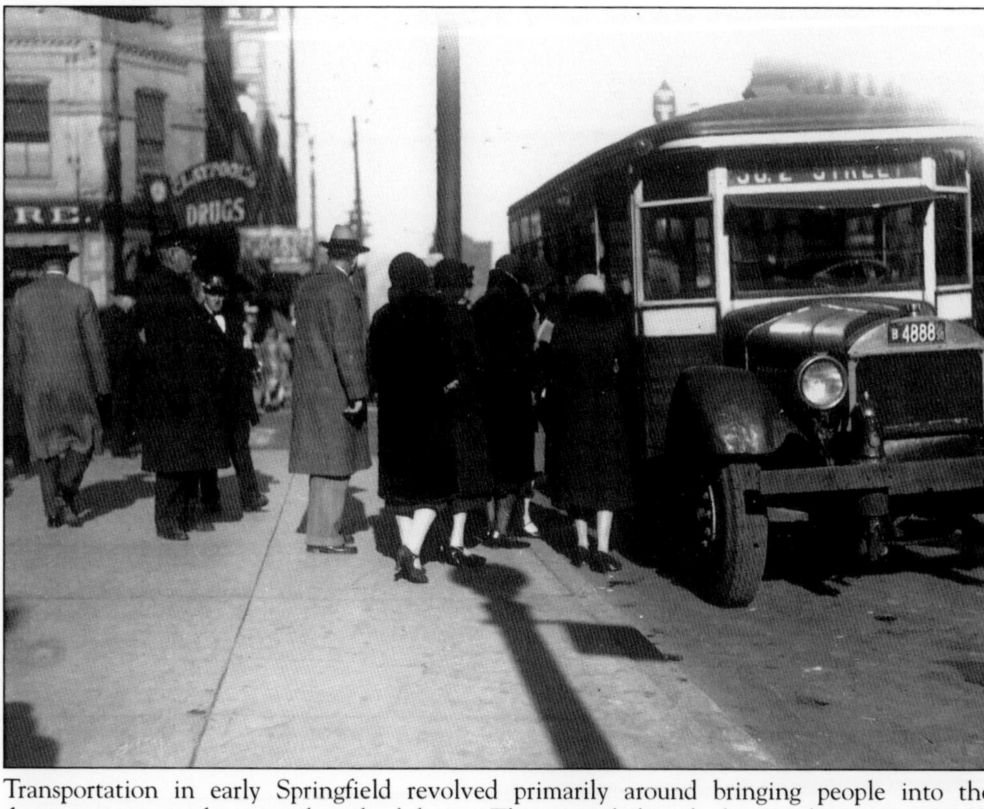

Transportation in early Springfield revolved primarily around bringing people into the downtown area and getting them back home. These people board a bus on the corner of Fifth and Monroe, an important stopping point for buses and streetcars.

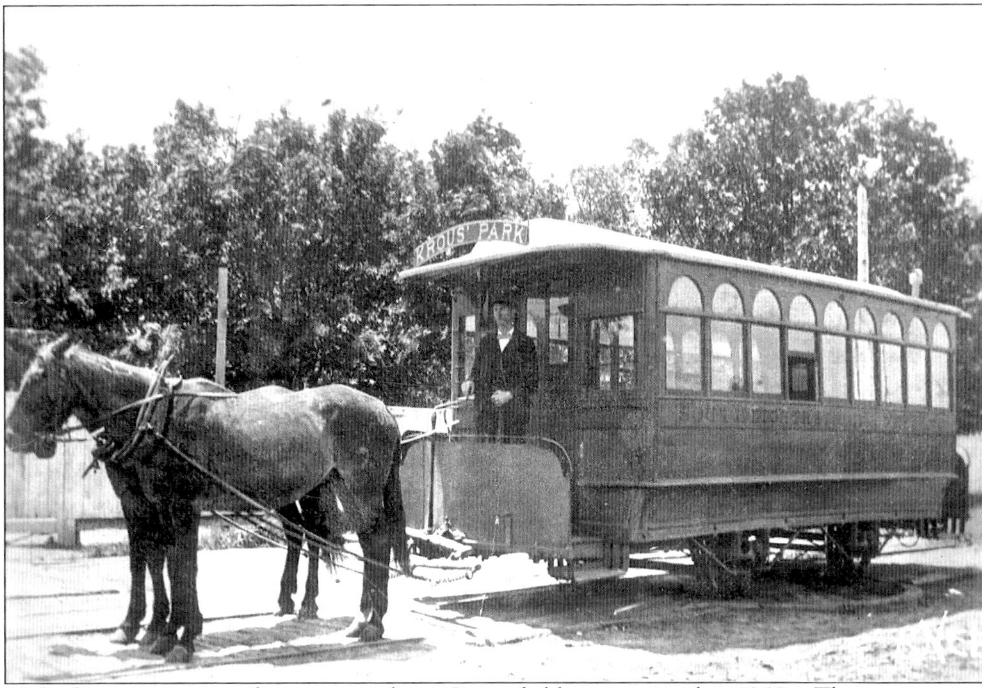

Mule-drawn streetcars first appeared on Springfield streets in the 1860s. The new system allowed the town to spread out physically as people could live further away from work but close to a convenient, inexpensive means of transportation.

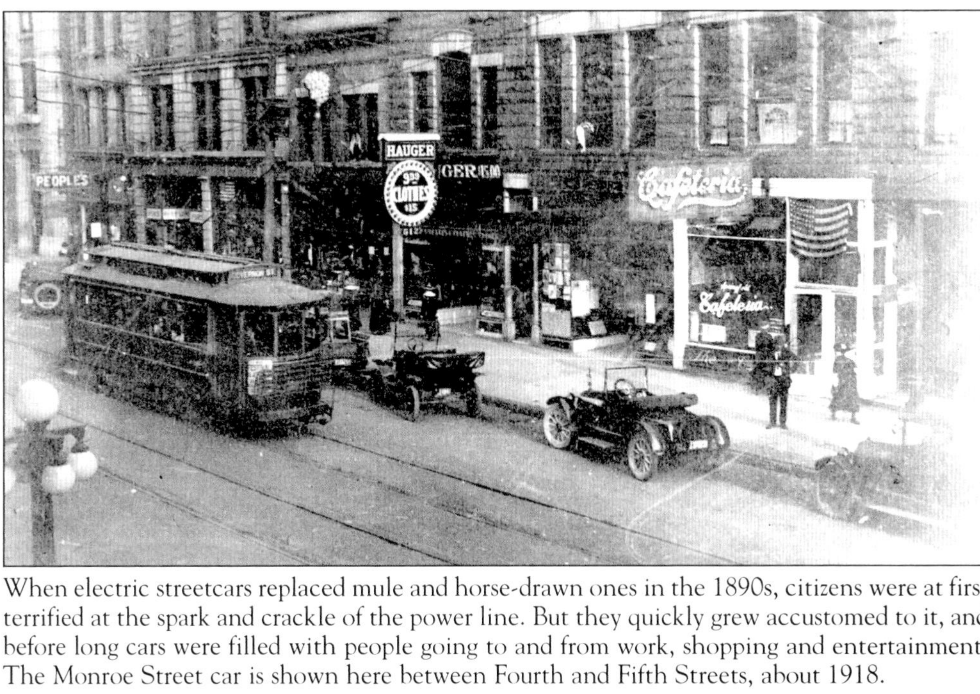

When electric streetcars replaced mule and horse-drawn ones in the 1890s, citizens were at first terrified at the spark and crackle of the power line. But they quickly grew accustomed to it, and before long cars were filled with people going to and from work, shopping and entertainment. The Monroe Street car is shown here between Fourth and Fifth Streets, about 1918.

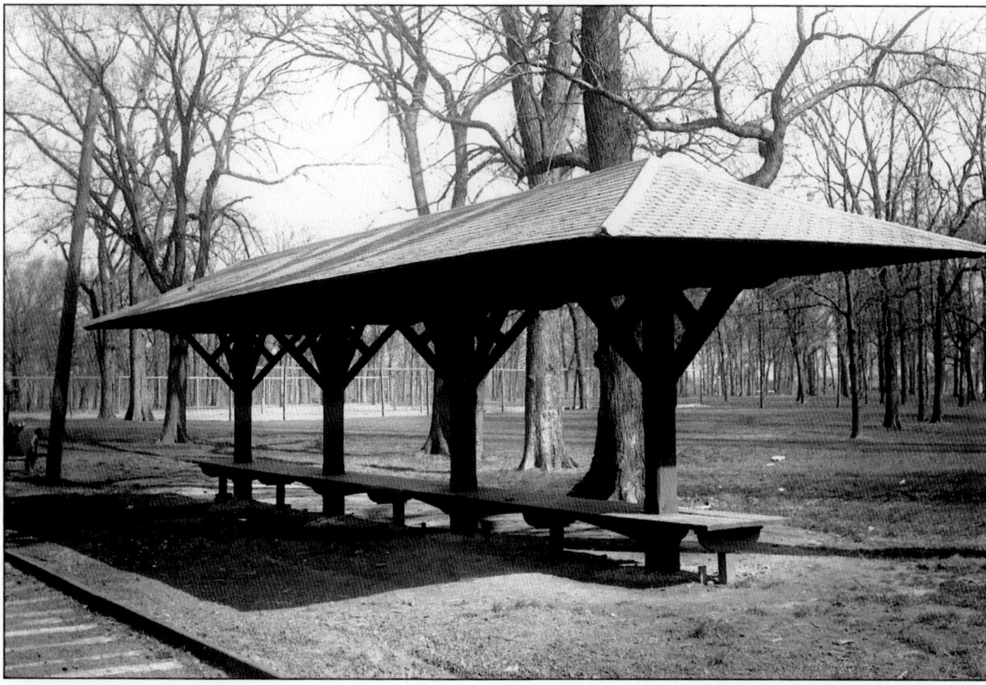

Waiting for the trolley in inclement weather was made infinitely more pleasant when a roof was available. This artfully-made shelter protected passengers at Springfield's Lincoln Park for many years.

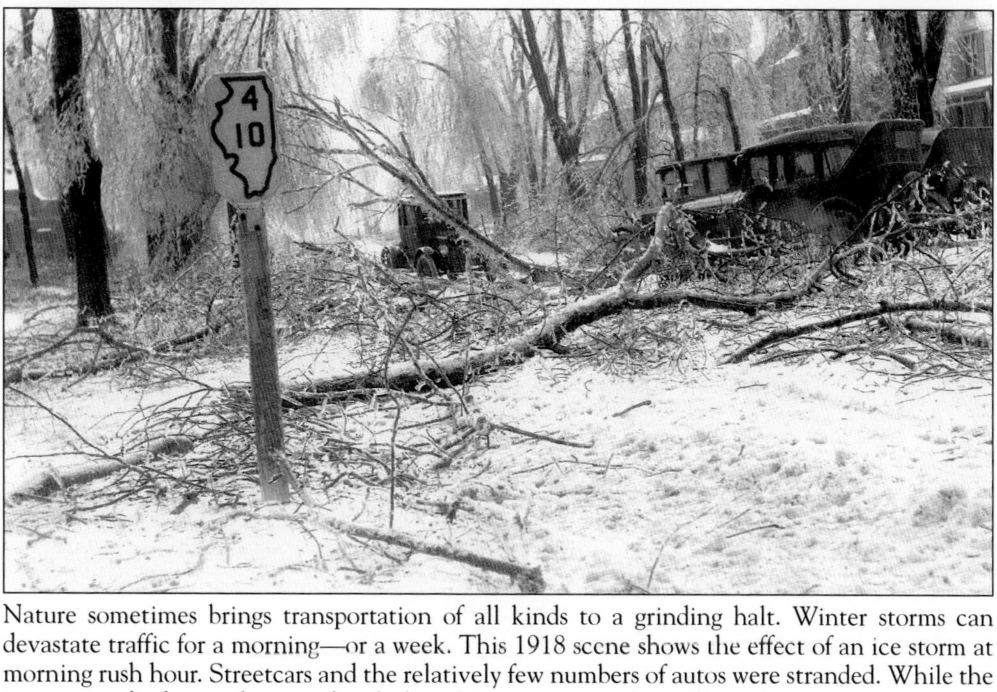

Nature sometimes brings transportation of all kinds to a grinding halt. Winter storms can devastate traffic for a morning—or a week. This 1918 scene shows the effect of an ice storm at morning rush hour. Streetcars and the relatively few numbers of autos were stranded. While the ice soon melted, it took many days before the streets were clear of branches.

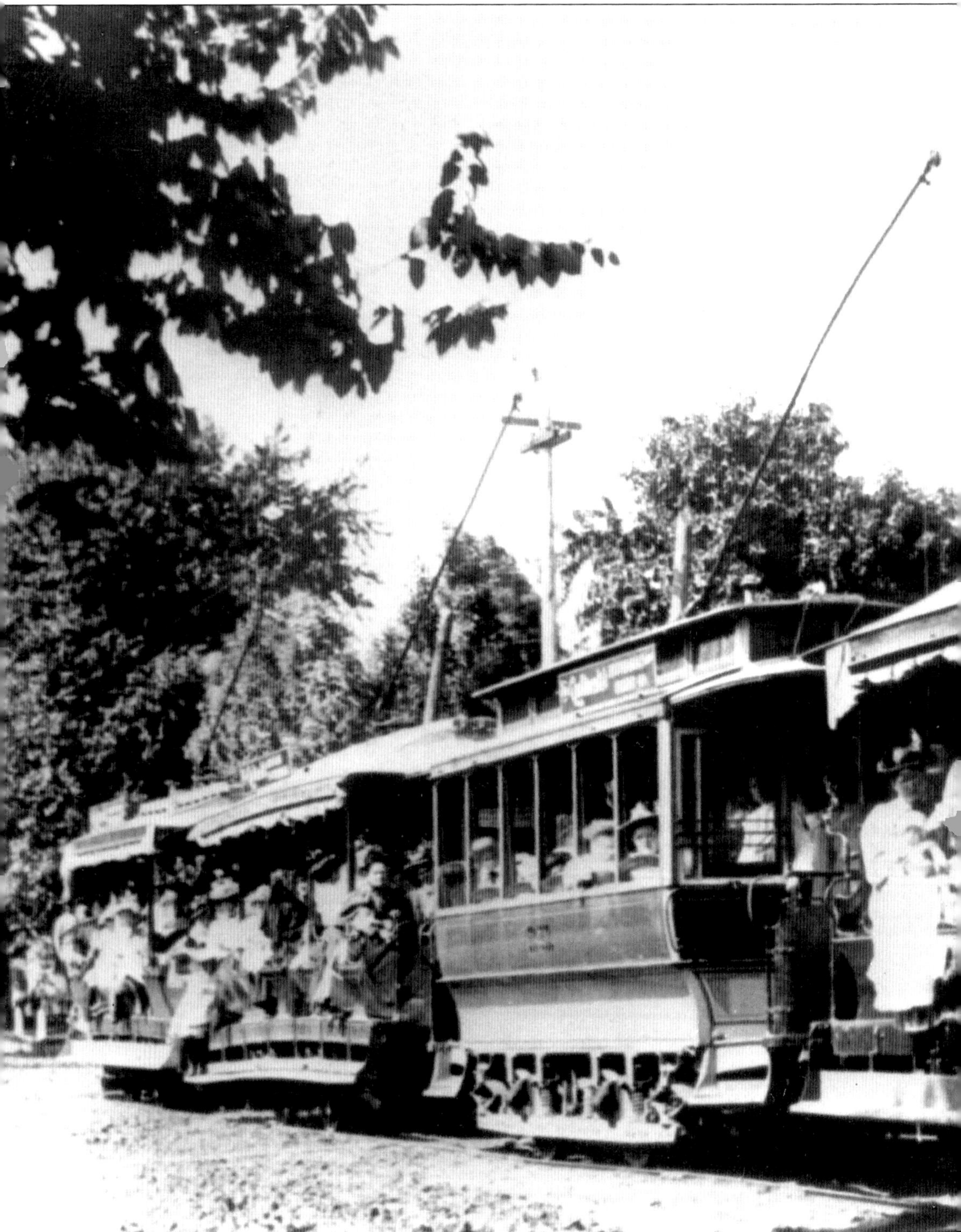

A day in the outdoors had great appeal to Springfield's urban dwellers in the early 1900s. Local trolley companies ran special excursions to the parks on Sundays; often the only day people did not

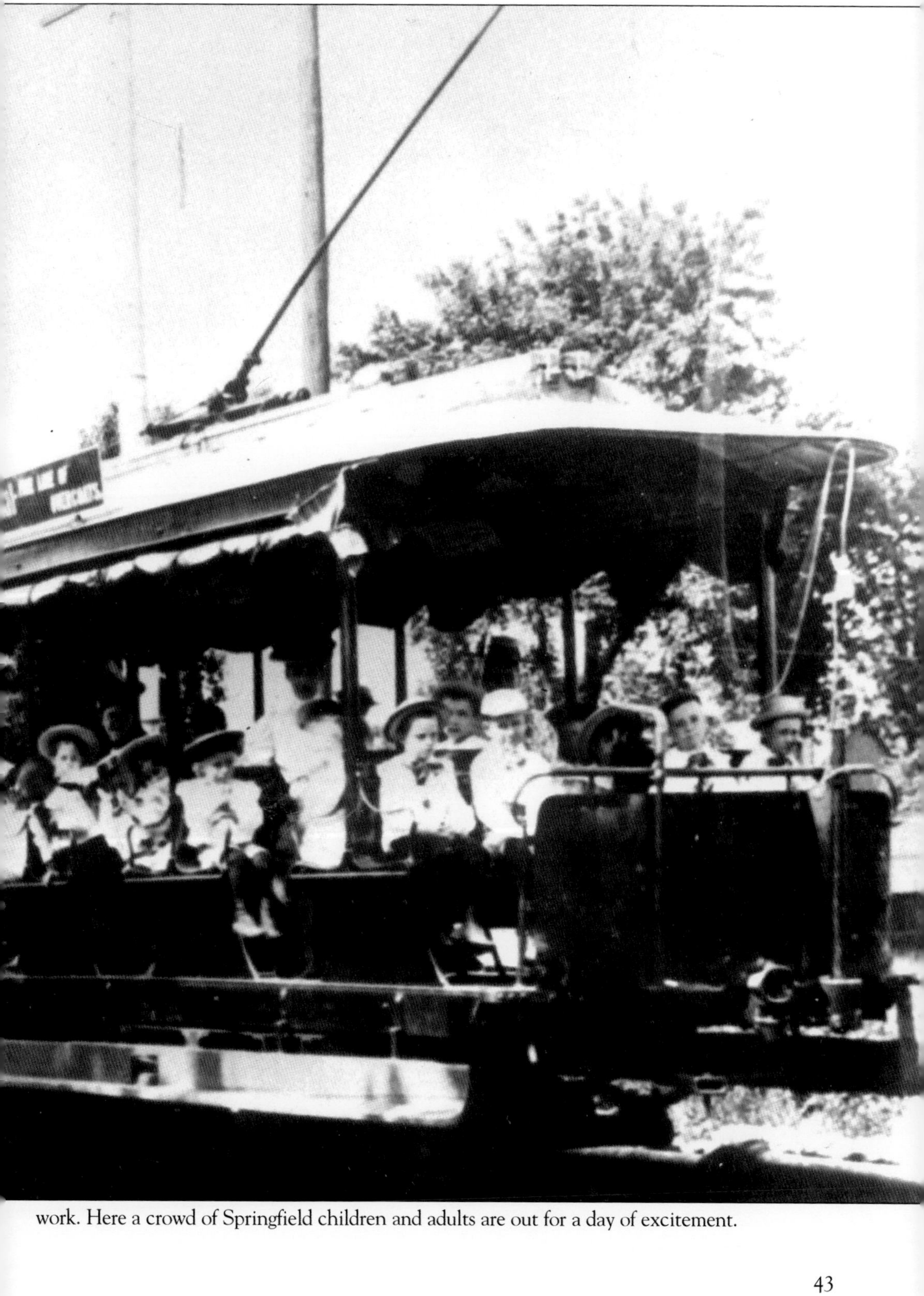

work. Here a crowd of Springfield children and adults are out for a day of excitement.

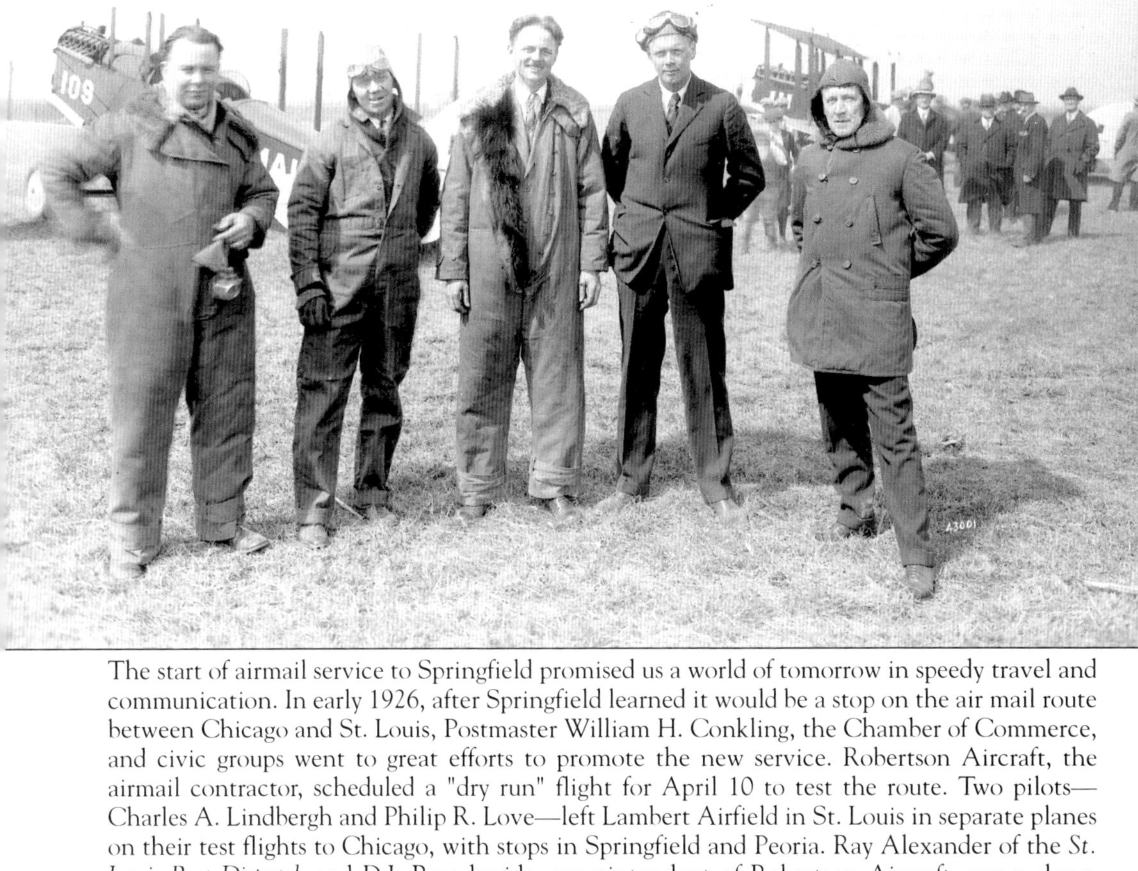

The start of airmail service to Springfield promised us a world of tomorrow in speedy travel and communication. In early 1926, after Springfield learned it would be a stop on the air mail route between Chicago and St. Louis, Postmaster William H. Conkling, the Chamber of Commerce, and civic groups went to great efforts to promote the new service. Robertson Aircraft, the airmail contractor, scheduled a "dry run" flight for April 10 to test the route. Two pilots—Charles A. Lindbergh and Philip R. Love—left Lambert Airfield in St. Louis in separate planes on their test flights to Chicago, with stops in Springfield and Peoria. Ray Alexander of the *St. Louis Post Dispatch* and D.J. Brandewide, superintendent of Robertson Aircraft, came along. Love flew alone. At Springfield, V.Y. Dallman, managing editor of the *Illinois State Register*, hitched a ride. In this photo, V.Y. Dallman is at the far right. Phil Love is second from the left, and the other two are Alexander and Brandewide.

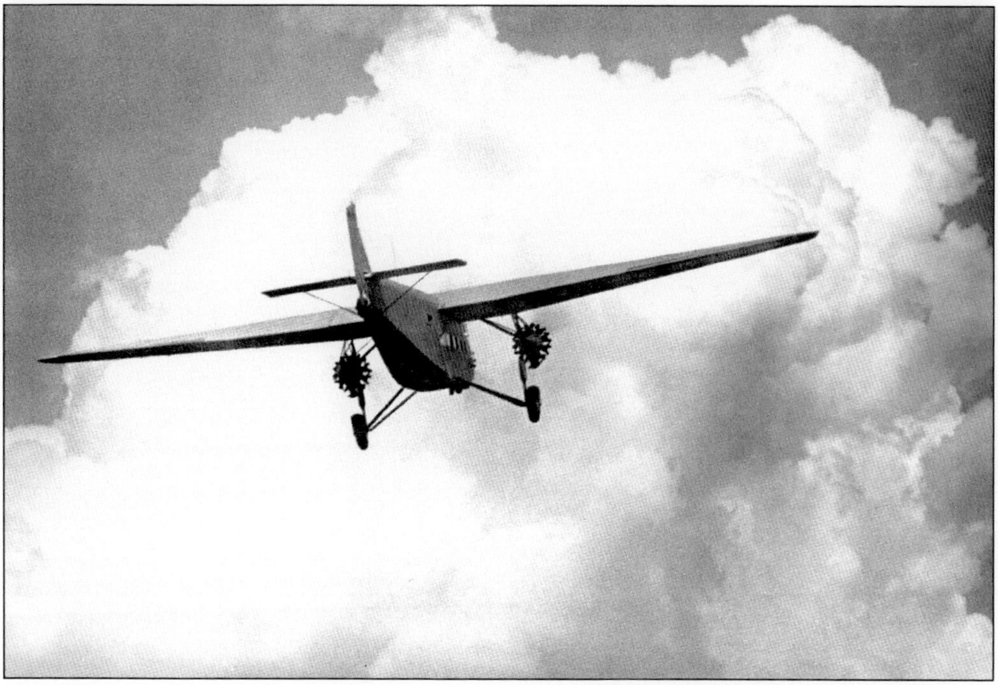

The Robertson Aircraft Corporation began passenger service at Springfield's Southwest Airport on August 20, 1928, using the Ford Tri-motor airplane, like the one shown here in flight.

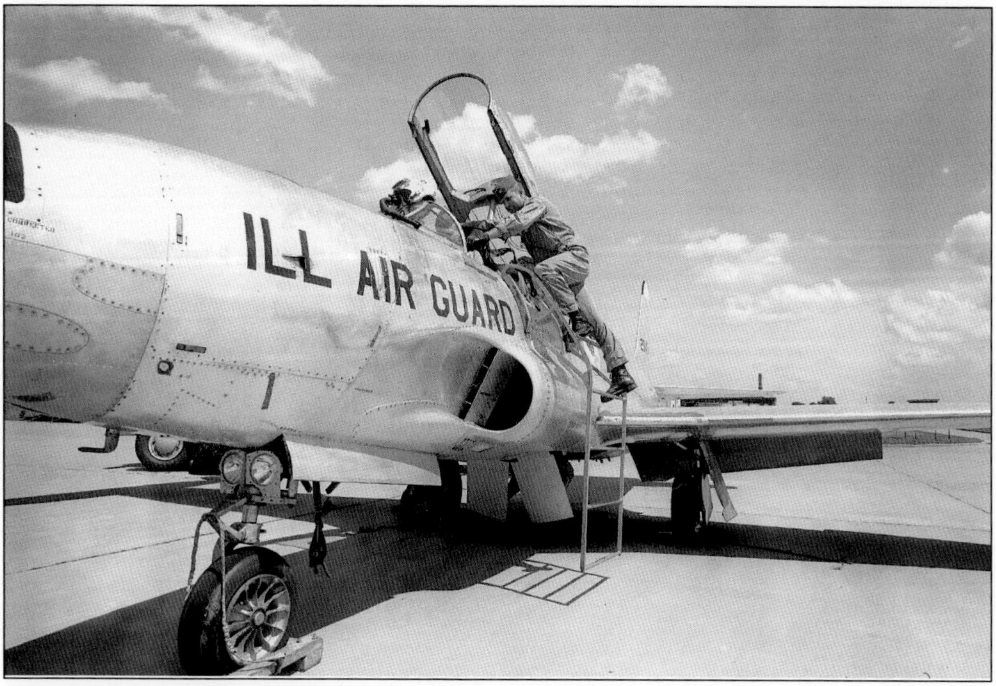

The 183rd Tactical Fighter Group of the Illinois Air National Guard has been stationed just north of Capitol Airport since 1948. Captain Harold Holesinger stares into the cockpit of a jet plane. William J. Davis is in the seat in this 1960s photo.

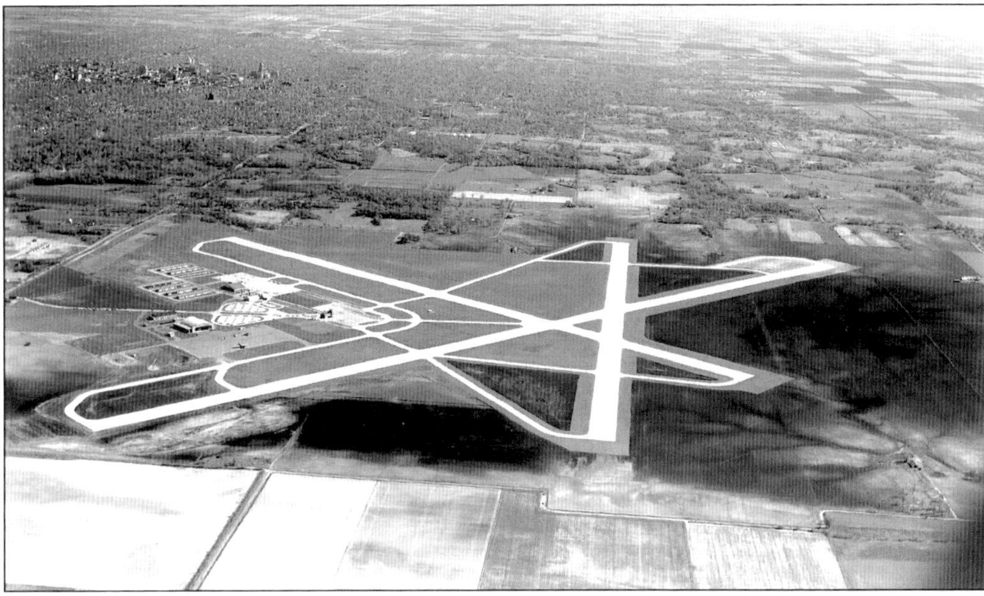

Springfield's new Capital Airport was dedicated November 2, 1947. The main runway seen here was 5,300 feet long, and most permanent buildings were not yet complete. American Airlines' "Flagship Springfield" plane was on hand for the ceremonies. Local crews vigorously polished its exterior much "as a debutante dabs her nose prior to her debut," according one local news story.

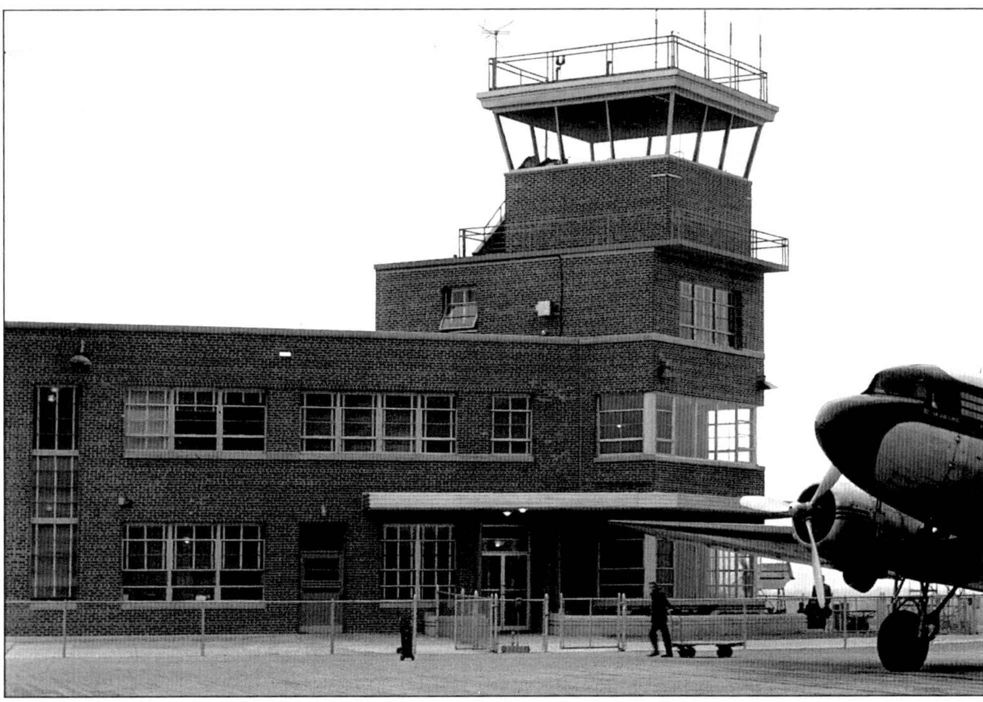

Capital's main terminal contained an octagonal lobby and offices of the State Department of Aeronautics, Civil Aeronautics Authority, American Airlines, U.S. Weather Bureau, Springfield Airport Authority manager, and a restaurant.

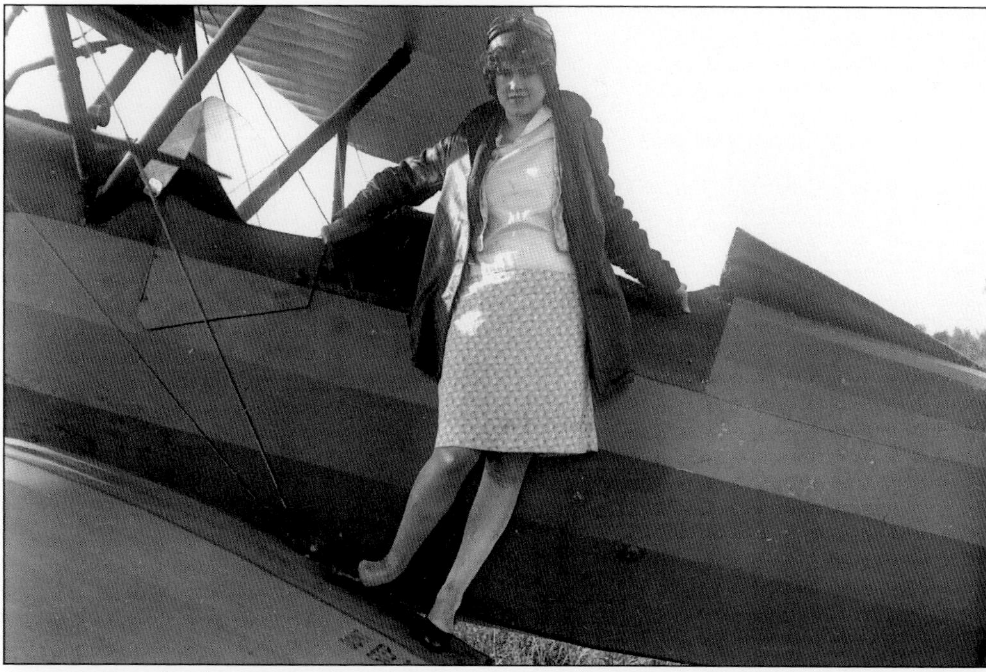

Air travel caught the imagination of young people of both sexes. Elizabeth Skadden, 18, was taking flying lessons at Springfield's Southwest Airport when she posed for this photo in 1929. "Just as soon as my chance comes, I hope to set a new endurance record for women flyers which will stand for a long, long time," she told reporters.

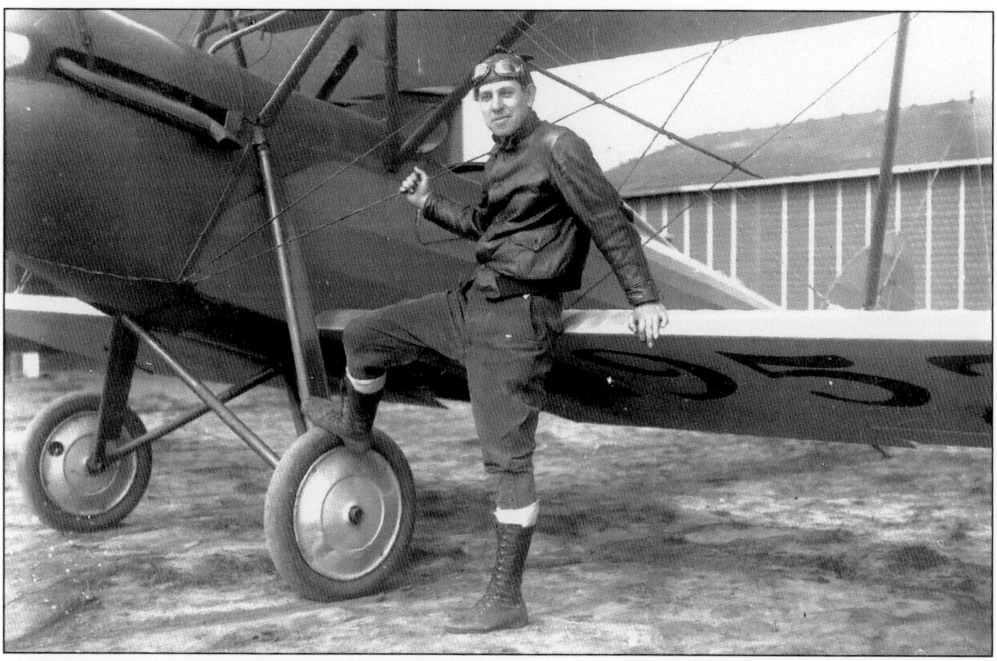

Gelder Lockwood, locally famed pilot and air-travel promoter, poses next to his plane in 1931. Lockwood and Craig Isbell established the old Southwest Airport, now part of the Westchester subdivision. Lockwood is well remembered for training numerous local pilots.

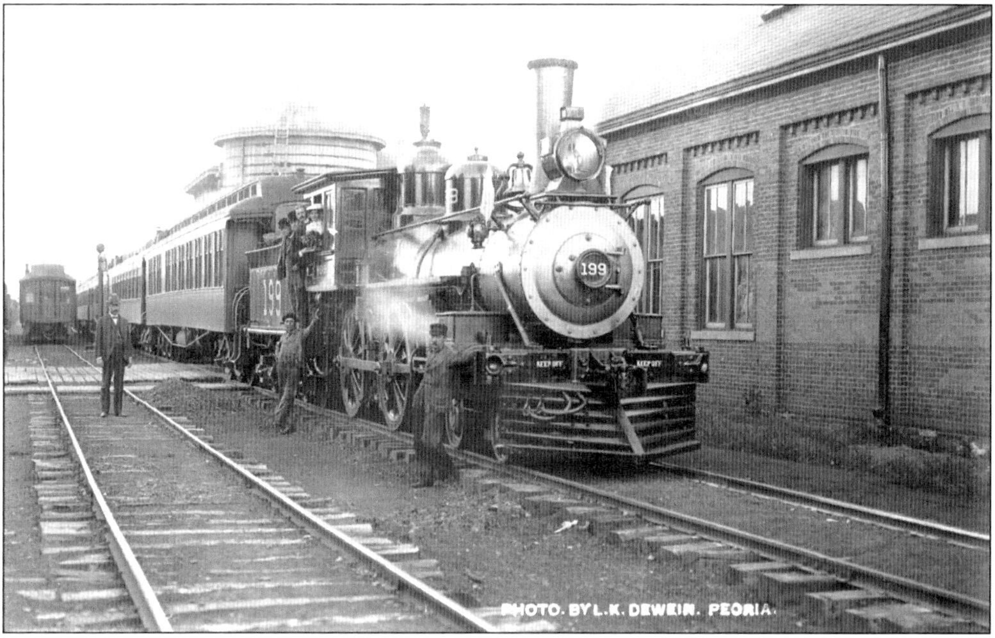

This special train, stopped in Springfield's Wabash rail-yards, had Governor Richard Yates and his wife in the engineer's cab. It is said the governor's wife requested the photo.

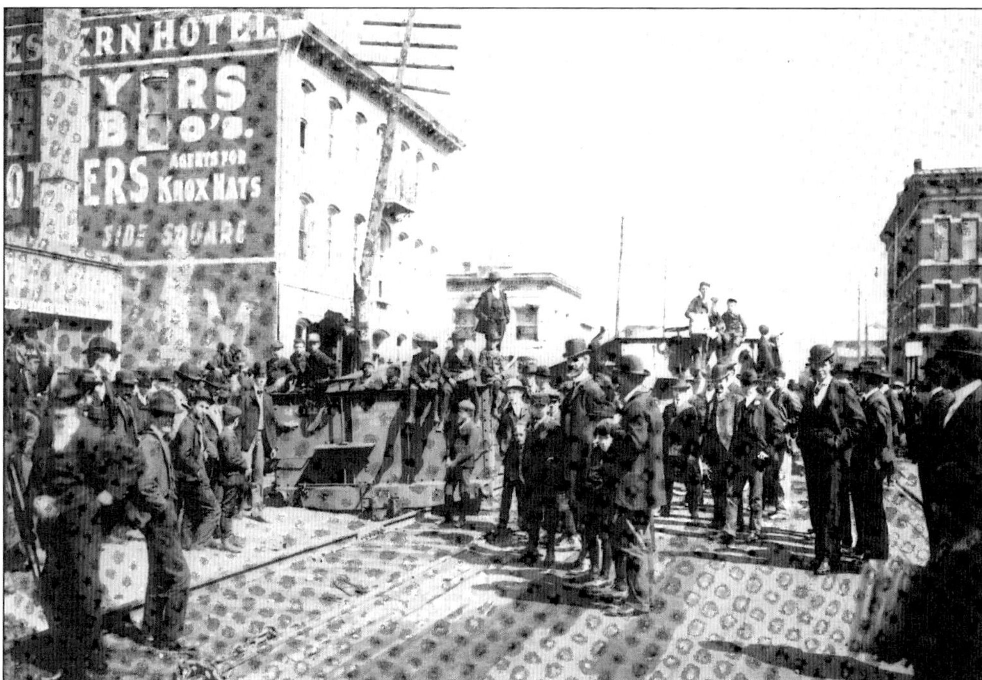

It was right in front of the Chicago and Alton (Amtrak) Station at Third and Jefferson Streets that these coal gondola cars derailed in 1901, spilling their contents and breaking telephone, telegraph, and power poles, generally disrupting life for the businesses, homes and apartment dwellers in the area.

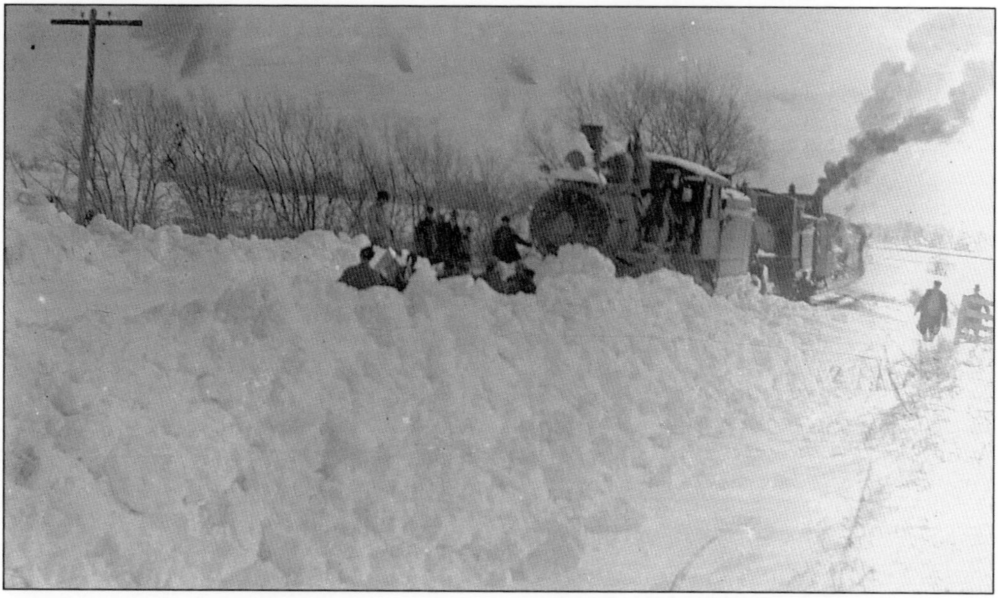

Travel across the snow-blown open prairie was usually not a problem for a locomotive until it came to brushy areas where high drifts often stopped the train on its tracks. It was up to a shovel-wielding crew to open the way. This scene from Springfield is from the early 1900s.

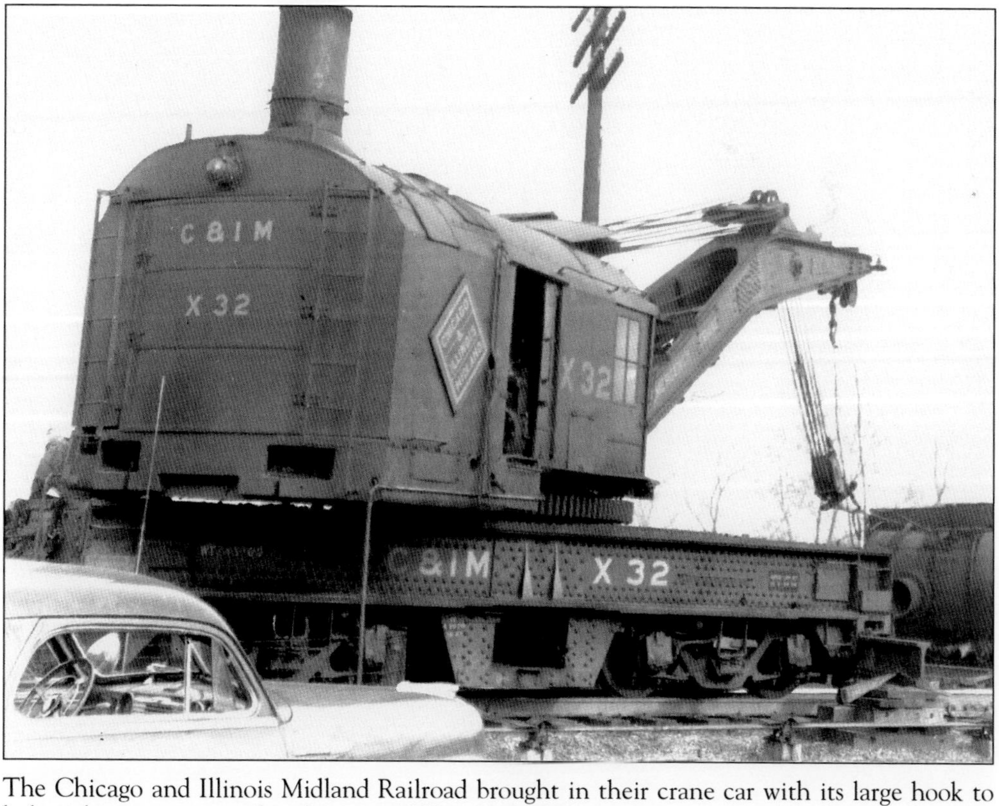

The Chicago and Illinois Midland Railroad brought in their crane car with its large hook to help right on overturned tank car in 1950.

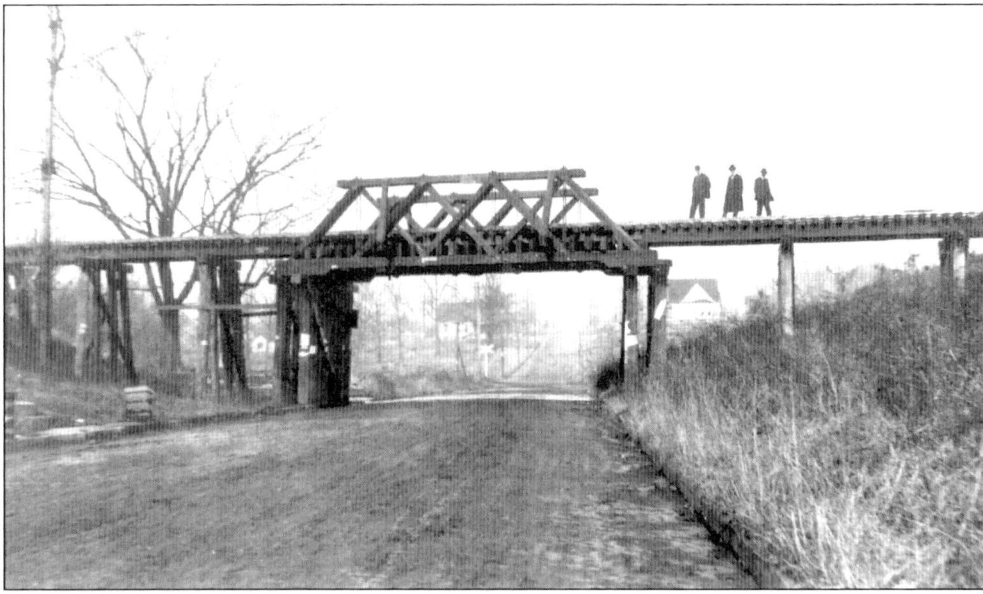

Bridges were often a necessity for railroads on central Illinois' rolling terrain. The bridge at top was located on North Walnut Street, and the one at bottom was on West Jefferson near Lincoln Avenue. Both photos are *c.* 1900.

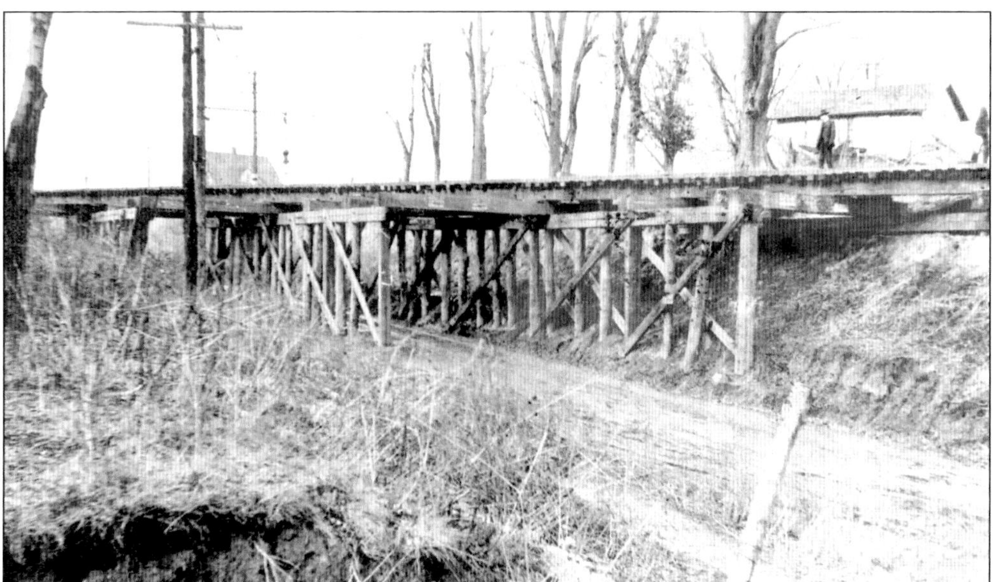

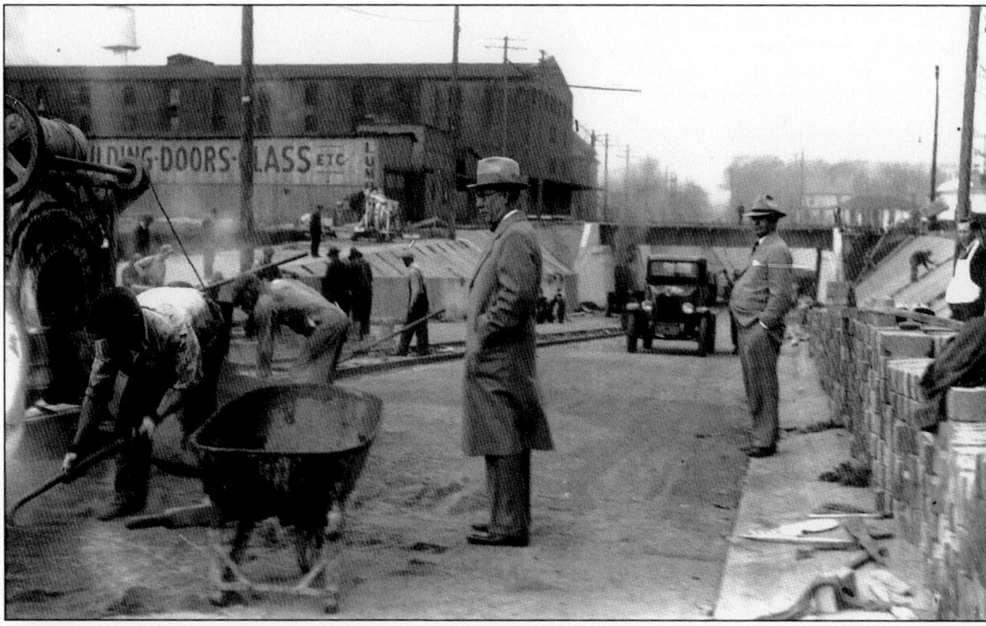

In 1931 merchants of the Southtown neighborhood were excited about the opening of a new subway underneath the Tenth Street railroad tracks at South Grand Avenue. Fred Horn of the Department of Streets and Public Improvements (center) watches workers complete brickwork on the pavement. Trains would no longer delay increasing auto traffic and many motorists would pass their business doors as people used the new underpass to avoid delays.

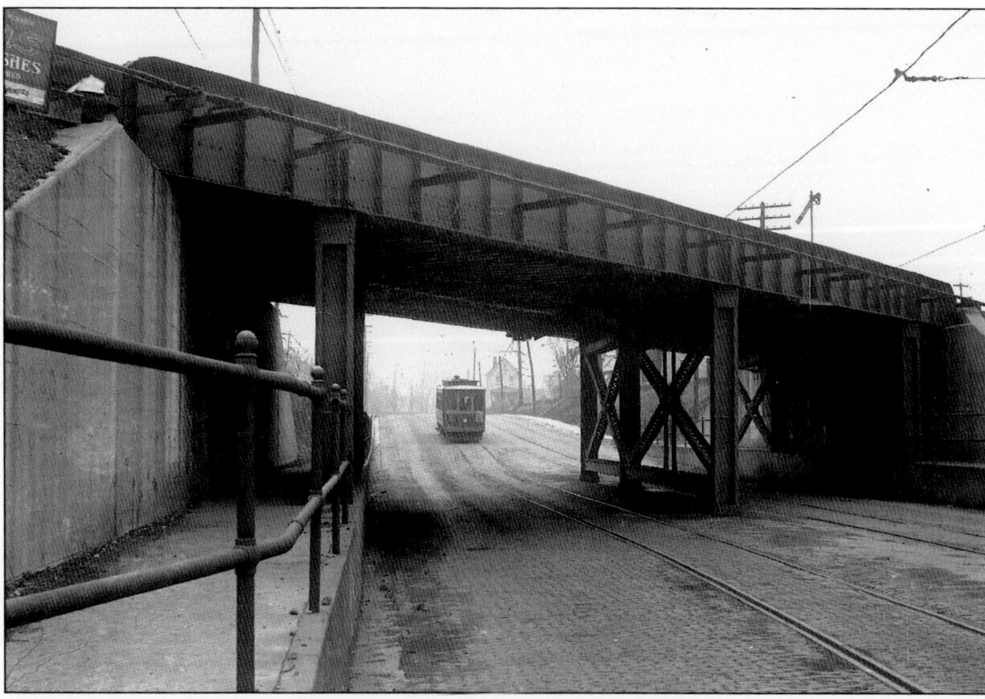

A Springfield streetcar is about to pass under the railroad bridge at Ninth Street north of Converse Avenue in the 1920s.

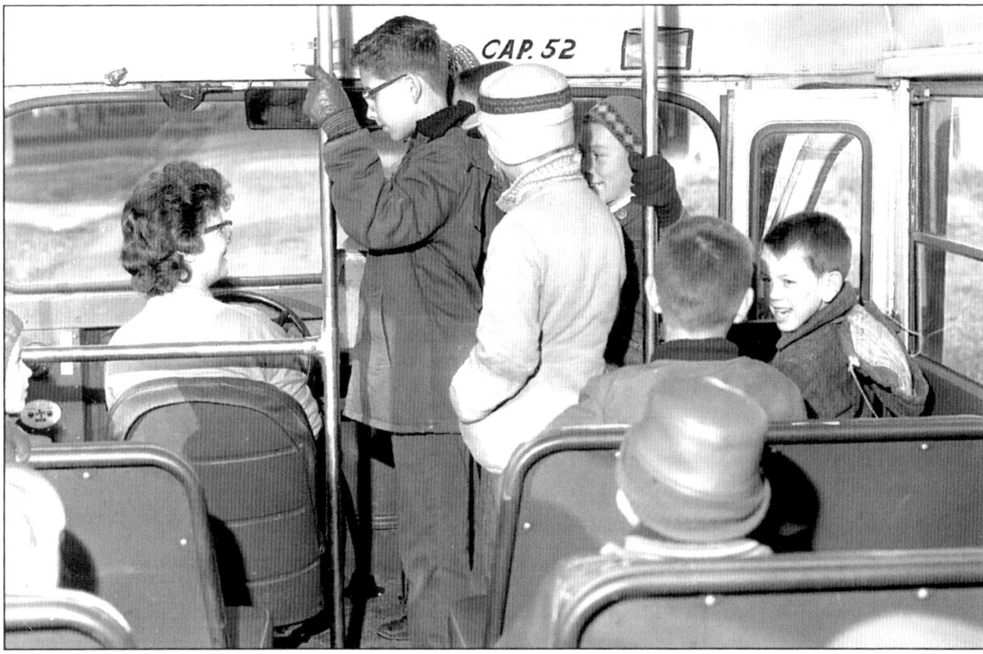

Riding the bus to school is a tradition for city and country children. This group of Springfield school kids climbs aboard in a 1950s scene.

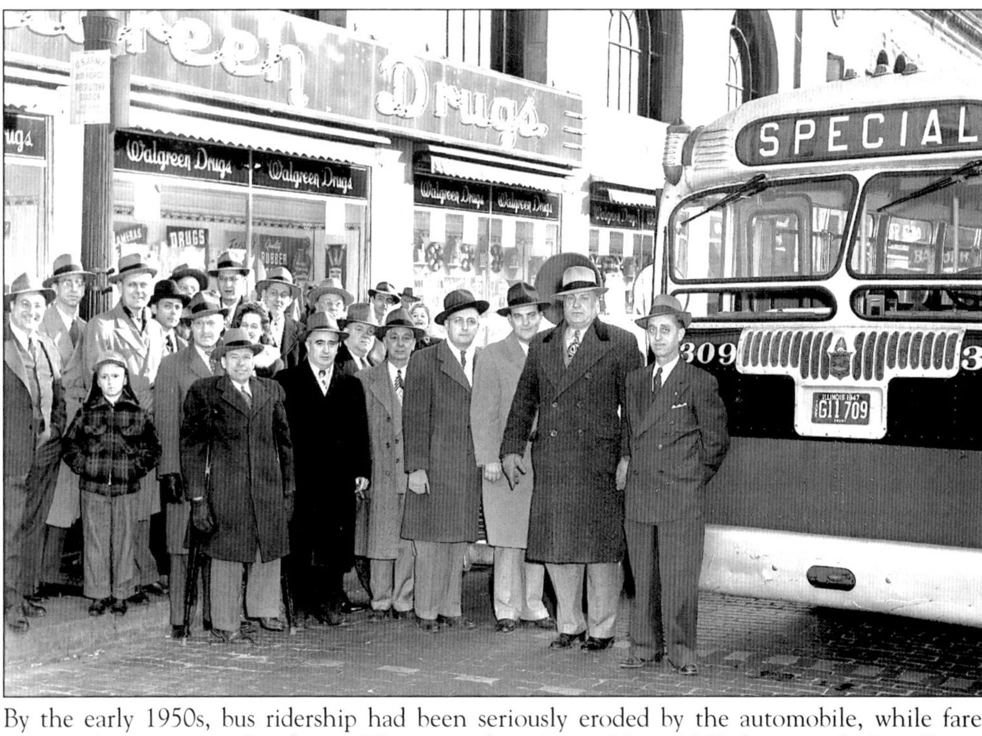

By the early 1950s, bus ridership had been seriously eroded by the automobile, while fares increased to keep up with inflation. They went from 11¢ to 15¢ in 1953, for example. Insufficient revenues dogged the Springfield Transportation Company for many years. Company officials are posed here.

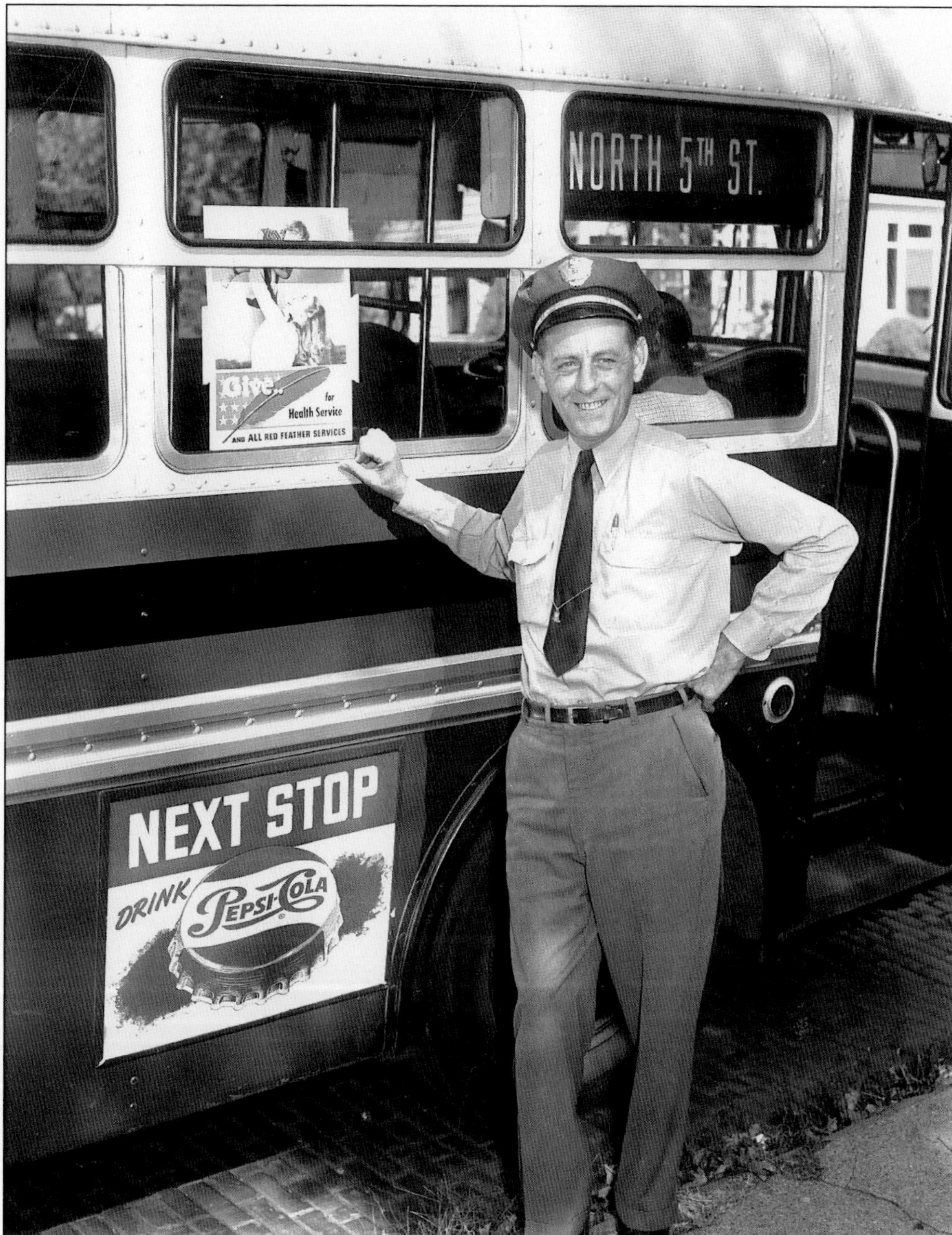

Bus driver Charles Seaborn strikes a jaunty pose in front of his North Fifth Street line bus in the 1950s. Seaborn had been a streetcar driver and made the transition to bus service. The Springfield Transportation Company experienced severe financial pressures in the 1950s, aggravated by a drivers' strike in 1955. The company refused also to pay a franchise fee to the city, the loss of which caused the layoff of 43 city Street Department employees who were paid from that fund. The big news for riders, however, were new wood and concrete benches painted with advertisements.

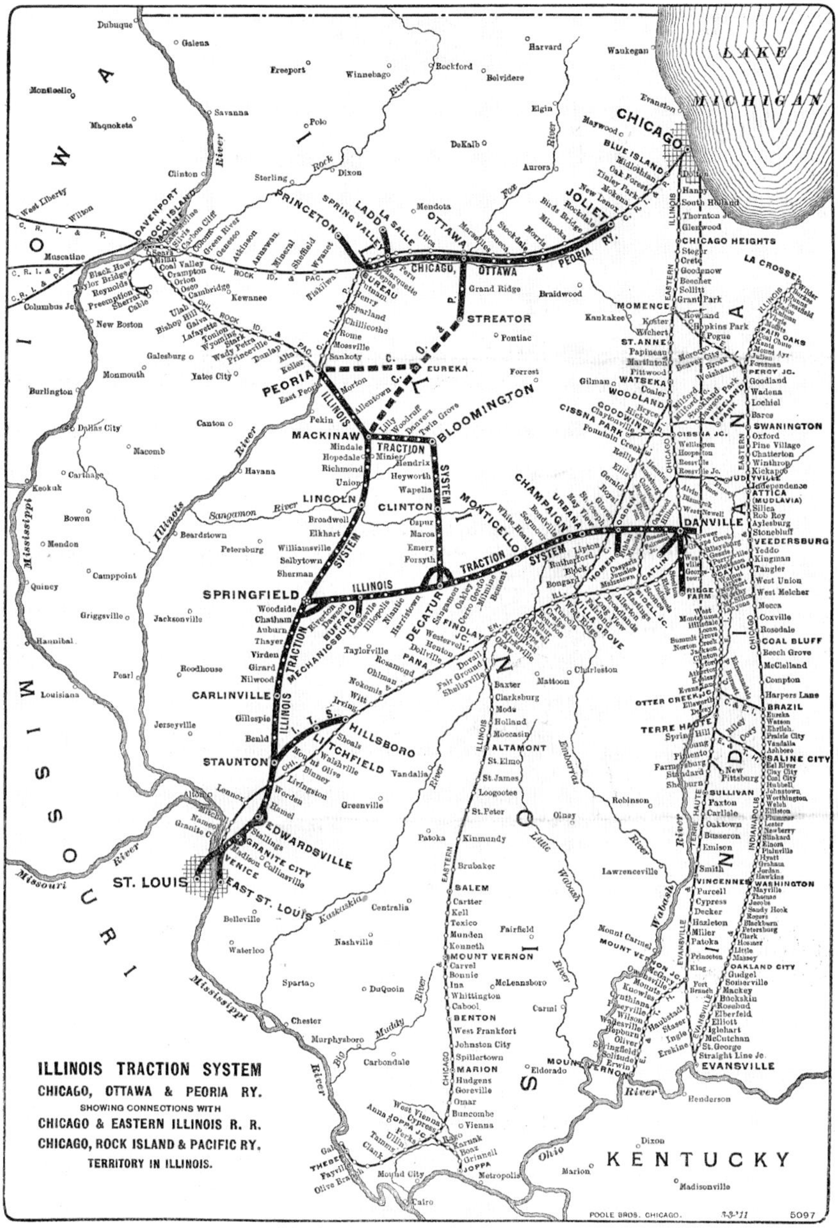

The Illinois Traction System, later known as the Illinois Terminal Company, was initially built as a passenger line running between communities and called by the new term Interurban. I.T.S. was one of the few electric rail systems that featured parlor and sleeping cars on its longer runs. This map shows its Illinois coverage.

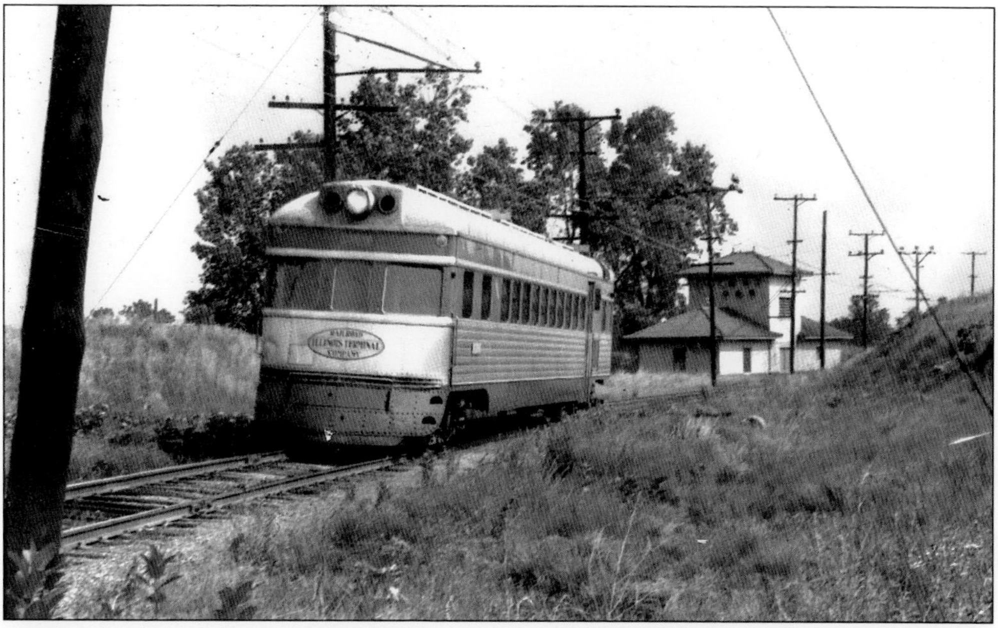

In 1948 the first of the streamlined cars were introduced on the Illinois Terminal Company's lines. Unfortunately, the stylish new cars could not save the company from its demise in the late 1950s as automobile travel prevailed. The train pictured here is pulling away from the Ridgely Depot on the city's north side.

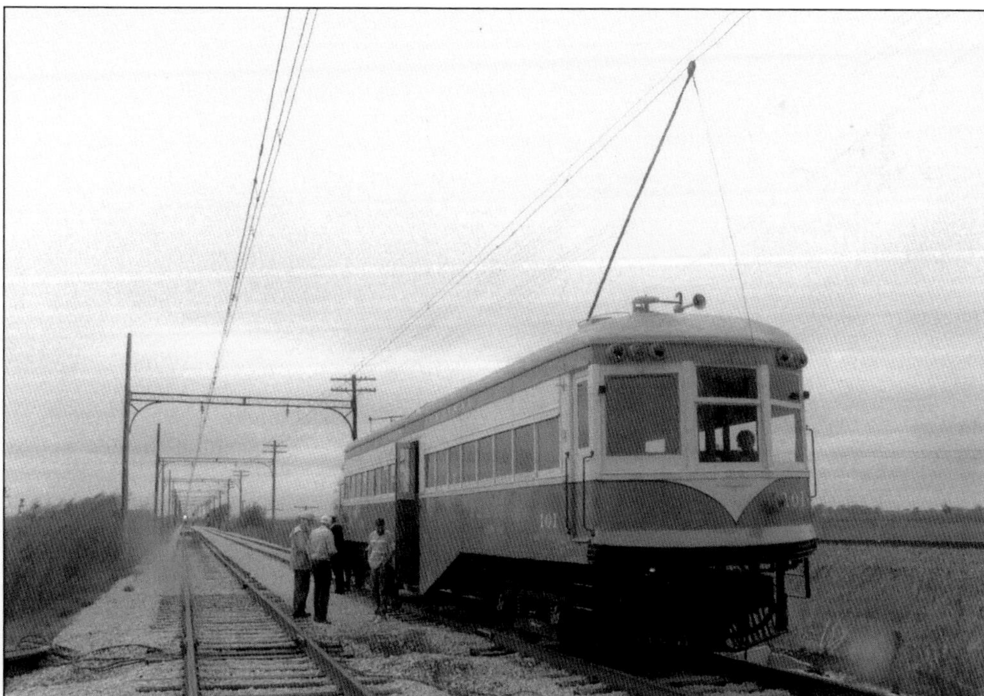

Some I.T.S. customers stretch their legs while awaiting repair for their electric train car that was temporarily stranded because of a power outage.

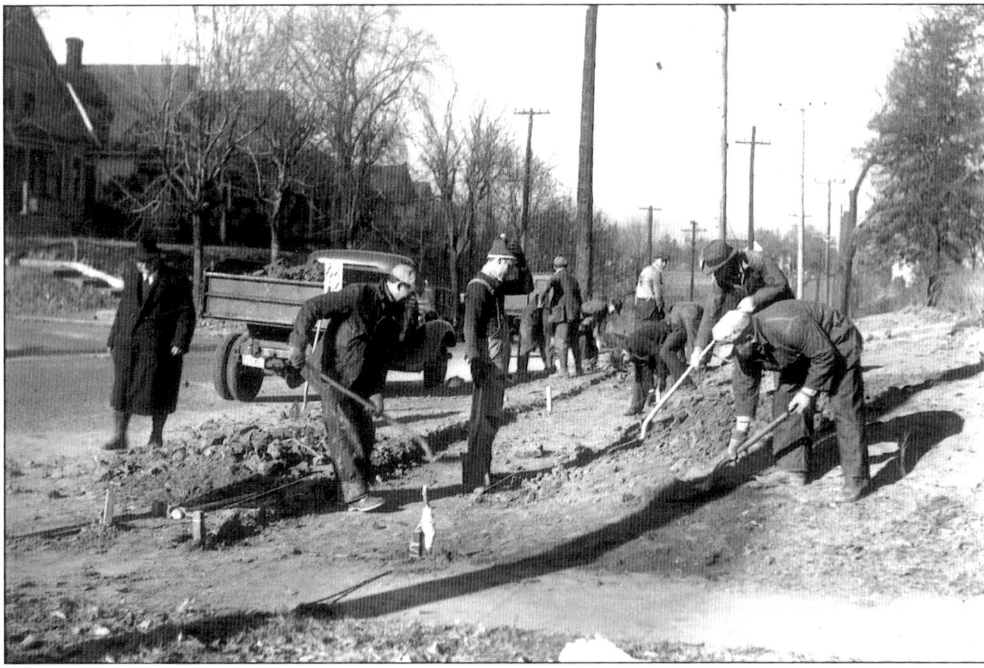

These men found useful employment during the Great Depression by working on a WPA project in Springfield. This group is busy leveling a place for a new sidewalk on North Walnut Street in 1935.

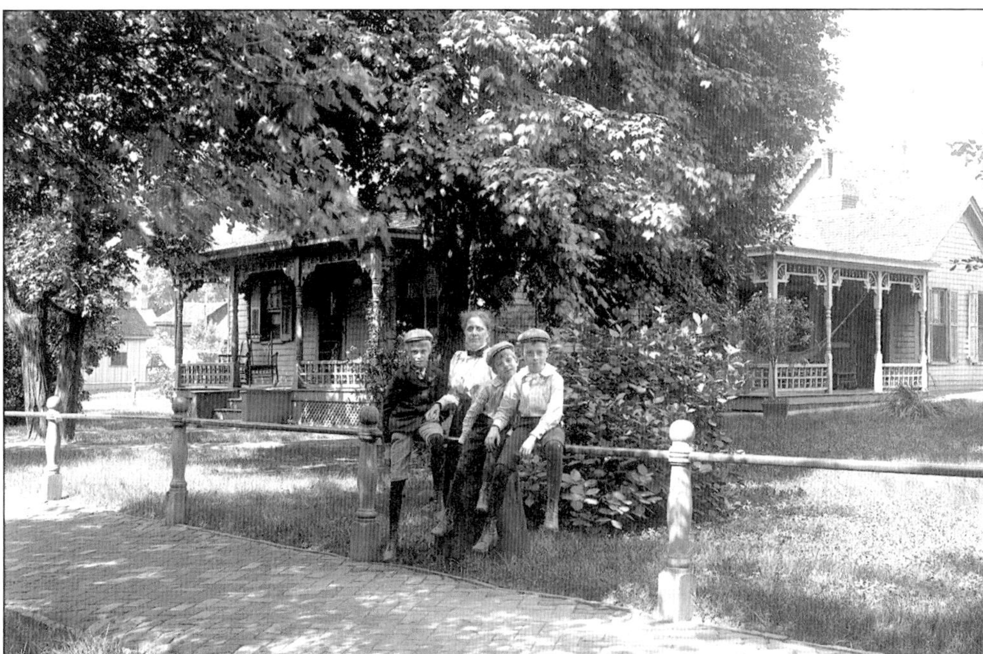

Well-laid brick sidewalks were quite an improvement over dirt or even plank sidewalks. Brick became common by the early 1900s. These Springfield children pose in front of an especially wide walk.

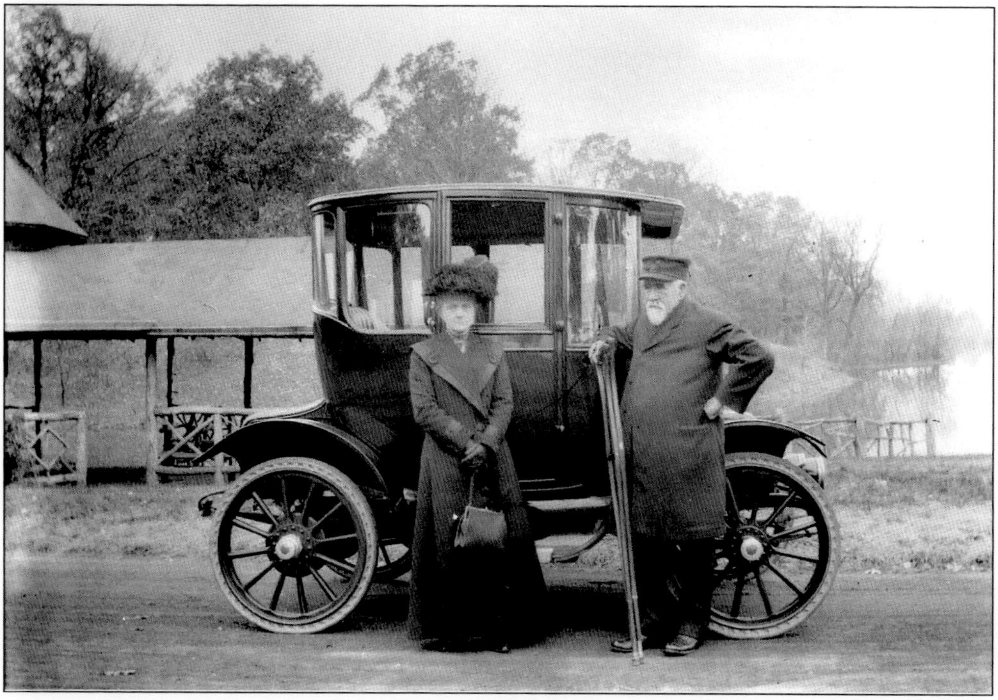

Springfield was once home to many wagon and carriage manufacturers. One of the largest was the firm of Booth and McCosker (below). Located at the corner of Eighth and Washington streets, this company produced hundreds of vehicles each year. Booth and McCosker sold their business in 1884 and moved into real estate investment. Amasa Booth traded in his horse and buggy for a new electric car by which he and wife stand proudly about 1908 (above).

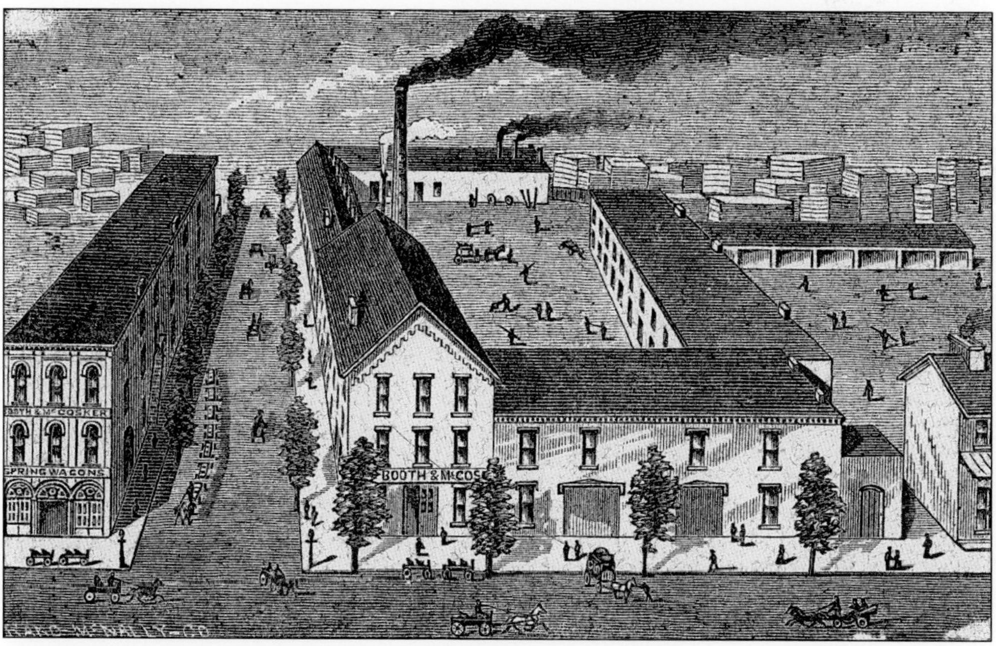

City streets undergo a constant process of change: paving, repairing, widening, and tearing up for sewer and other utility repairs. Some of it is subtle, but sometimes it's quite dramatic. The photo below shows 5th Street at Ash Street before the central green strip was removed in the 1950s (compare this scene with today). Commissioner Percy Darling (opposite, top) confers with other city officials on the state of storm sewers in a 1940s scene. Crews (opposite, below) repair South Grand Avenue about 1930.

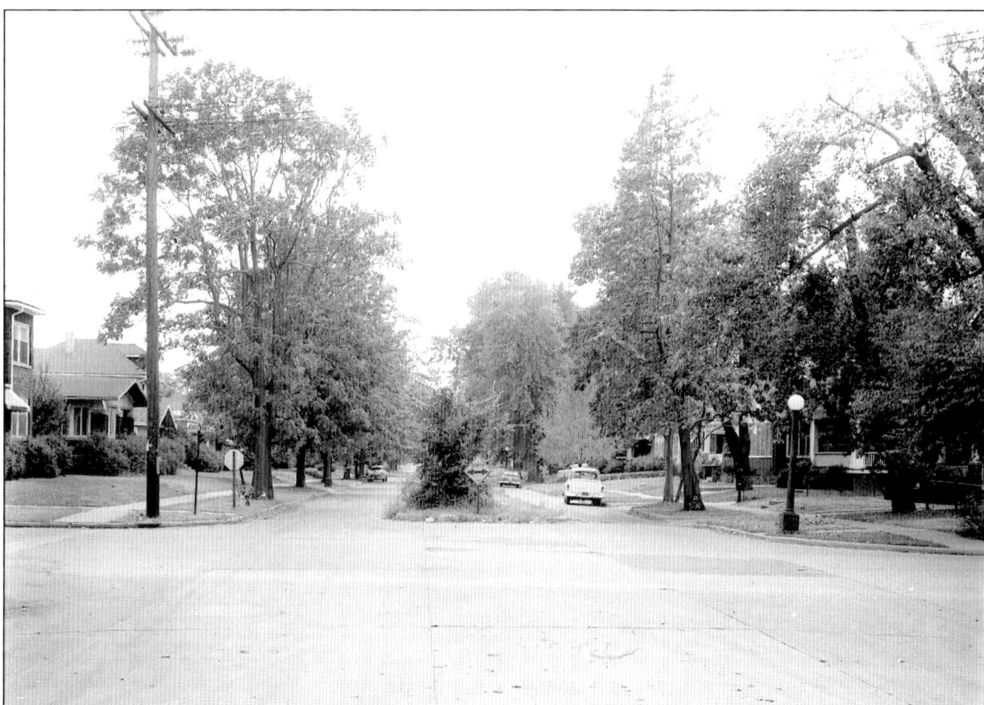

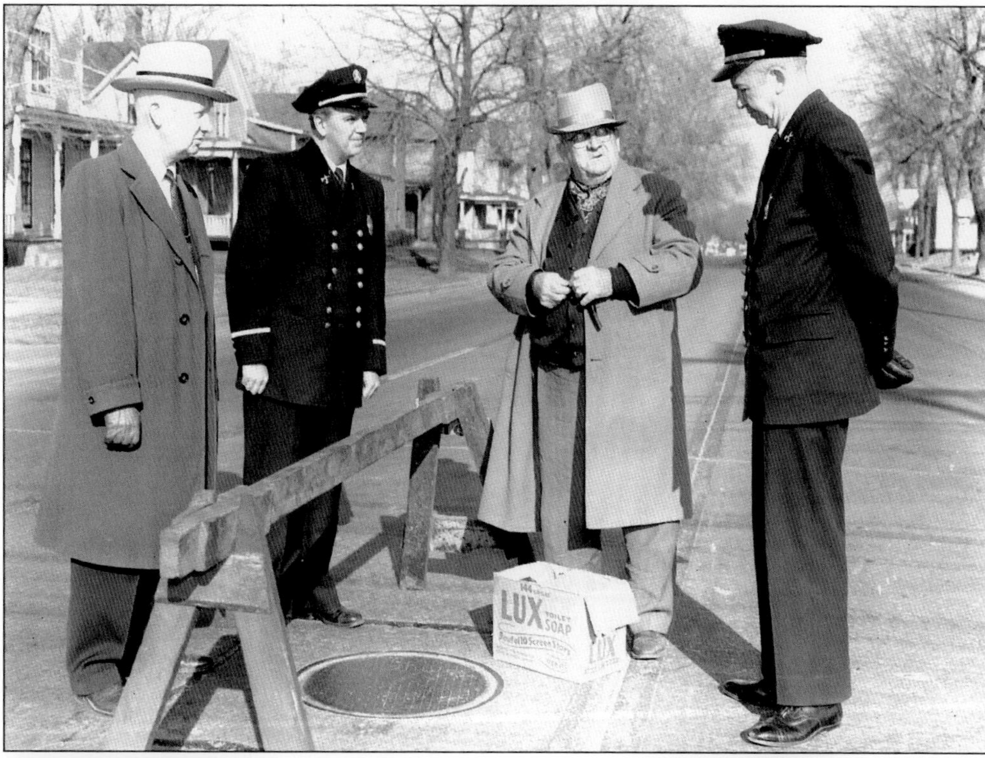
LUX
TOILET SOAP

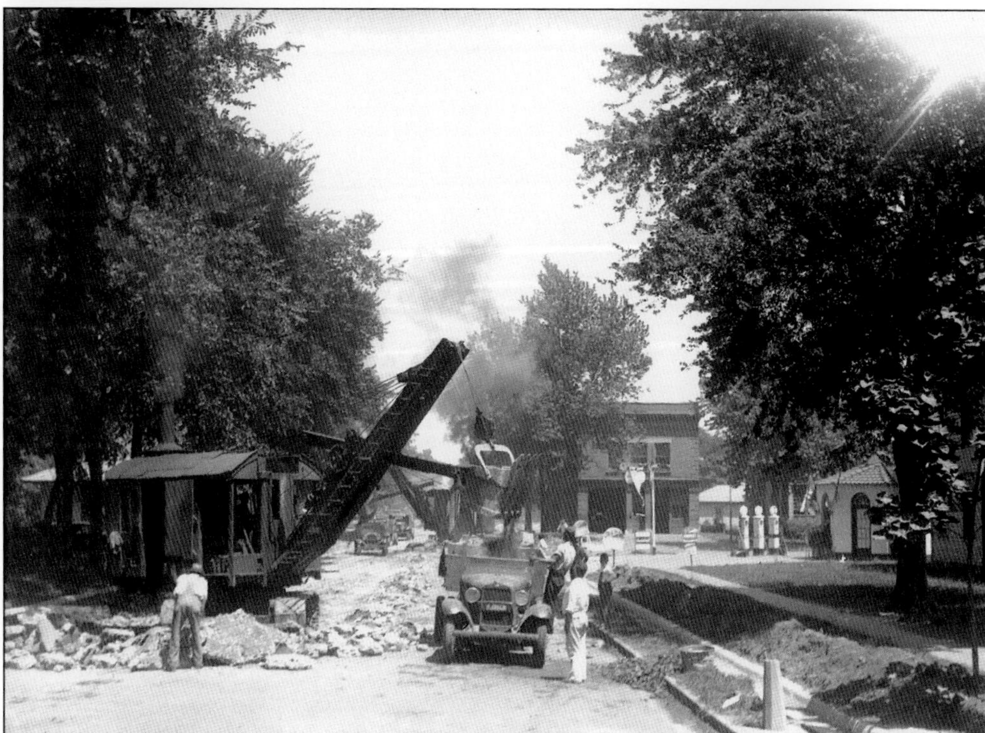

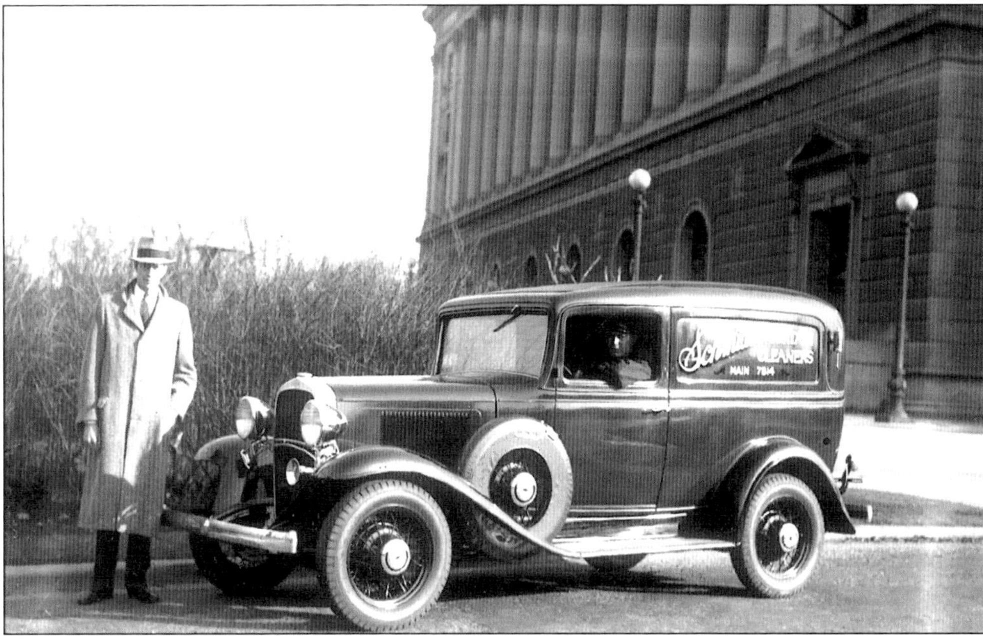

Connelly Chevrolet used a new 1933 delivery sedan purchased by Schmidt's Curtain Company in their ads to promote sales. The Centennial (now Howlett) Building can be seen on the right.

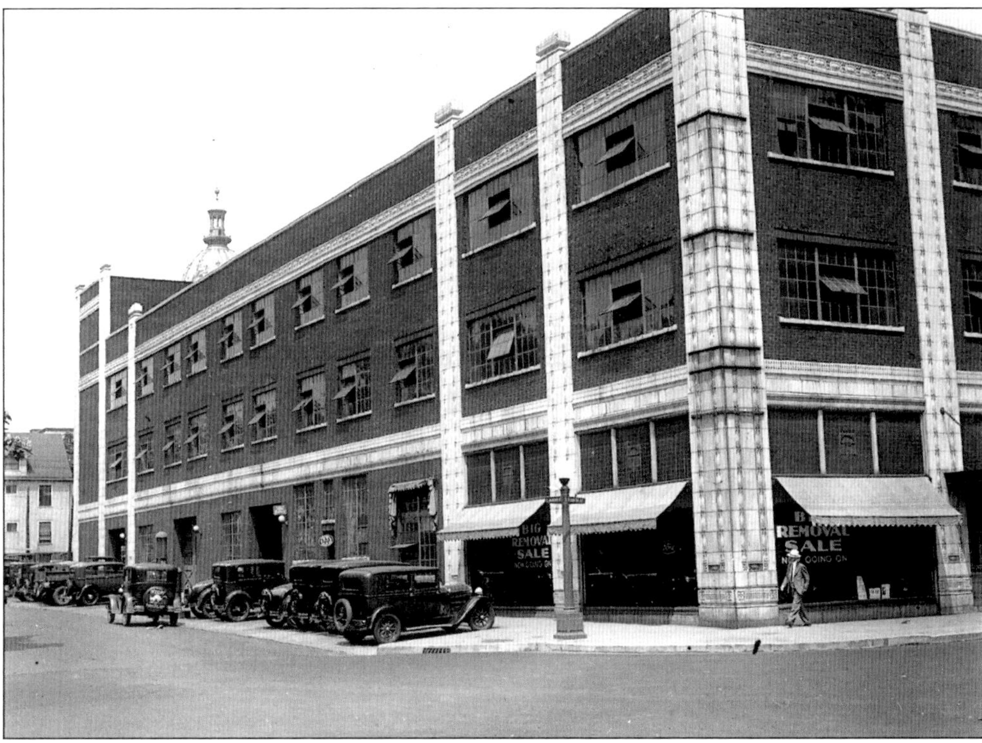

In 1933 S.N. Glisson, central Illinois car dealer, located his Springfield Ford and Lincoln service and sales center in the building on the corner of Fourth and Jackson Streets. Built as a Ford dealership about 1920, the building today houses State of Illinois offices

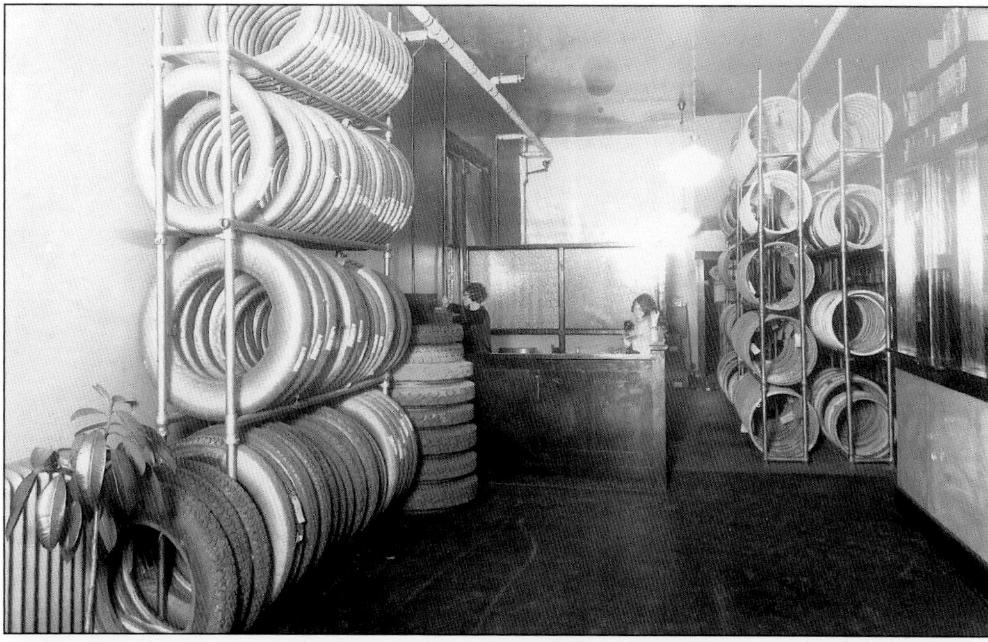

Racks of narrow tires ready for inner tubes and installation on 1920s cars surround the women working in the bookkeeping department of the Capitol 24 Tire Company at 208-210 North Sixth Street. Every square inch of space was crucial for the busy firm.

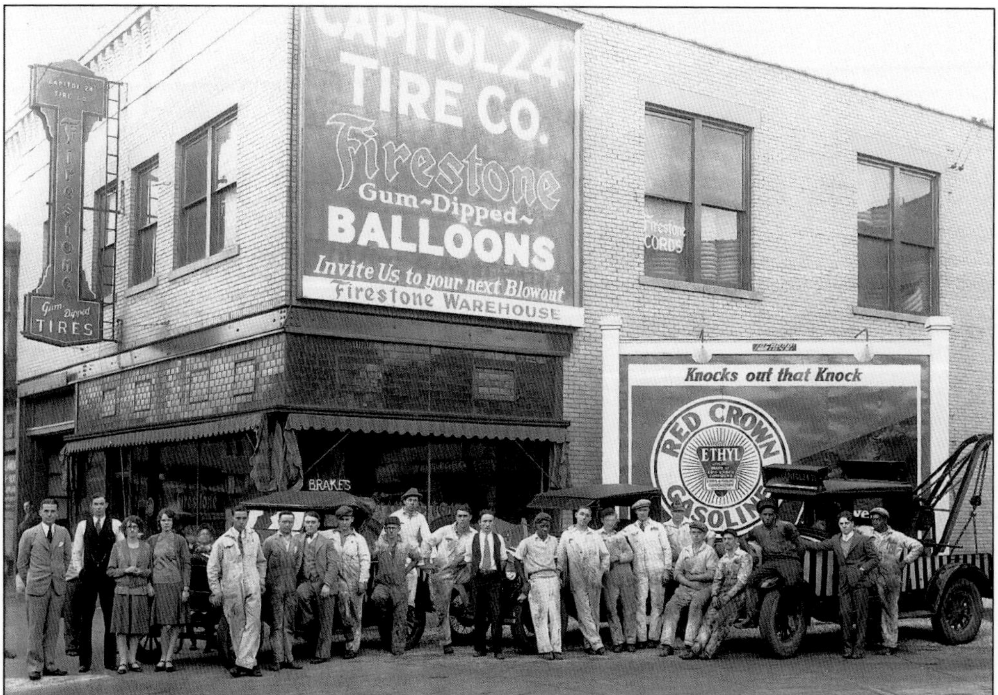

Capitol 24 employees pose for a group photo under a sign that encourages customers to invite them to "your next blowout." Thankfully, the days of frequent flat tires and inner tubes that need replacing or patching are long gone.

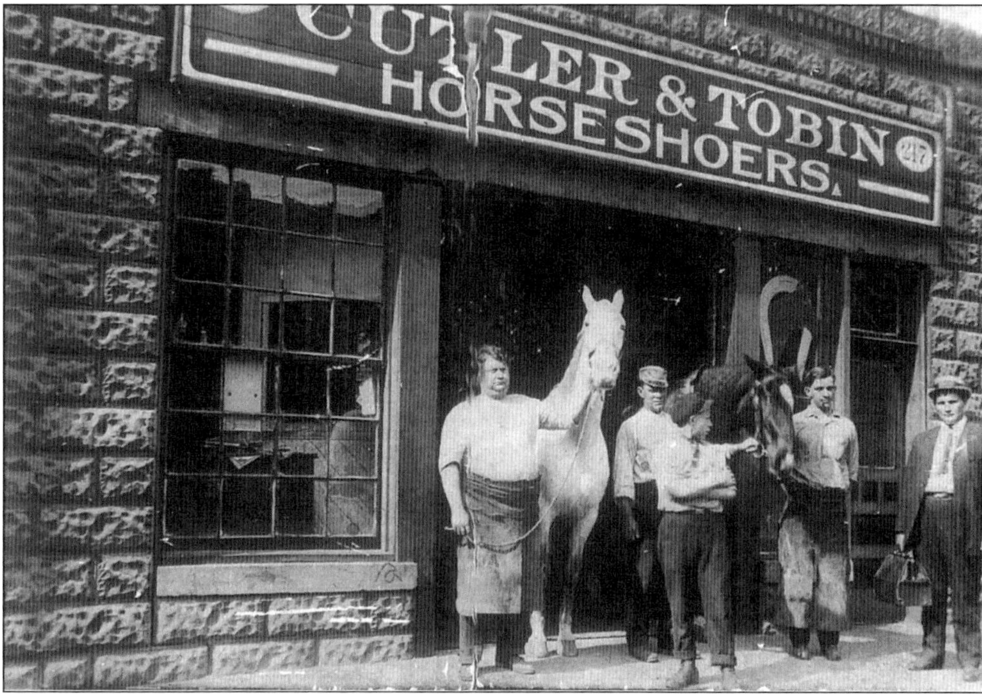

Horseshoers and blacksmiths were responsible for keeping Springfield horses and mules well shod. When Frederick Cutler opened for business about 1904, he joined 22 other smiths and horseshoers in Springfield. Cutler moved his operation to 217 East Washington and took on Edward Tobin as a partner about 1912. This partnership lasted less than two years before Cutler was murdered by his mistress in a Springfield boarding house in 1914.

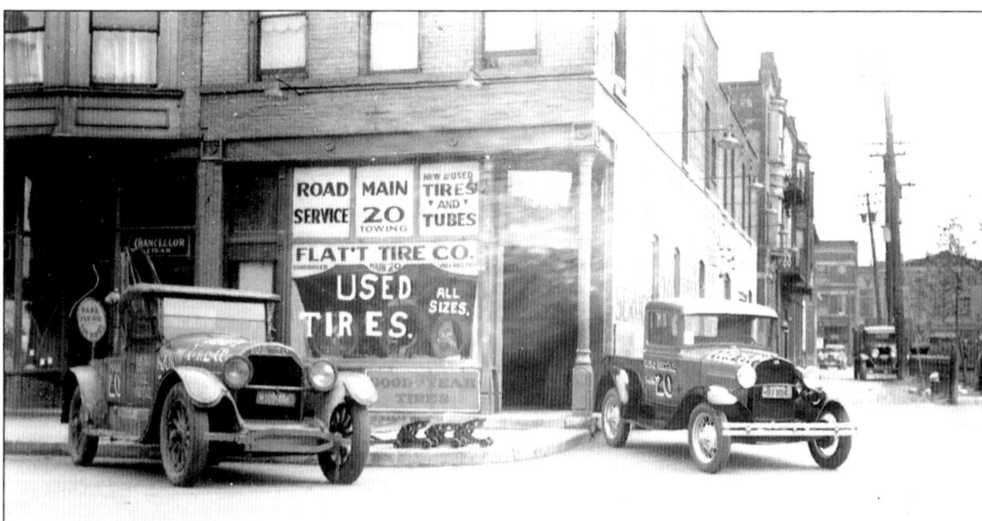

Stranded motorists with tire trouble had only to call the unfortunately named Flatt Tire Company for dependable and inexpensive service. The company's high-powered Cadillac truck at left was available for towing, while the light truck at right provided tire service on the spot.

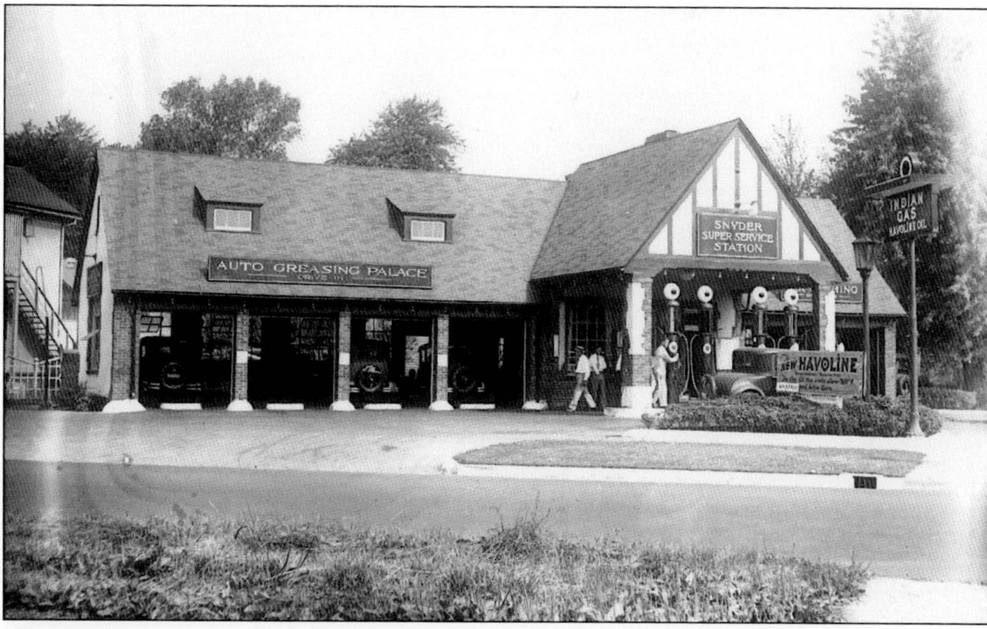

Many early gas stations had their own distinct style of architecture aimed at blending in with residential neighborhoods. This Tudor Revival structure was used by the Indian Gas and Oil Company in Springfield at its station located on the northwest corner of Fifth Street and South Grand Avenue.

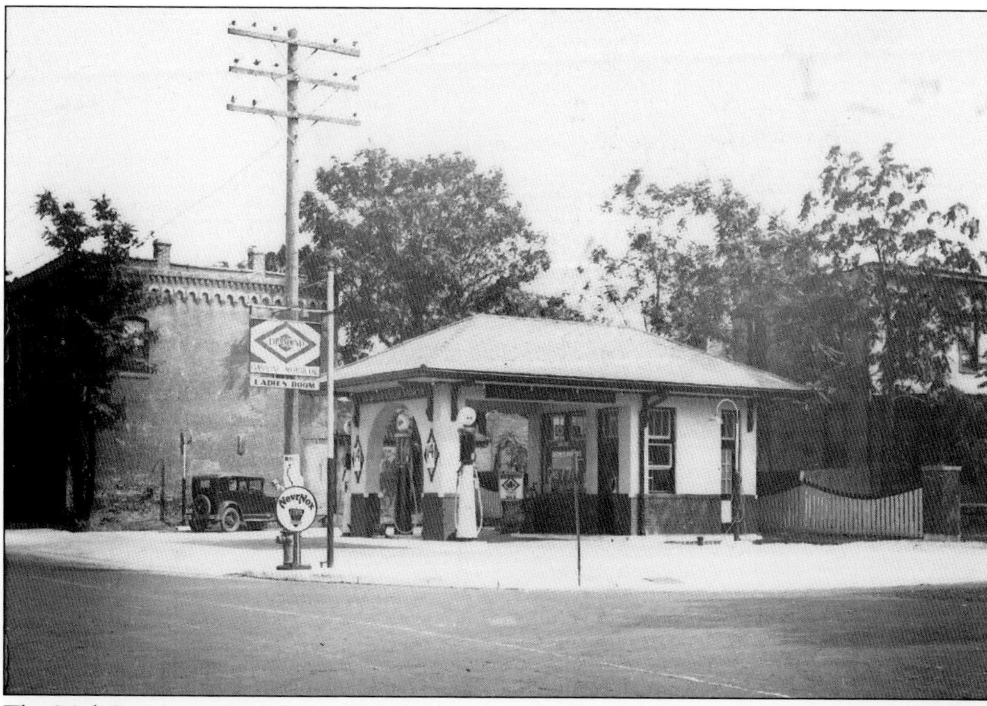

The Mid-Continent Petroleum Corporation was just one of many oil companies that opened a string of service stations in Springfield in the 1920s and 1930s. Ralph S. Rodgers sold the company's Diamond brand of gasoline at his station at 800 East Jefferson.

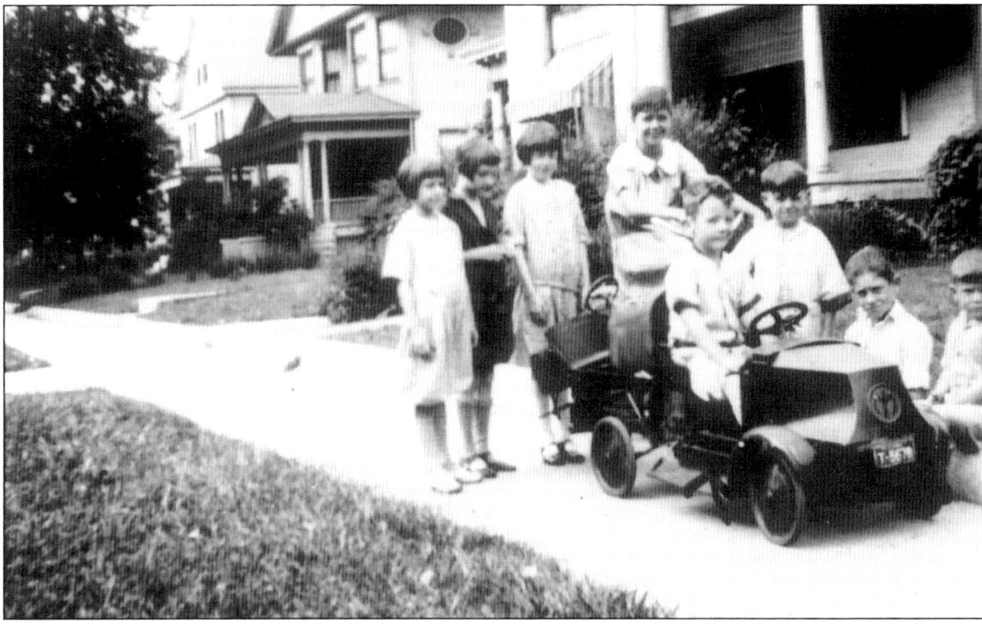

These neighborhood kids on Holmes Avenue in the 1920s are getting their first experiences behind the wheel. The automobile fascinated children from its first days, and then, just as now, few could resist its siren call when they were old enough to drive.

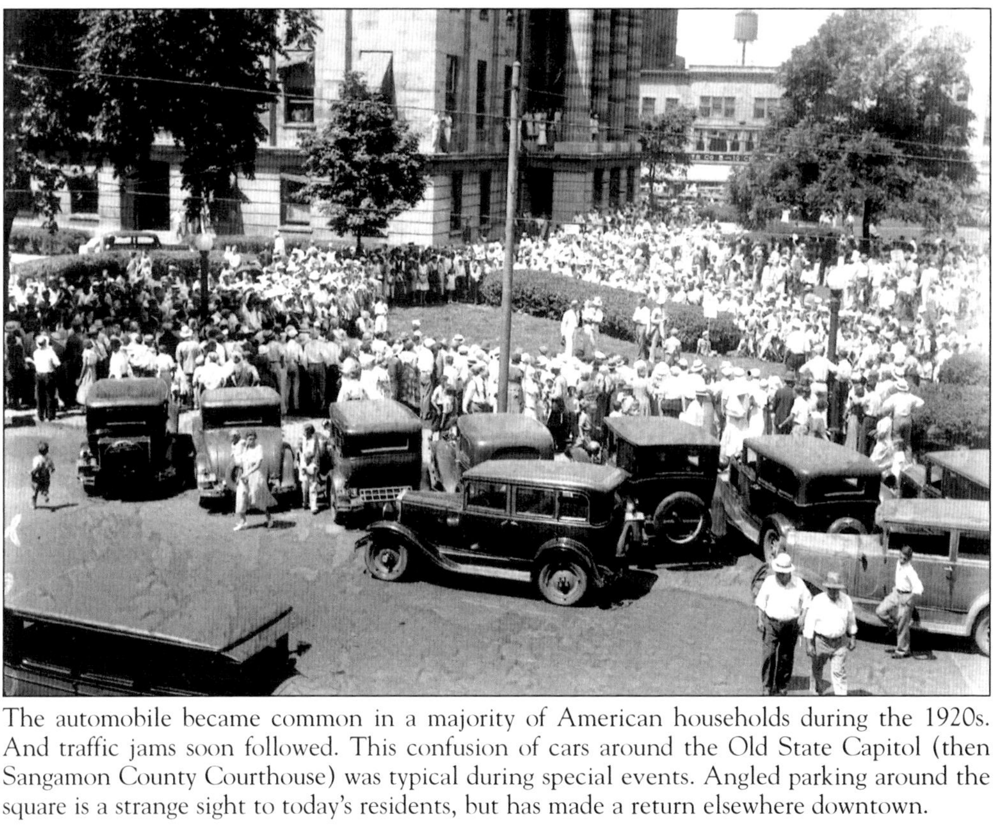

The automobile became common in a majority of American households during the 1920s. And traffic jams soon followed. This confusion of cars around the Old State Capitol (then Sangamon County Courthouse) was typical during special events. Angled parking around the square is a strange sight to today's residents, but has made a return elsewhere downtown.

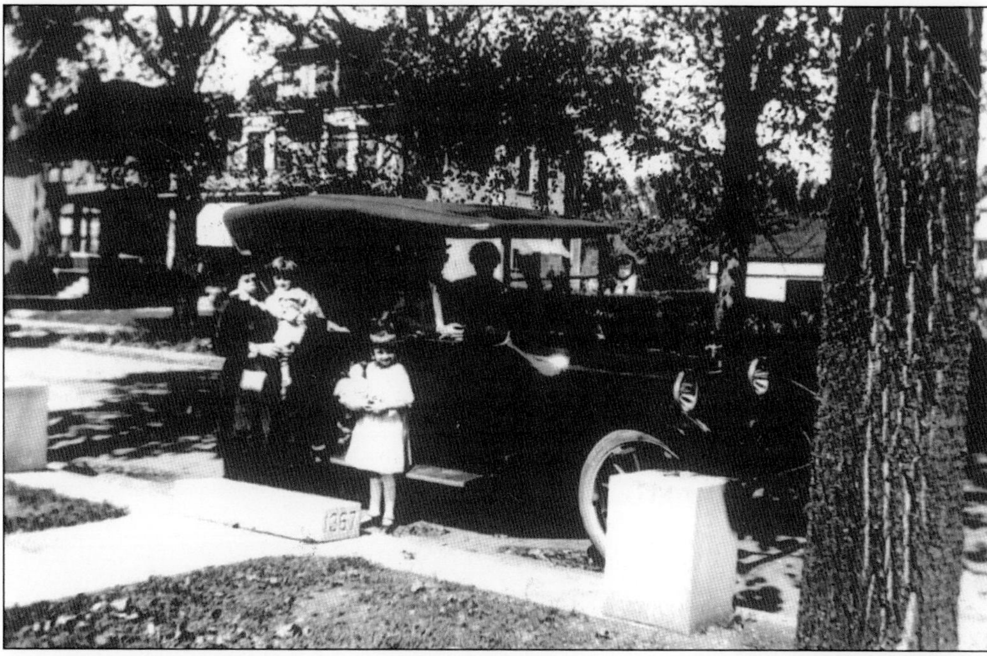

A "touring car" was the ancestor to today's family sedan. There was room for the entire family or a group of friends. The canvas top could be lowered on a nice day or side curtains hurriedly attached when it rained. The Dr. Clarence Milligan family alights in front of their home at 1427 Holmes Avenue after a pleasure ride in the 1920s.

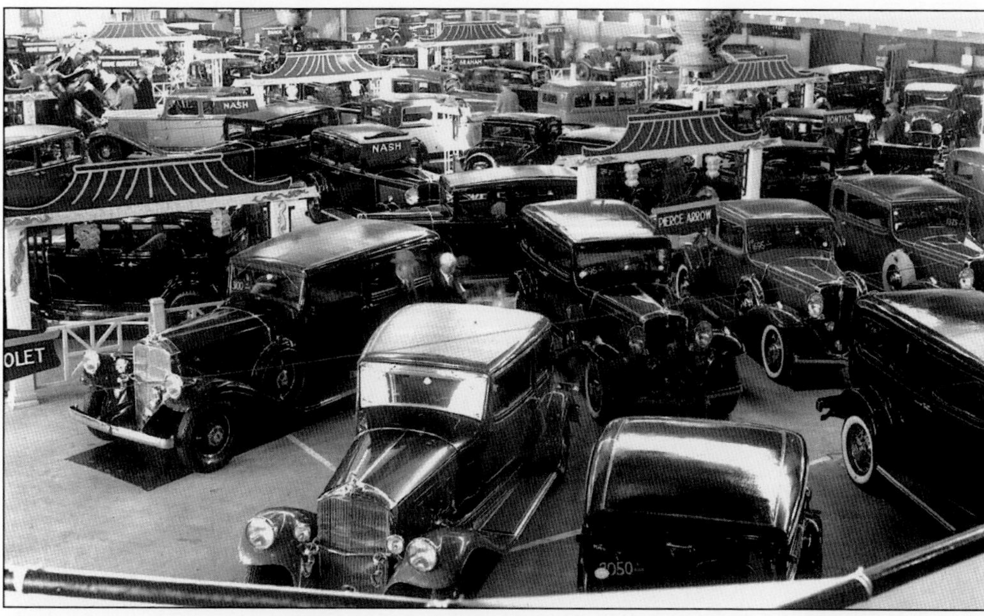

Shiny paint and chrome polished to perfection have long been part of the appeal to new car buyers. But the auto show, where dealers parade their new models, can be almost overwhelming to prospective purchasers. This show of about 1928 was one held annually in the old State Arsenal Building, where the current Armory stands at Second and Adams. Nearly every Springfield dealer participated in the popular event.

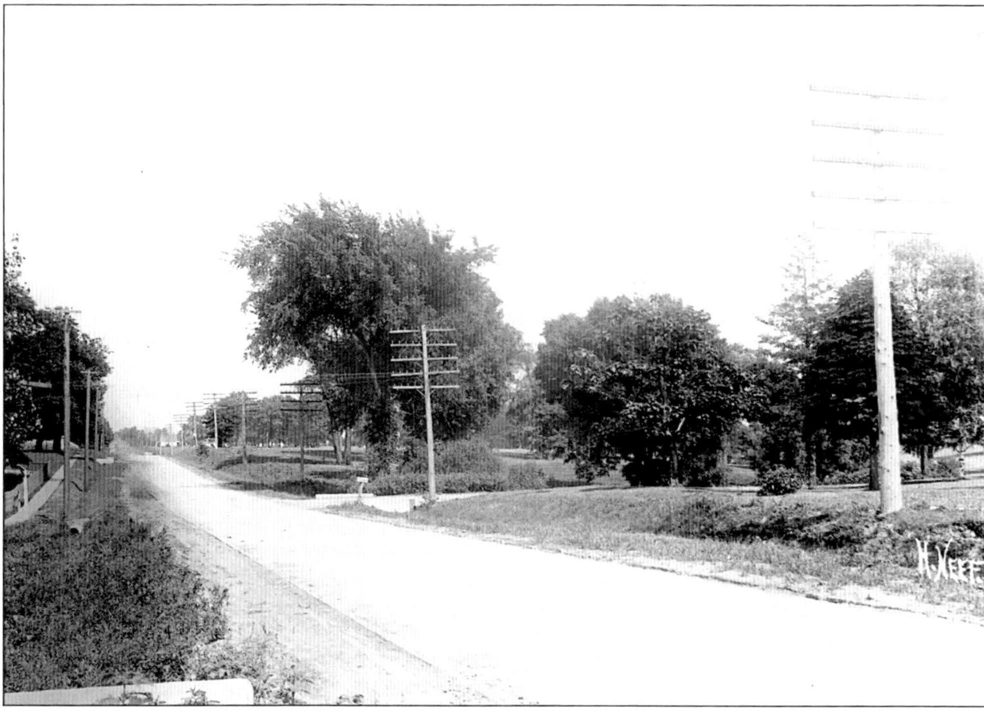

Today's busy, paved, four-lane Chatham Road is all but unrecognizable in the 1920s scene. The oiled dirt road was then a quiet country lane. The photo is looking south near Old Jacksonville Road.

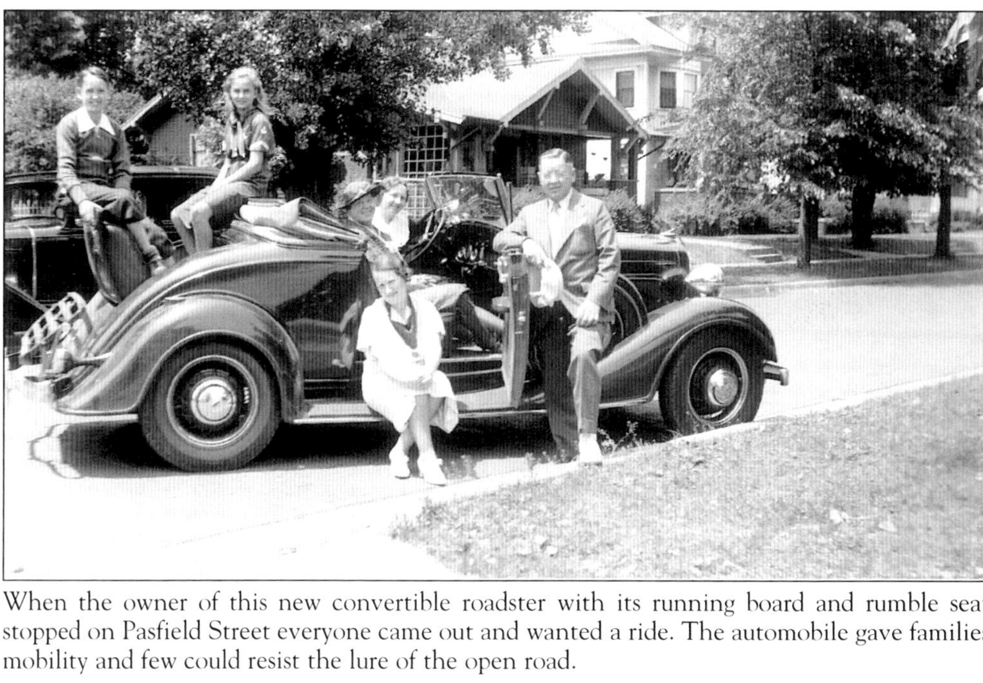

When the owner of this new convertible roadster with its running board and rumble seat stopped on Pasfield Street everyone came out and wanted a ride. The automobile gave families mobility and few could resist the lure of the open road.

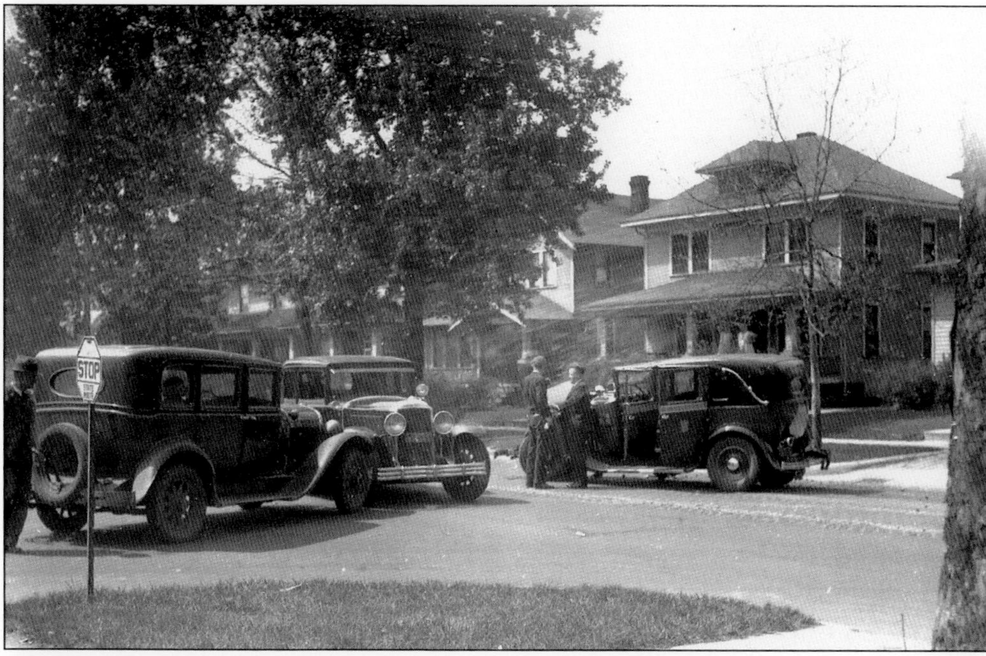

Who has the right of way appears to be the question at hand in this quiet neighborhood about 1930. Auto accidents were one of the consequences of growing automobile congestion in the United States.

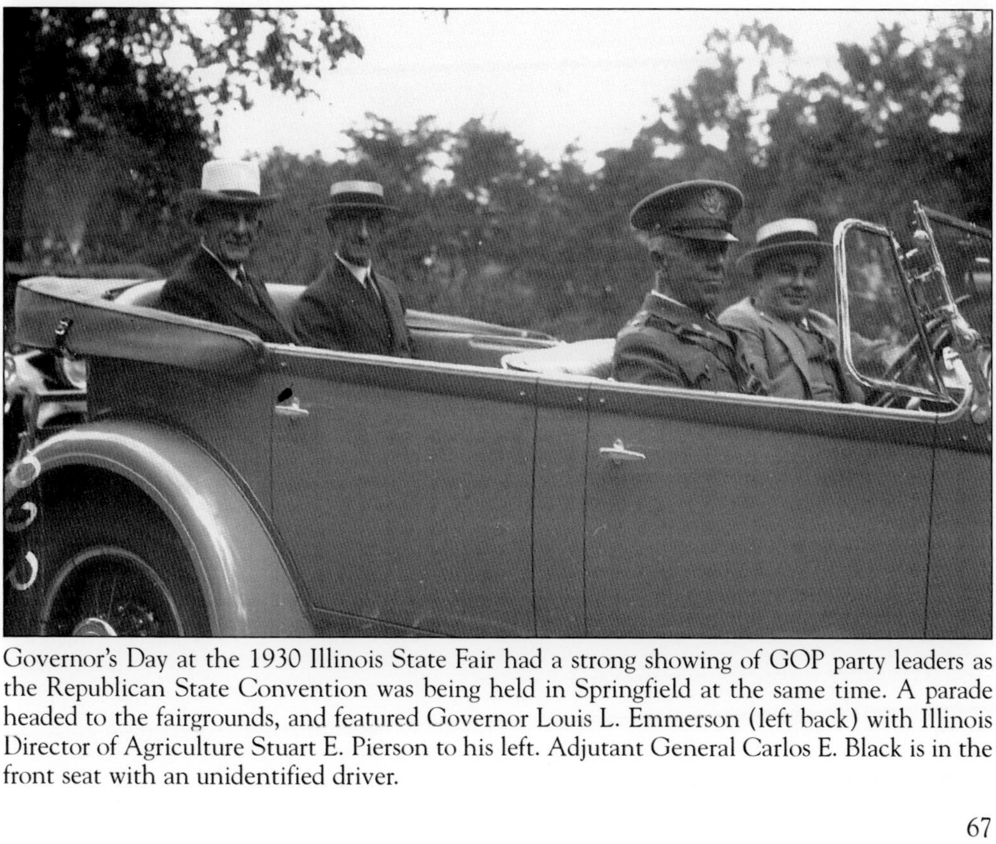

Governor's Day at the 1930 Illinois State Fair had a strong showing of GOP party leaders as the Republican State Convention was being held in Springfield at the same time. A parade headed to the fairgrounds, and featured Governor Louis L. Emmerson (left back) with Illinois Director of Agriculture Stuart E. Pierson to his left. Adjutant General Carlos E. Black is in the front seat with an unidentified driver.

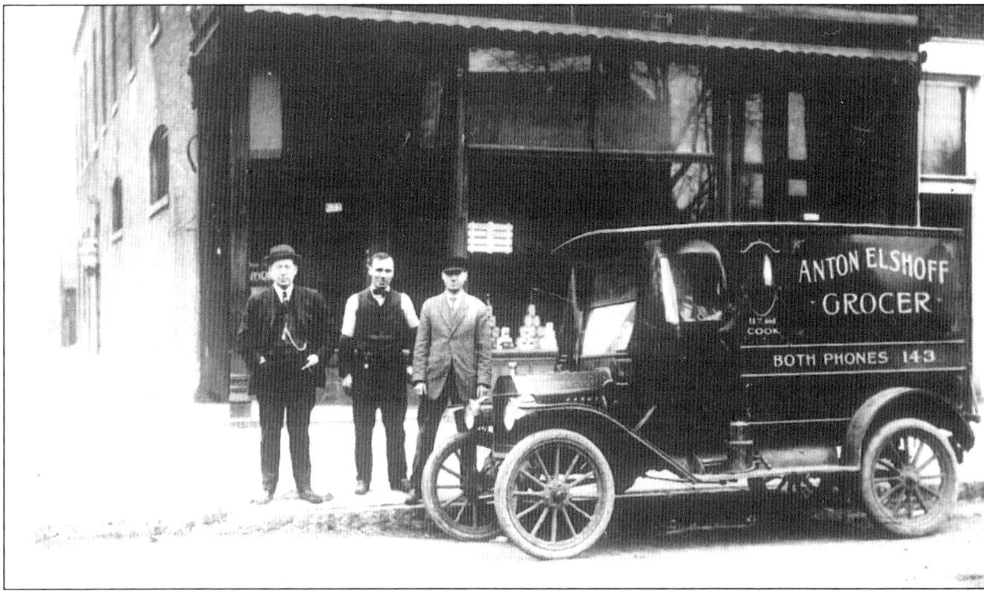

The horse-drawn delivery wagon was replaced by the arrival of the automobile in the early 1900s. Springfield businessmen, especially grocers like Anton Elshoff, quickly took advantage of the new mode of transportation. Elshoff stands by his delivery truck at in front of his store at the northwest corner of Eleventh and Cook Streets in this scene.

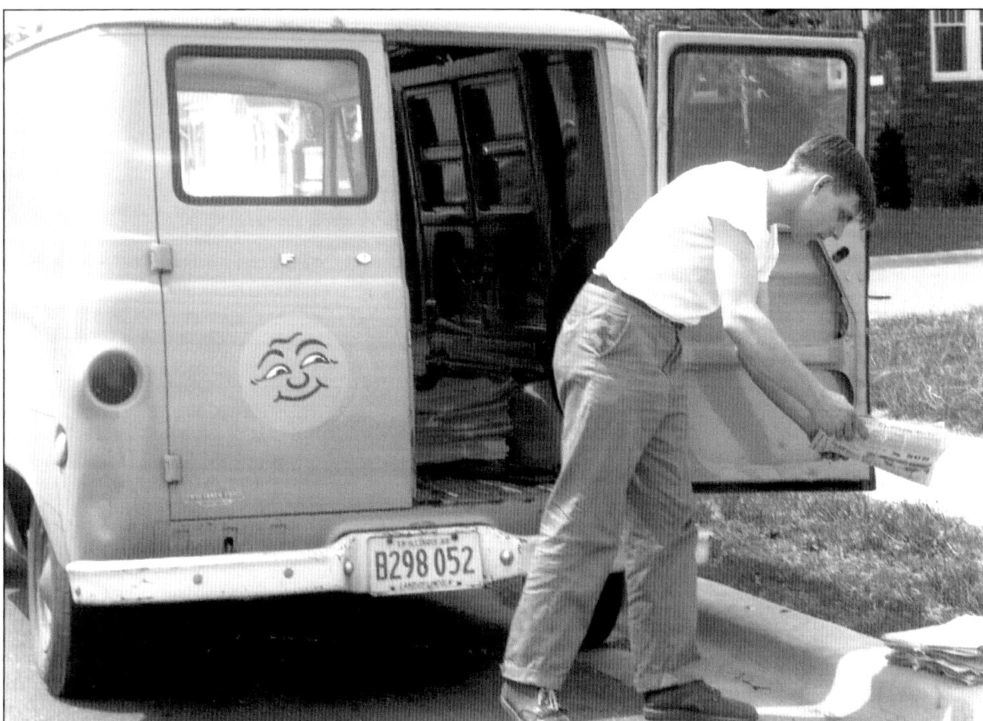

This employee of the *Springfield Sun* newspaper drops off bundles of papers to be delivered to homes throughout the city. The paper operated in the 1960s and closed its doors in 1973.

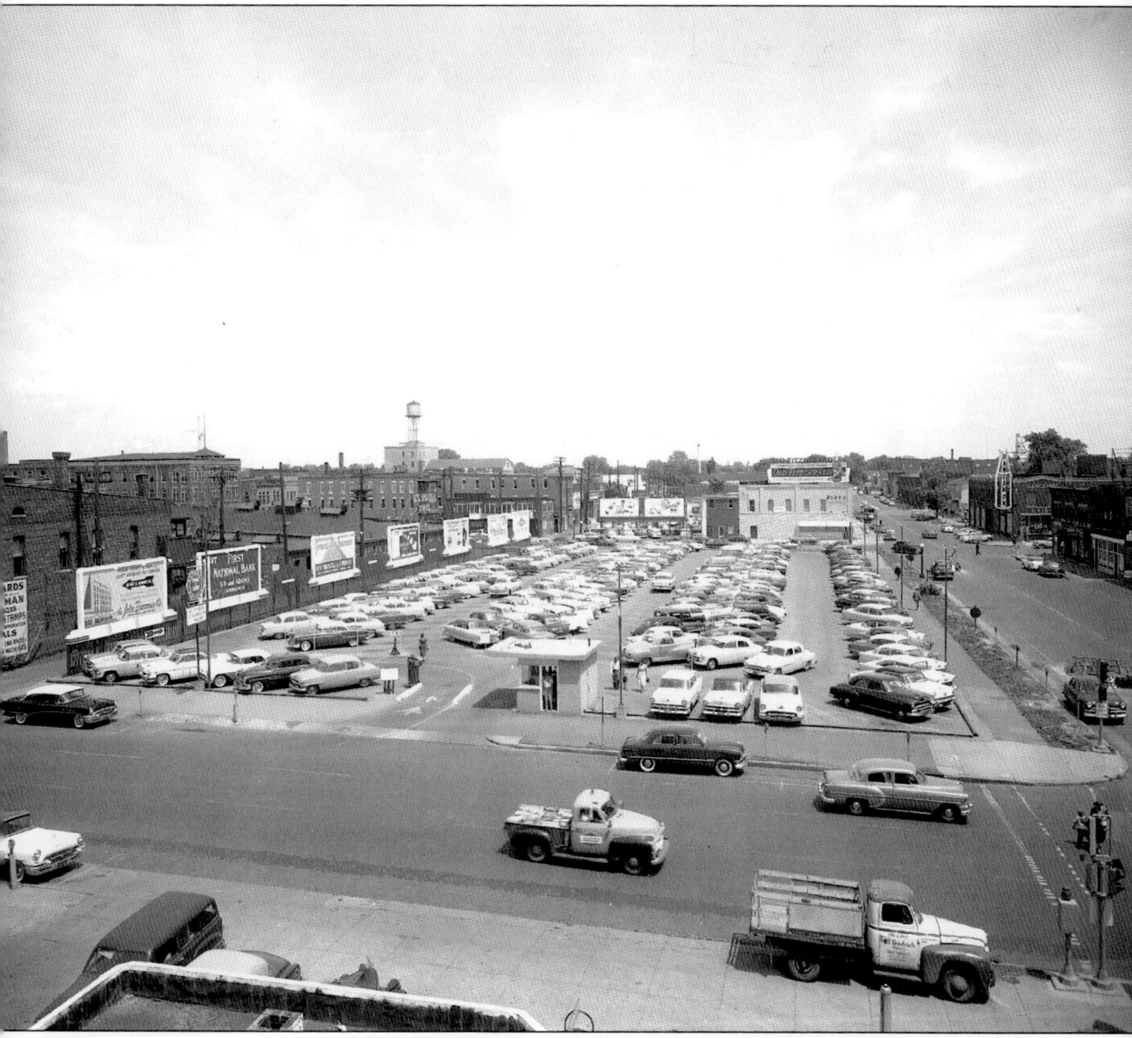

The automobile has been responsible for dramatically changing the landscape of downtown Springfield over the past 75 years. As more and more people commuted to work in Springfield, more parking spaces were needed. Older buildings were demolished to make way for parking lots. This lot at the northeast corner of Seventh and Monroe streets was once the site of a Catholic Church. The nearly surreal view makes stunningly clear the auto's effect on downtown.

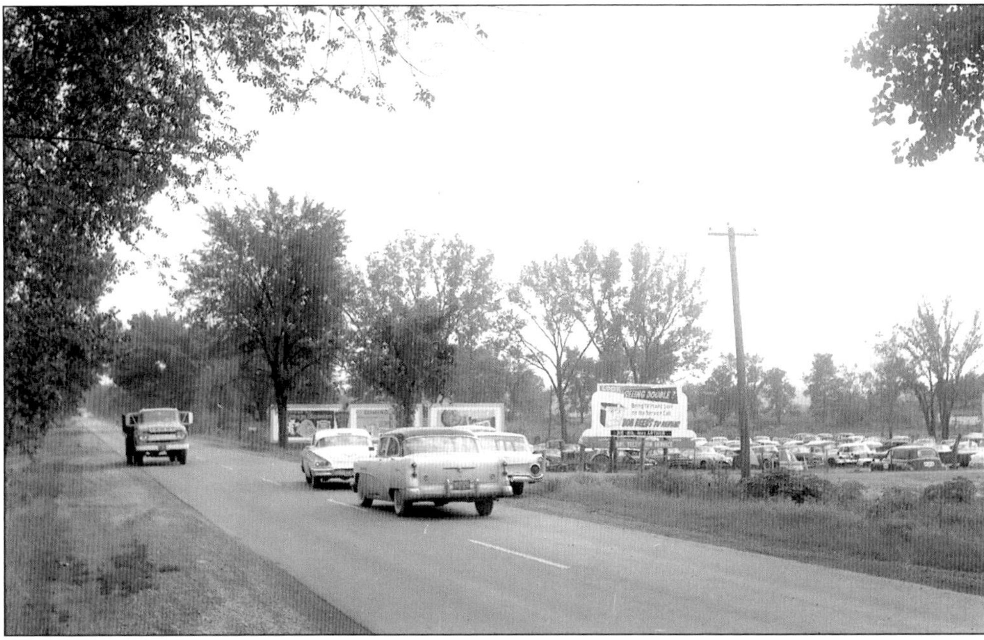

Cars made great inroads into our daily lives after World War II. The "super highway" system of the 1950s, built allegedly as an evacuation route in case of nuclear attack, became a great escape route in another way. Millions of people headed off exploring the country, but our automania came at a price. Auto graveyards, for example, like this one near Springfield, despoiled countryside nationwide. . .

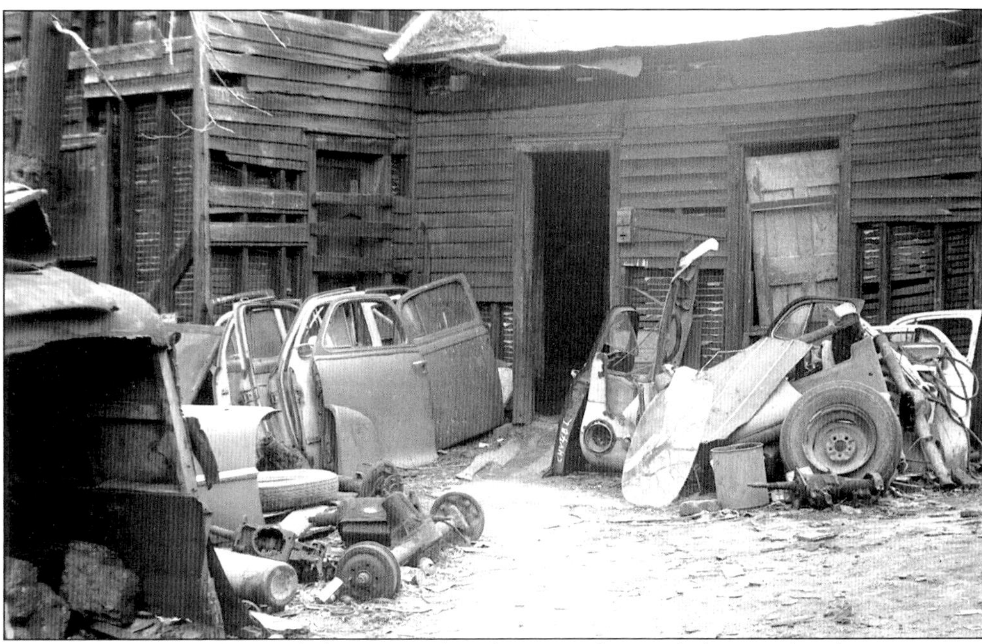

. . .and the detritus of cars piled up in "junkyards" everywhere—skeletons of no longer exciting autos were tossed aside as we raced to embrace the latest model. This photo was made as part of a survey of Springfield's substandard housing in the 1950s.

Three

SPRINGFIELD AT PLAY

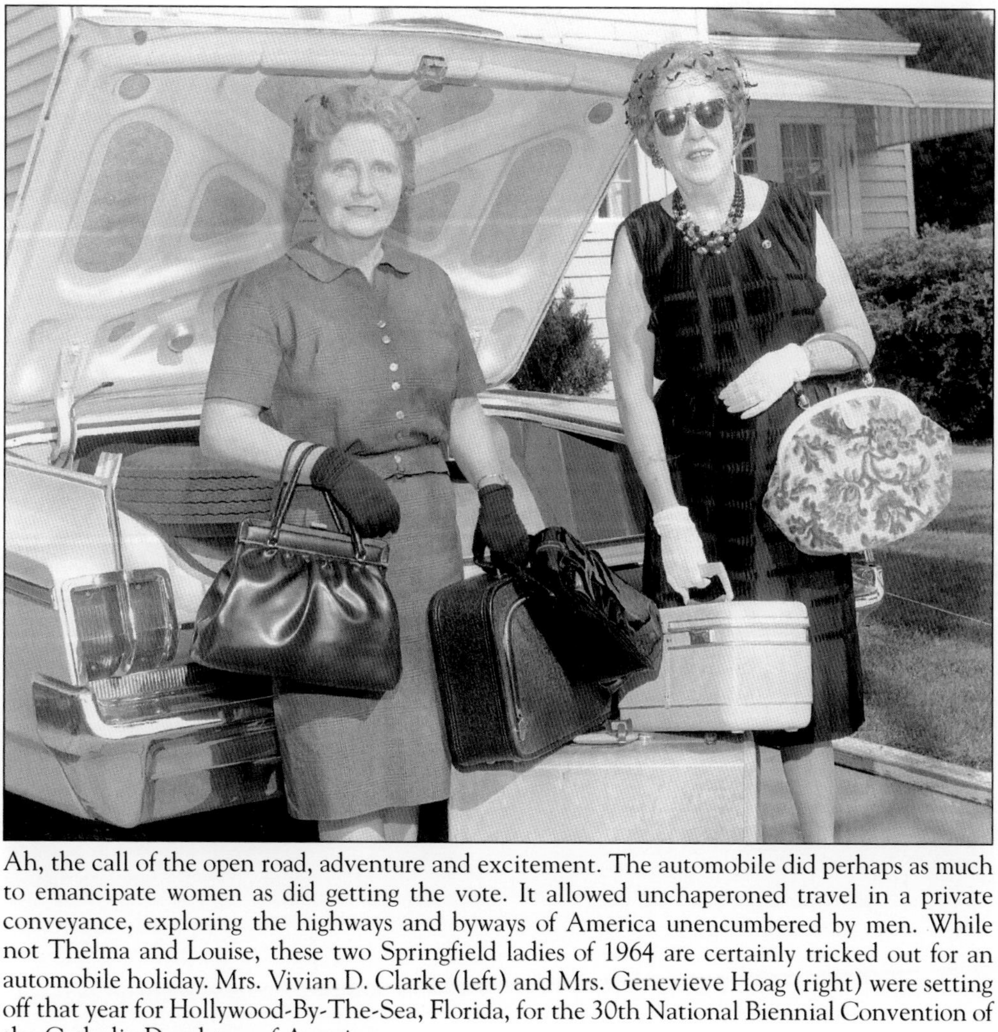

Ah, the call of the open road, adventure and excitement. The automobile did perhaps as much to emancipate women as did getting the vote. It allowed unchaperoned travel in a private conveyance, exploring the highways and byways of America unencumbered by men. While not Thelma and Louise, these two Springfield ladies of 1964 are certainly tricked out for an automobile holiday. Mrs. Vivian D. Clarke (left) and Mrs. Genevieve Hoag (right) were setting off that year for Hollywood-By-The-Sea, Florida, for the 30th National Biennial Convention of the Catholic Daughters of America.

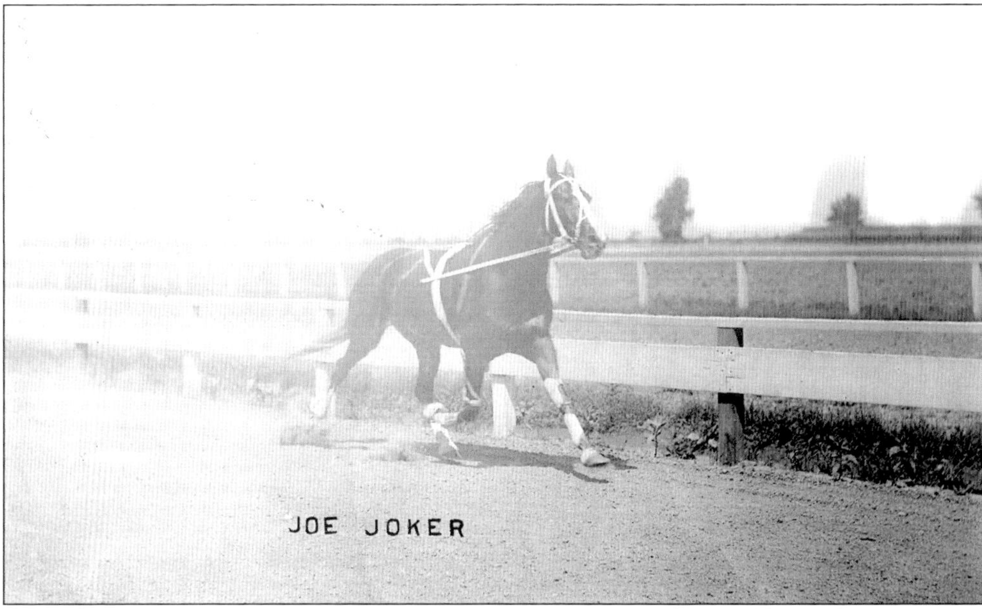

Joe Joker was a popular novelty attraction at county and state fairs throughout the Midwest in the 1890s. Joe's talent was racing himself around the track without a rider or driver, and he is shown here performing on the old fair racetrack about a century ago.

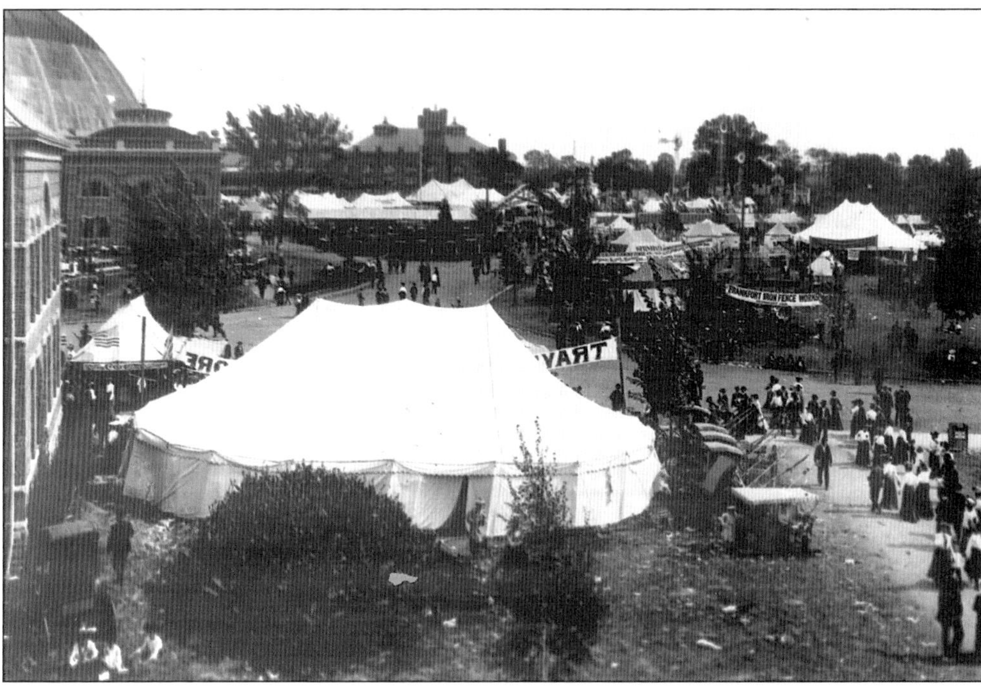

The Illinois State Fair once traveled around the state, but became permanently located in Springfield in 1893. Hundreds of thousands of dollars were expended on permanent buildings, streets and landscaping. During fair week, it becomes a city of tents, crowded with visitors looking for entertainment from carnival rides to livestock judging. This early 1900s photo captures the fair mood exactly.

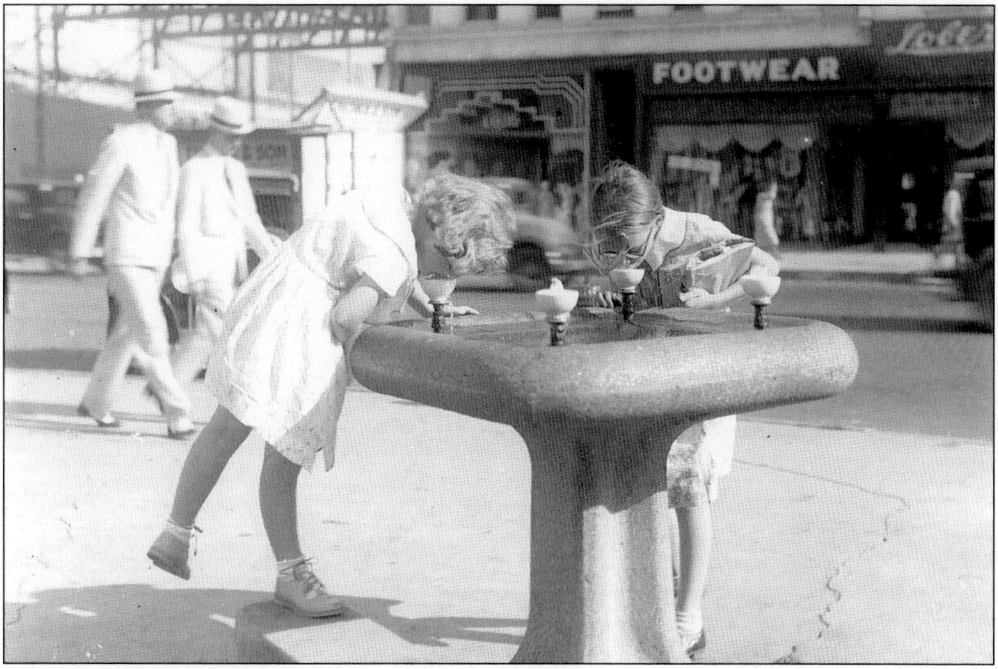

Sometimes the simple pleasures like a drink of cool water on a hot summer's day are the most enjoyable. These children visit a water fountain that once gurgled on the south side of the Old Capitol (then County Courthouse) square in the 1930s.

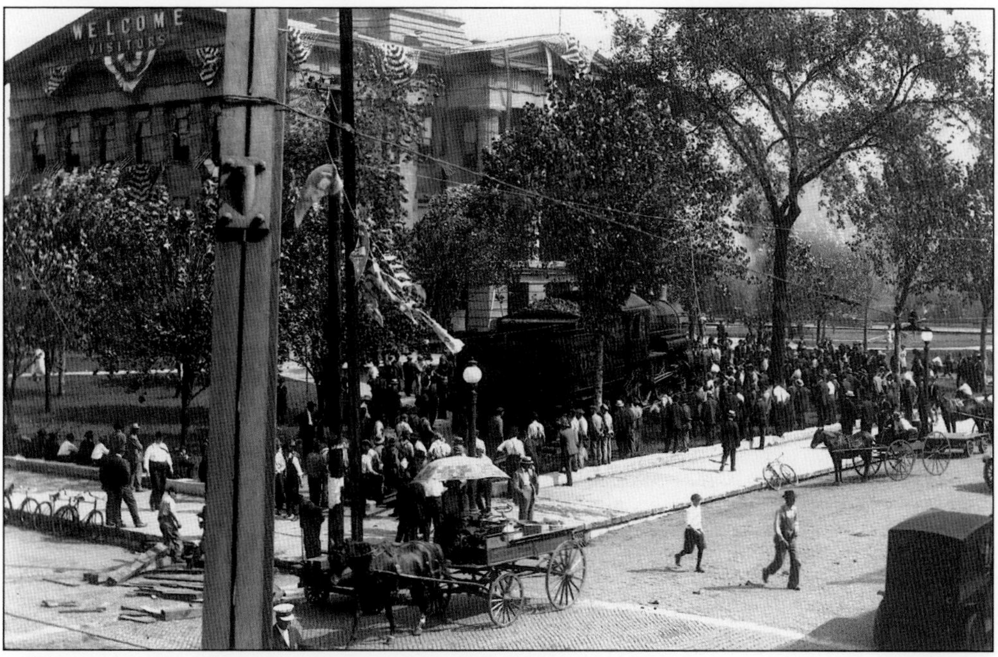

Publicity for this demonstration of the early 1900s called it "one of the most novel and interesting sights..." A steam locomotive, moved to the courthouse grounds, sent steam vapor to special plumes on the building. Colored floodlights lighted the escaping steam with an "indescribably beautiful" effect.

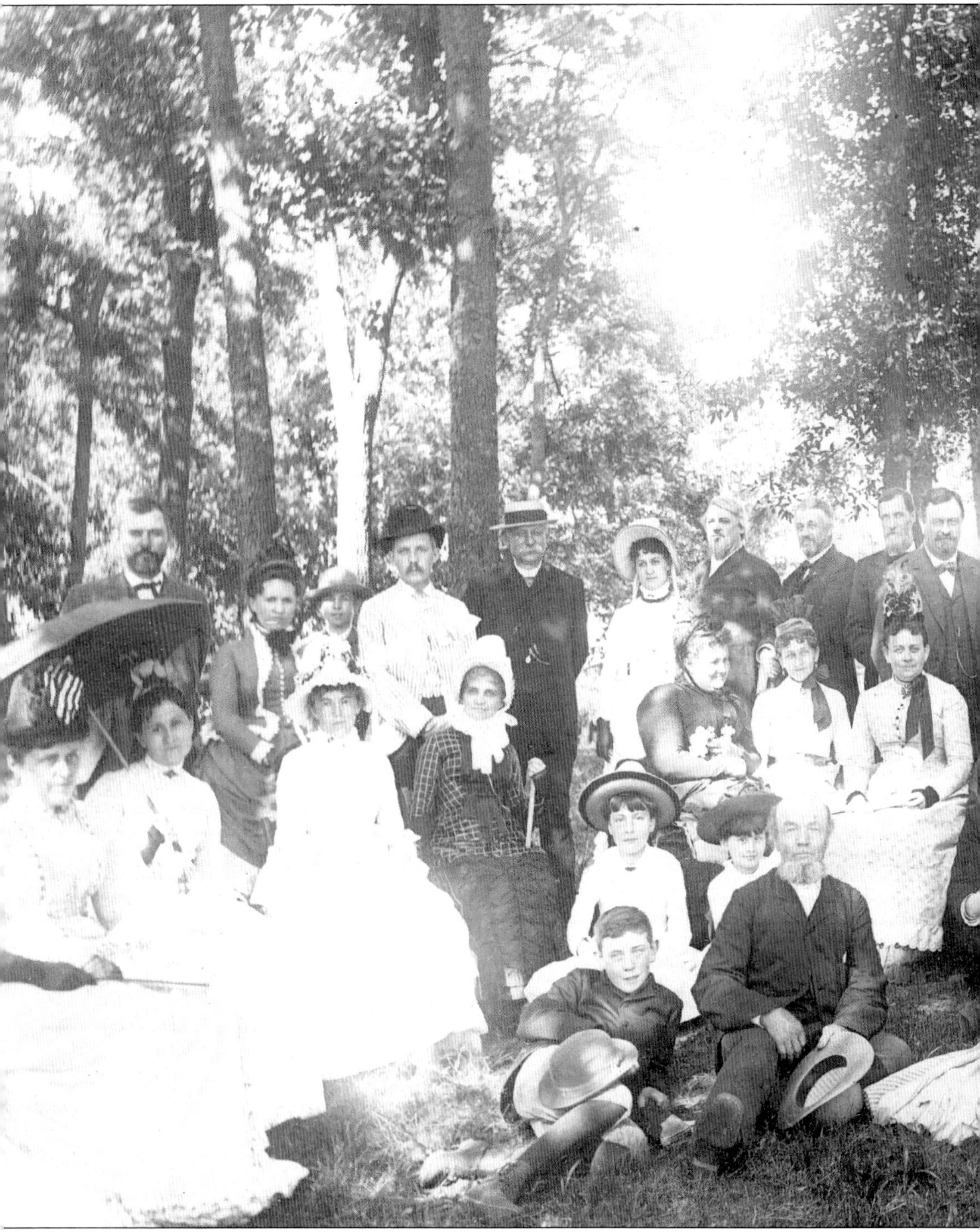

Convention-going is one reason many people join organizations, and it was probably always thus. Attending a convention in another city was and still is a great opportunity for adventure, travel, sight seeing, and meeting new people from other parts of the country. Thoughts of their upcoming journey was on the minds of this group of dapper delegates and wives from Sangamon

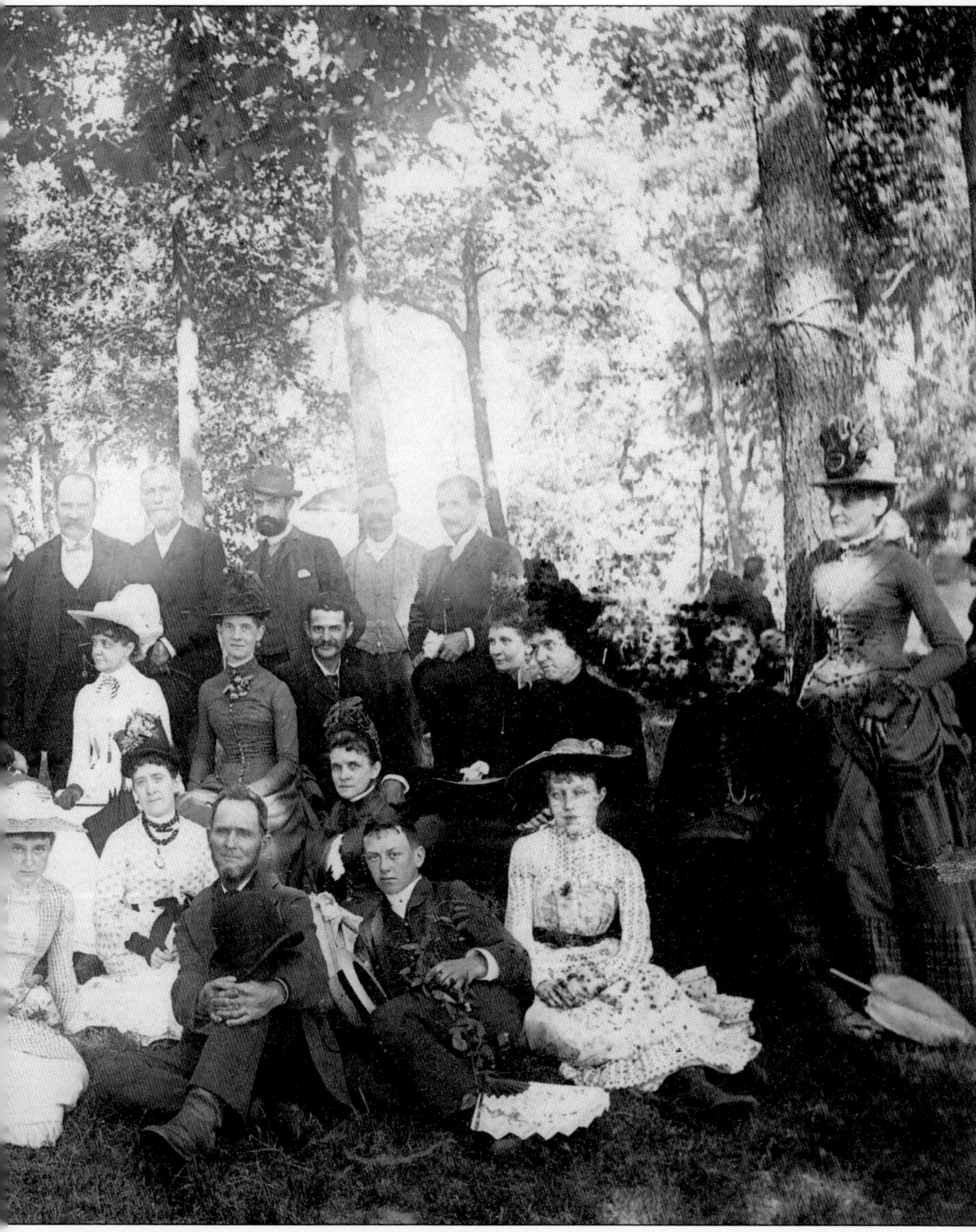

County in the 1890s, shown here ready to leave for a national Masonic convention. Freemasons were the first fraternal order to establish a lodge in Springfield, doing so in 1822 after several prominent Sangamon County residents petitioned the Grand Lodge of Missouri for a charter. The organization is still well represented in the city.

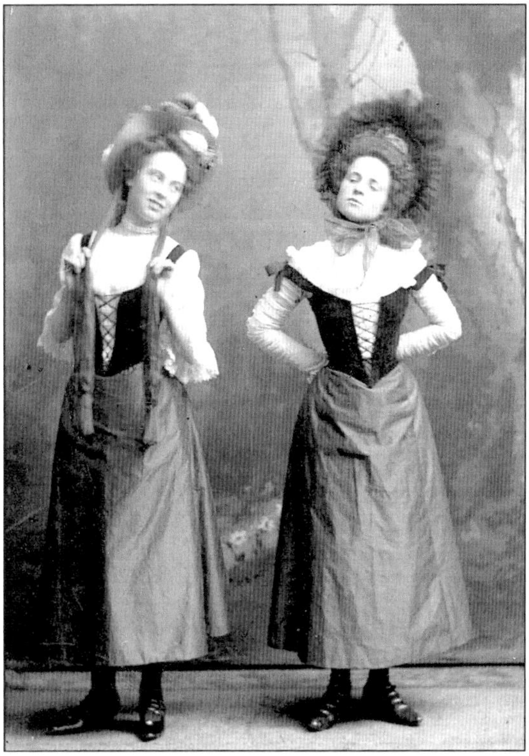

Period costumes, numerous rehearsals and good local talent made the Springfield Opera Club's performance of The Three Musketeers memorable. The ladies are identified only as Miss Selby and Mrs. McCoy in this early 1900s shot.

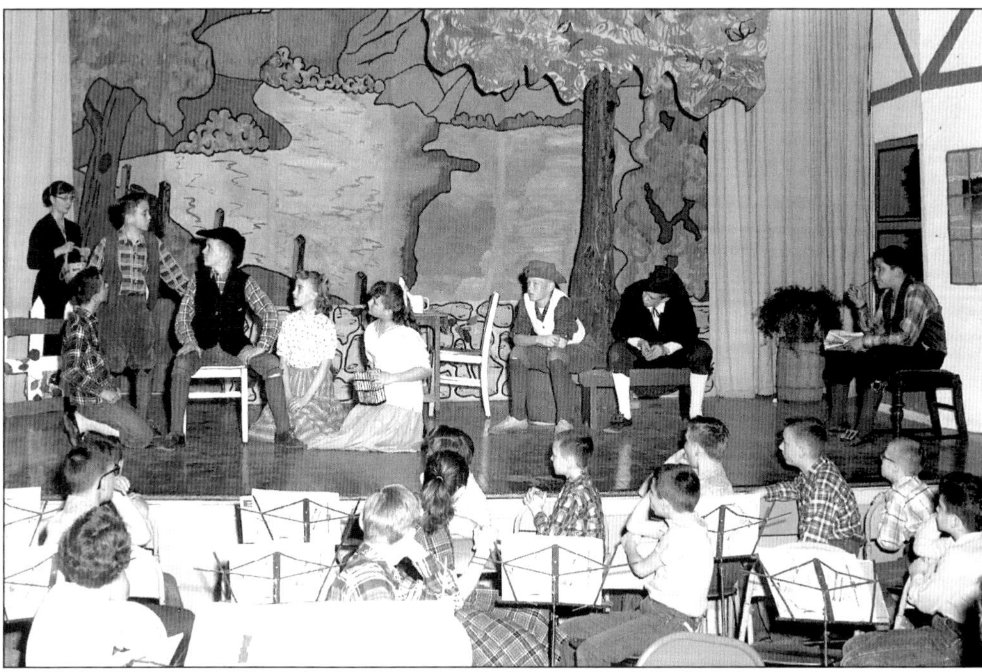

The 1957 class at Hay-Edwards school learned something about the Colonial time period and had fun entertaining family as well as friends with their school program. They also learned about the cooperation, patience, and work it takes to get sets created, costumes made, and lines and music learned before a performance.

The working title for the gone, but not forgotten Orpheum Theatre complex, was Lincoln Square Theatre. As a part of the Great State Theaters on the Orpheum Circuit, promoters spared no expense in providing Springfield with a luxurious facility in which to enjoy both stage and movie productions. The photograph is from 1926.

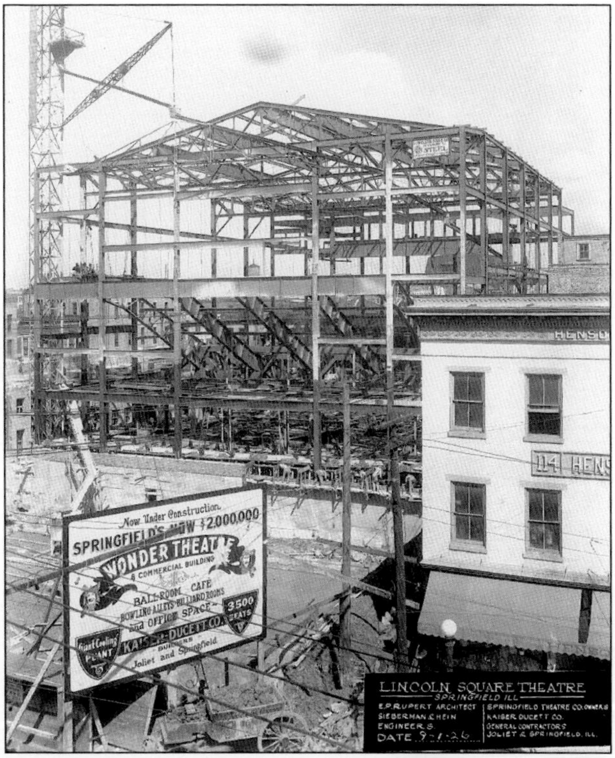

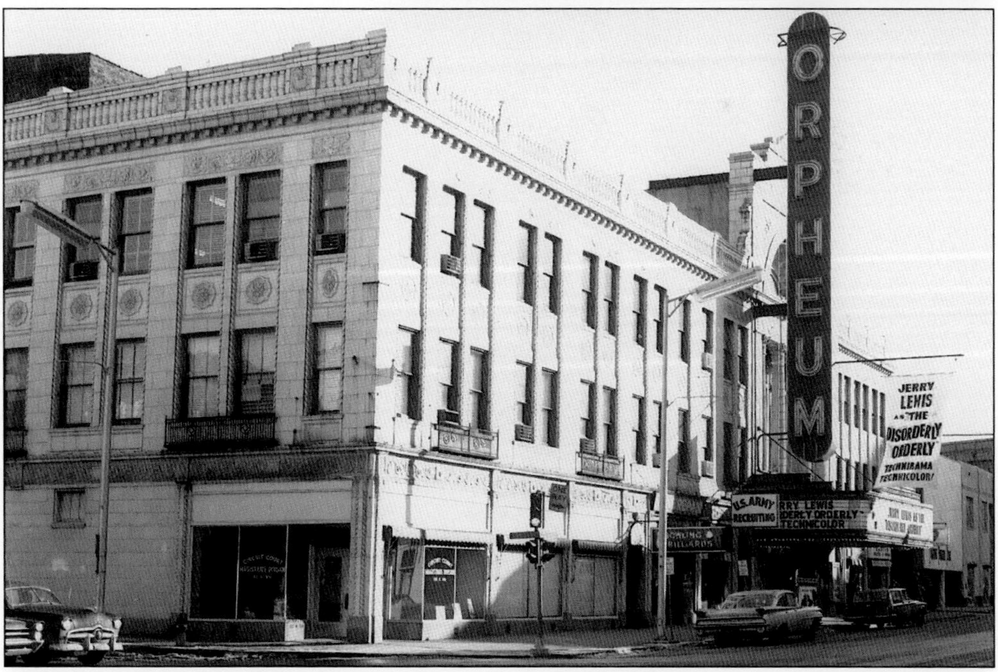

Once located on the east side of the100 block of North Fifth Street, the Orpheum Theatre with its marble floors, sweeping staircases, crystal chandeliers, rich draperies, and upholstered chairs opened in 1927 and was demolished in 1965 before it was even 40 years old. It is shown here in its last days

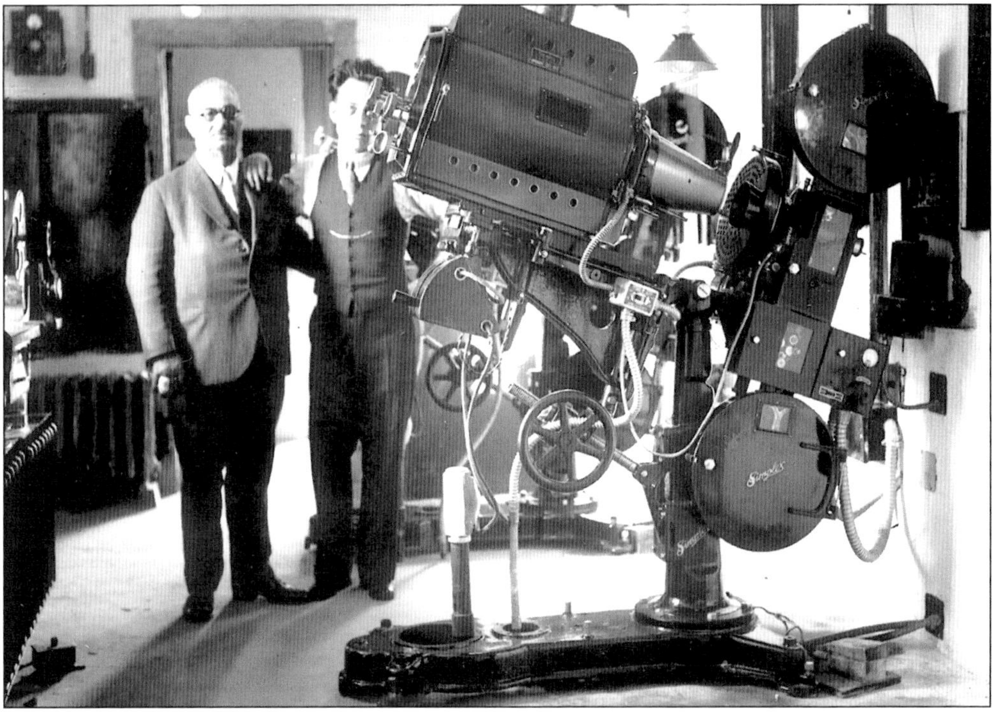

Motion pictures were an important form of escapist entertainment during the Great Depression, and any theater-related news usually received local press coverage. When the Strand Theater got new projection equipment in 1931, it was worthy of having a formal portrait made with theater owner and projectionist.

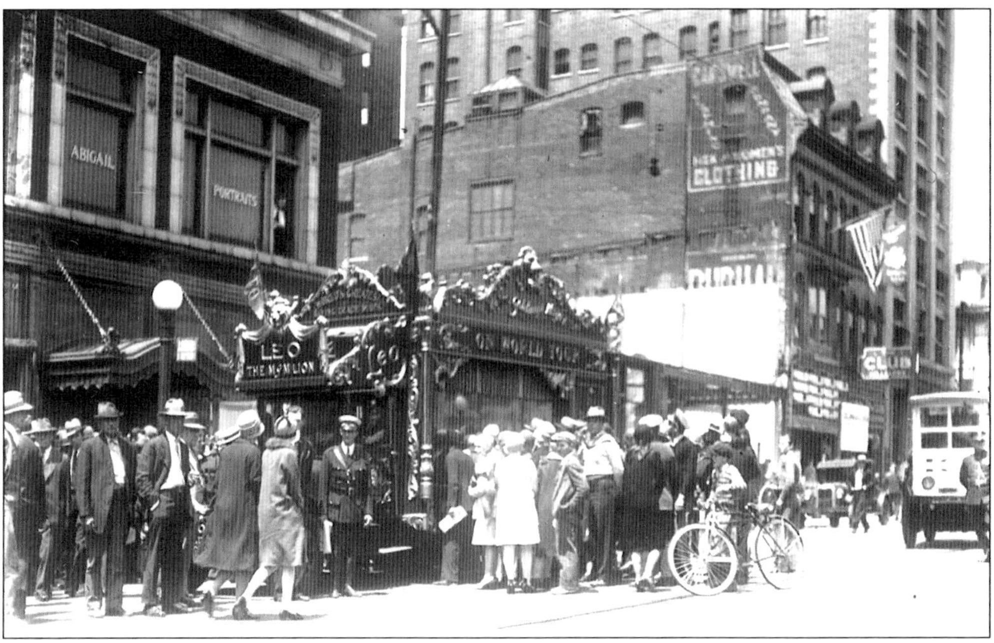

MGM Pictures brought a caged lion to Springfield in 1929 representing their mascot "Leo the Lion." The confined lion was doubtless quite tired of gawking crowds by the end of the tour.

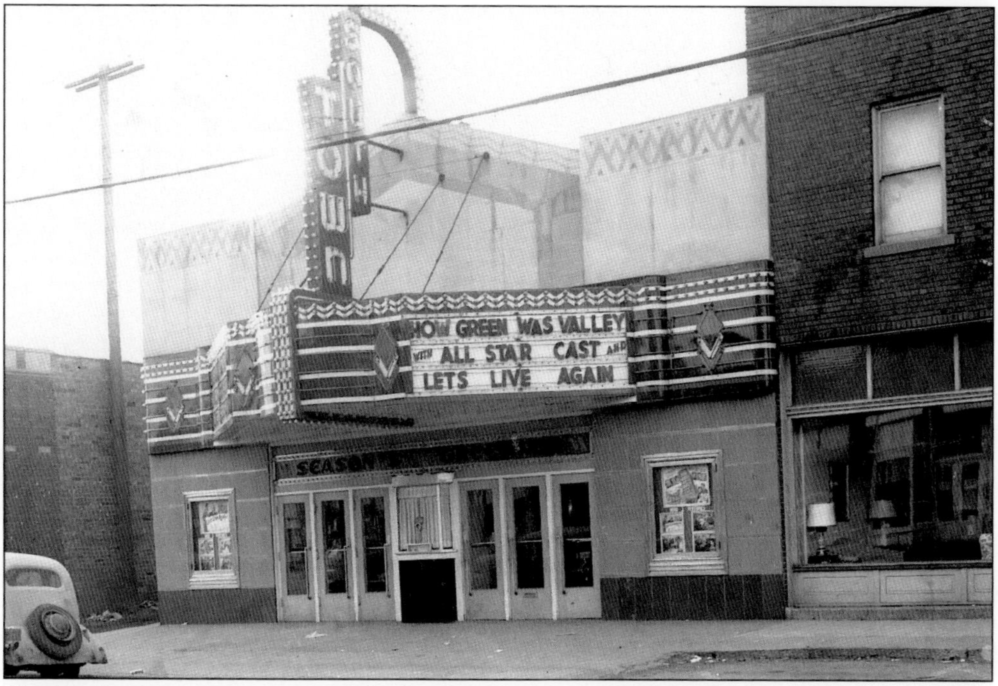

The Southtown was once one of the few motion picture theaters not located downtown (the Esquire, which still operates, and Pantheon were others). Southtown was anchored in a strip of neighborhood shopping on South Grand Avenue, east of Eleventh Street. Neighborhood theaters like this were often second-run houses fondly remembered for their Saturday morning serials and cartoons.

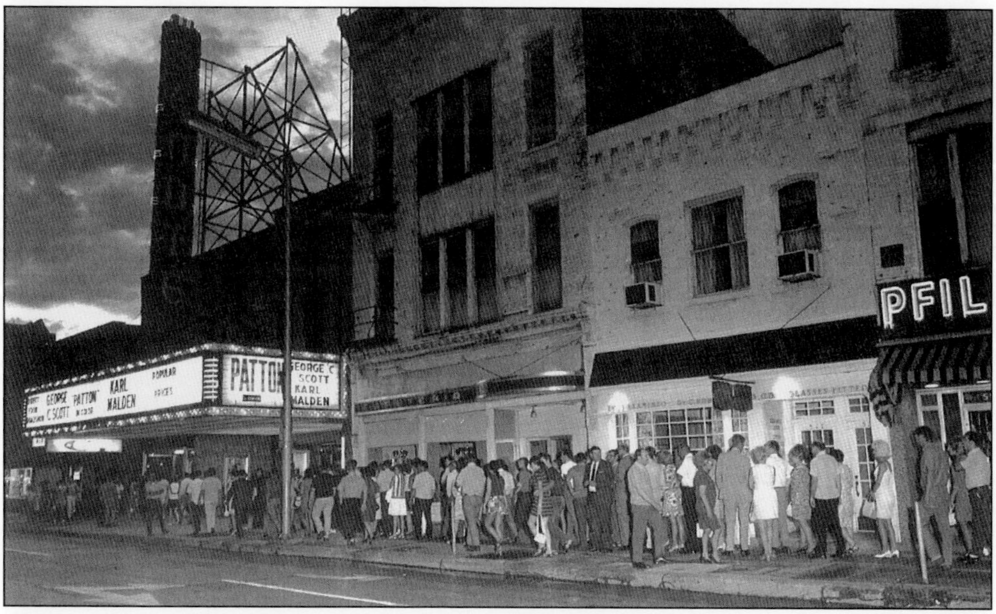

The Last Picture Show. When the Senate, Springfield's last downtown theater, closed in 1983, it was an important marker for a changing community. By then the film houses had all gone further out to places with plenty of parking. Crowds lined up to see Patton that year.

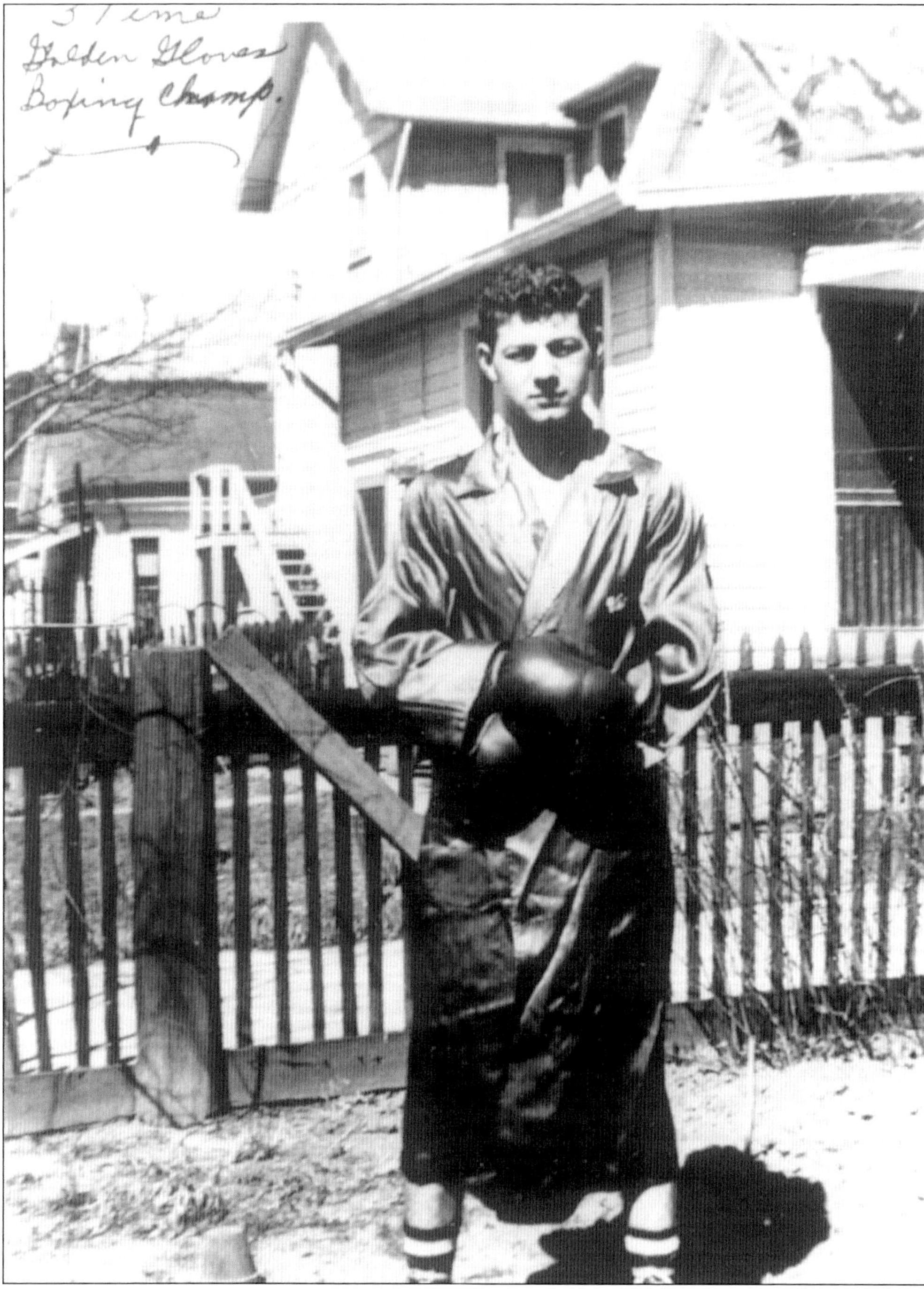

Oh, tough guy, eh? Yes, actually. Springfield's Vince DiGiovanna was a scrappy high school student when he struck this pose for the camera in the back yard of his North Fourth Street home about 1939. The 120-pound DiGiovanna wasn't cut out for football, his first love, but found instead local fame as an amateur boxer. Some gym class buddies introduced him to the world of Golden Gloves boxing. Golden Gloves was THE amateur boxing championship in the U.S. from the 1930s through the 1950s.

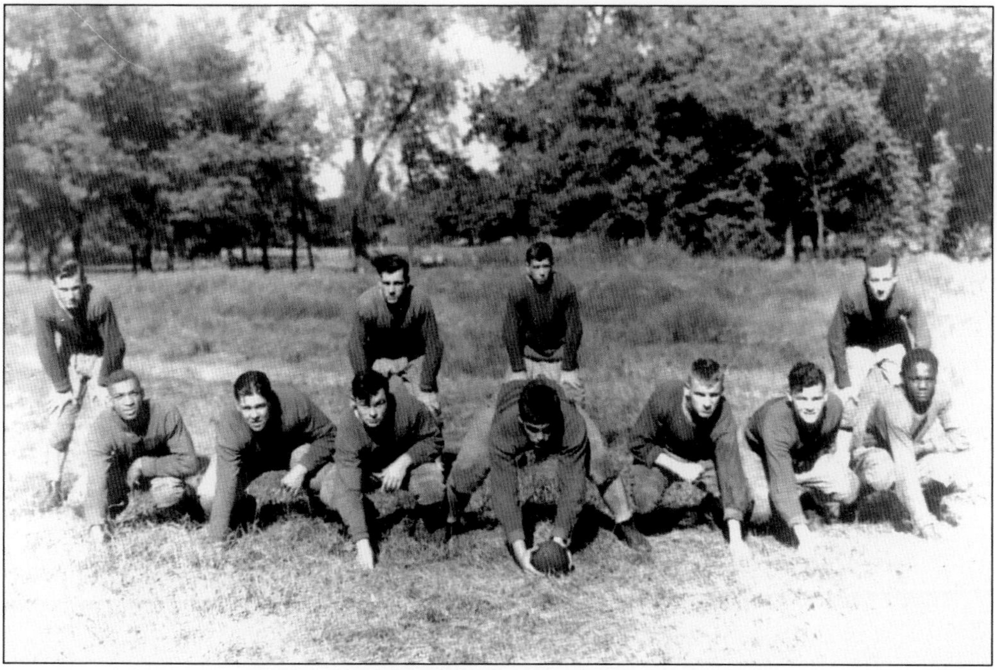

With few pads and no helmets for protection, these early football players at Feitshans High School in Springfield had to be tough to endure the blocks and tackles of this contact sport.

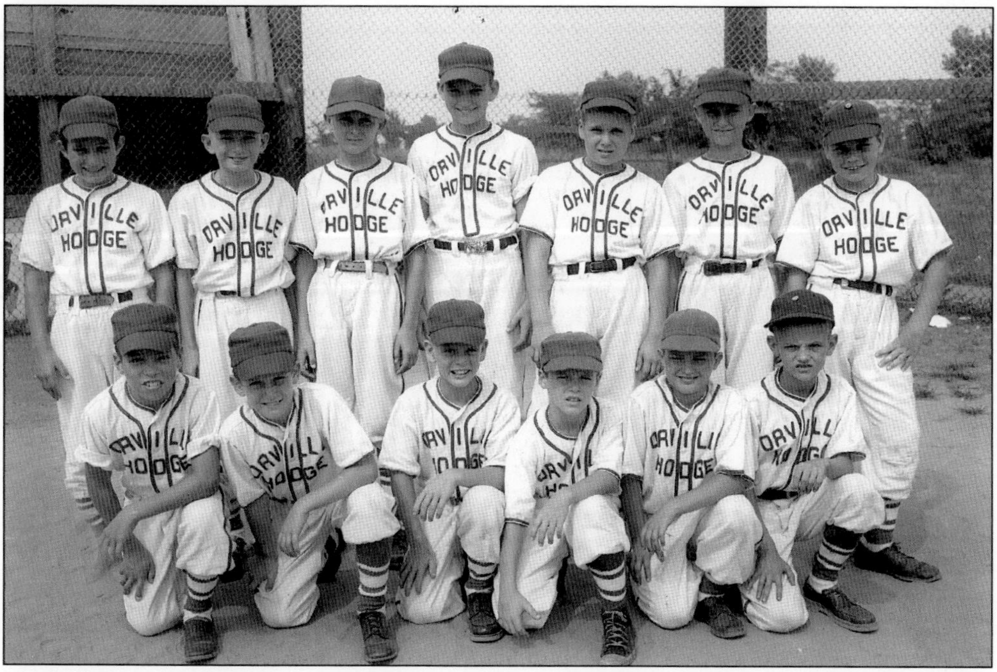

Baseball was one of the first organized sports in Springfield. It was also a popular pastime for young boys after school and during summer. This group comprised the Orville Hodge junior baseball team in 1954.

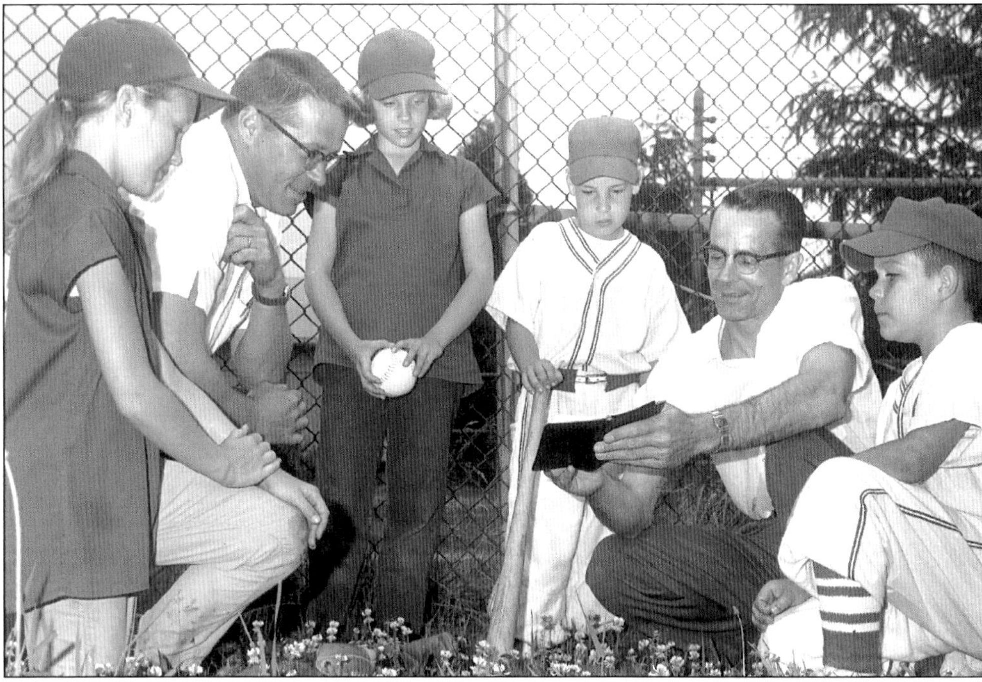

Summer means it's time to play ball. A couple of young female helpers listen in as the baseball league coaches go over the line-up with a some of their players.

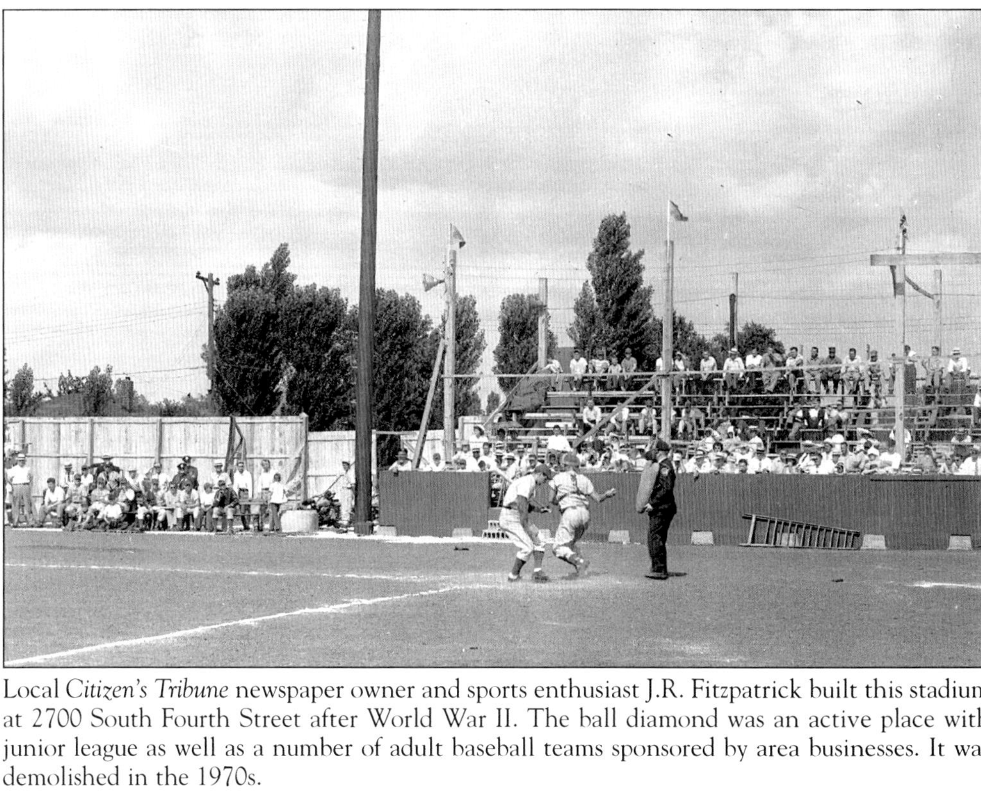

Local *Citizen's Tribune* newspaper owner and sports enthusiast J.R. Fitzpatrick built this stadium at 2700 South Fourth Street after World War II. The ball diamond was an active place with junior league as well as a number of adult baseball teams sponsored by area businesses. It was demolished in the 1970s.

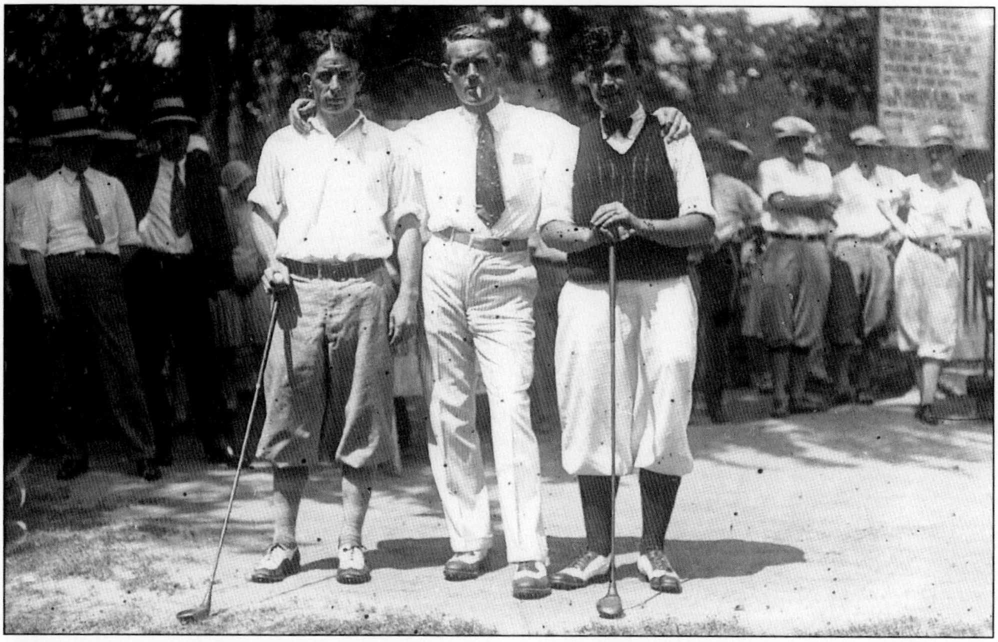

Illini golf pro Alex Ayton (center) poses with Leslie Whipple (left) winner and Cliff McKelvey (right) runner-up in the first Illinois State Journal sponsored central Illinois golf tournament in 1929. Knickers were the fashionable golf course wear for men at the time.

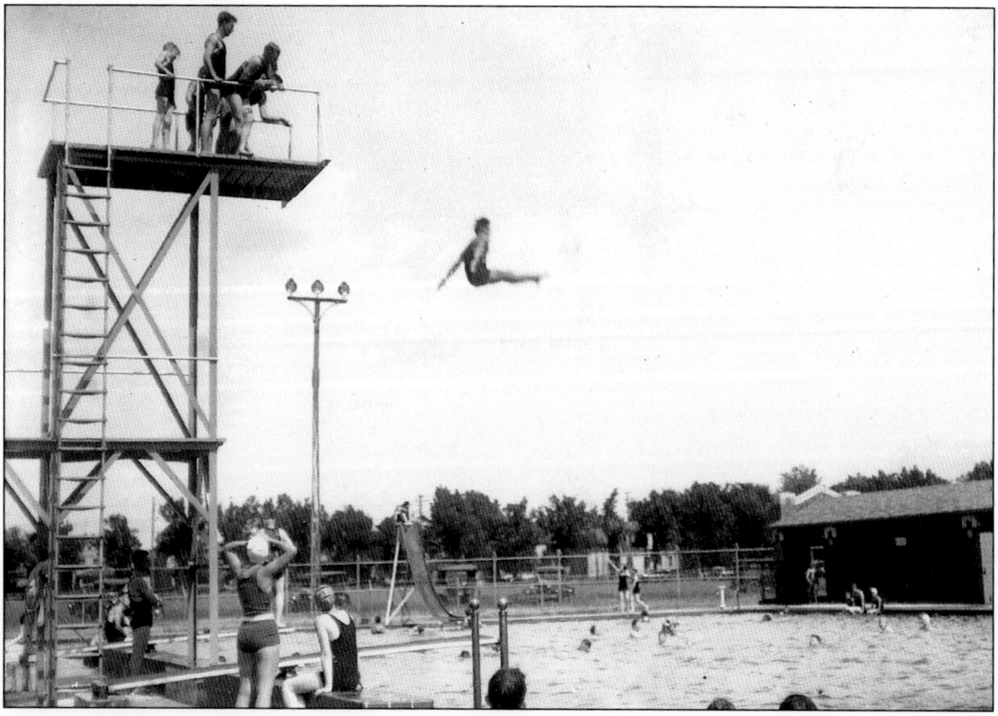

The nearly 14-foot-high diving board at the deep (11 foot) end of Soldiers and Sailors Memorial Pool gave divers a chance to perfect double somersaults and a variety of other challenging dives. The pool at Ninth and Converse streets is shown about 1930.

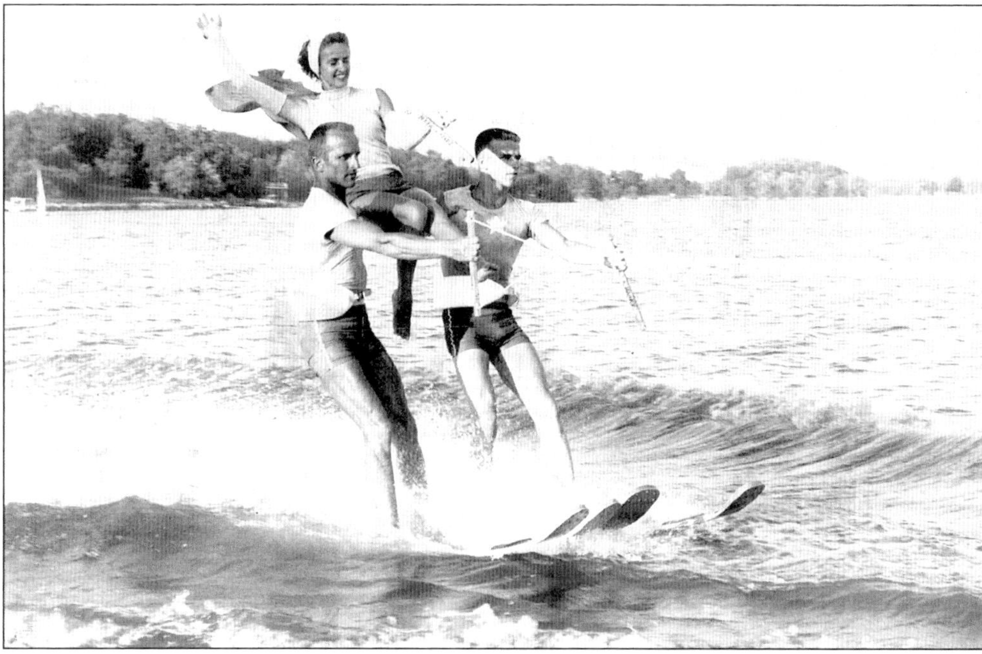

Members of the Terry family perform at a show given at the Springfield Ski and Boat Club on Lake Springfield in August of 1964. Mother and wife Margaret Terry sits atop the arms of her husband Harry, at left, and son Mike, at right.

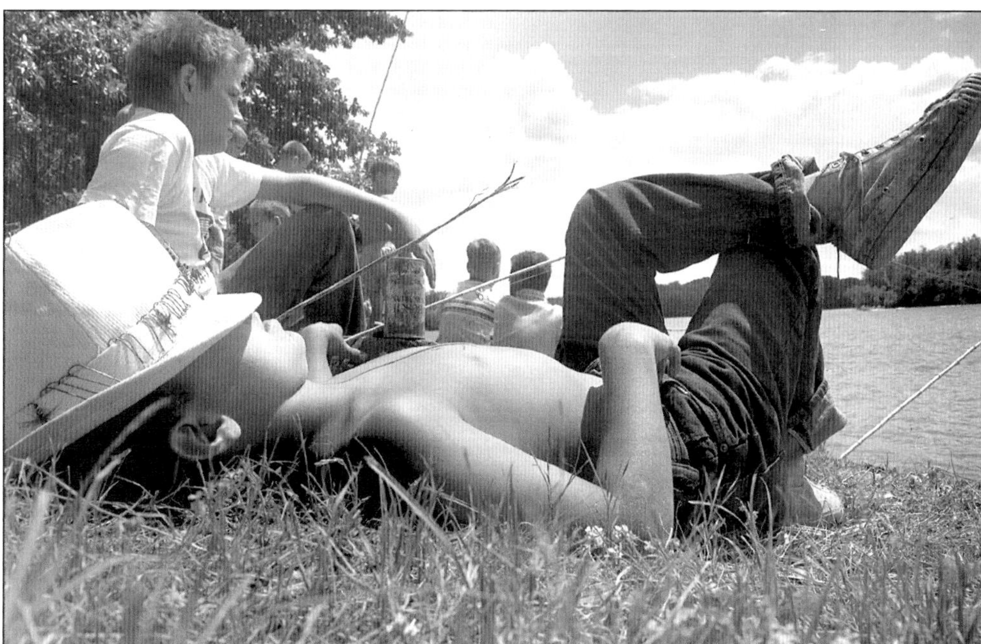

Summer and relaxing went hand-in-hand when school was out. These kids enjoy a warm, sunny day at Lake Springfield about 1960. Though only a couple of generations have passed, this scene seems like ancient history compared to today's teens, many of whose tightly scheduled summers are filled with work, sports, lessons, and hours at a computer terminal.

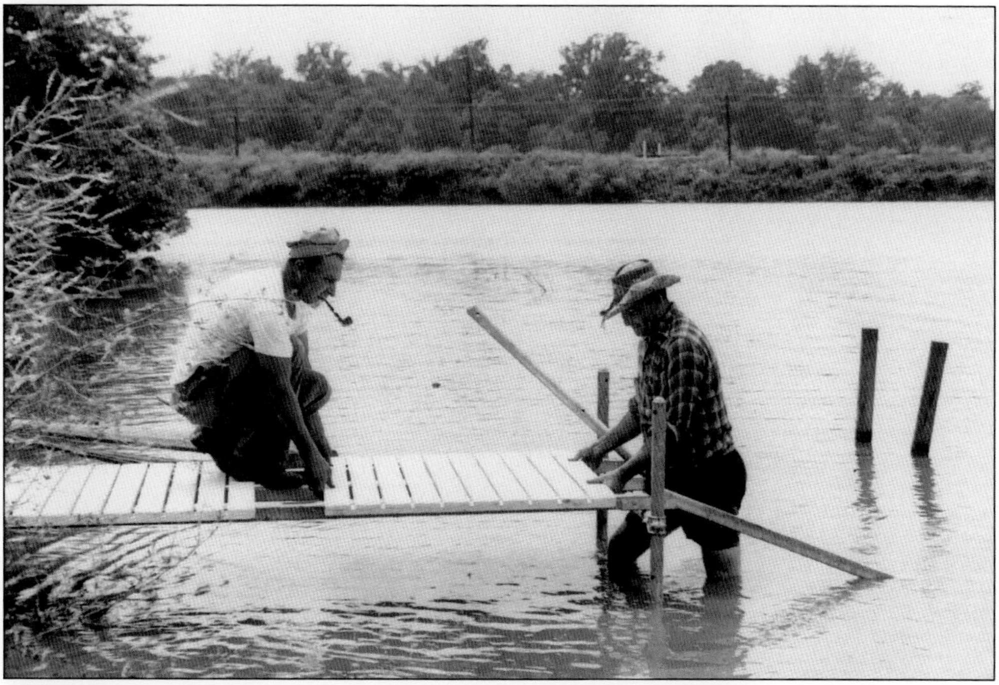

Although it's work, these men repairing a dock at Lake Springfield in the 1950s, suggest two boys at play, Somehow being in the water on a balmy day just doesn't qualify as "real" work to many of us.

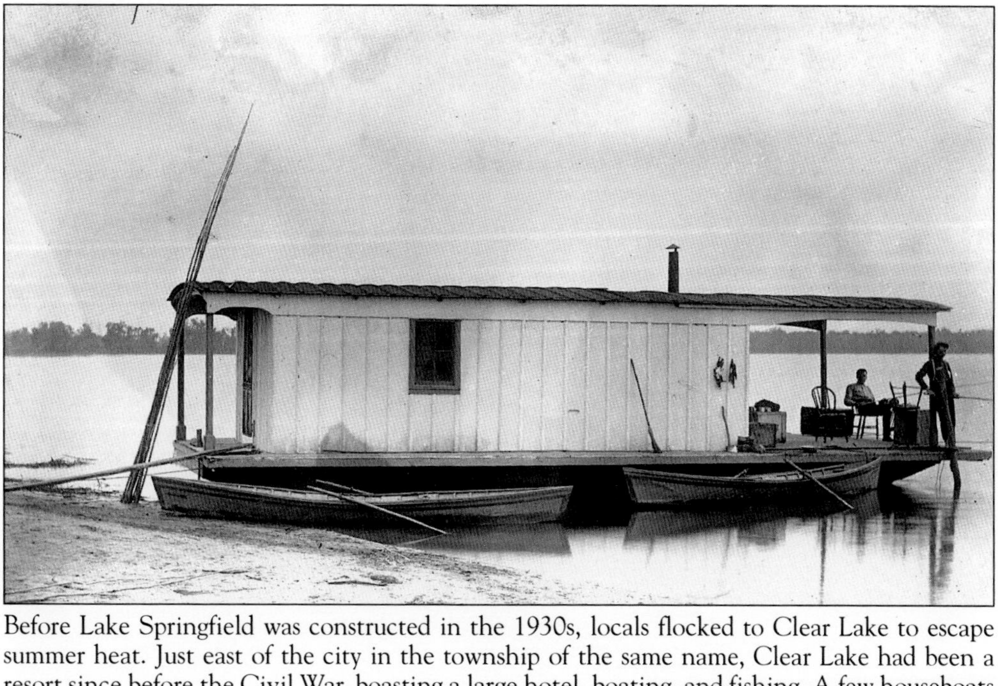

Before Lake Springfield was constructed in the 1930s, locals flocked to Clear Lake to escape summer heat. Just east of the city in the township of the same name, Clear Lake had been a resort since before the Civil War, boasting a large hotel, boating, and fishing. A few houseboats like this one were used for overnight "camps" for fishermen. The lake closed by the 1920s and the hotel burned.

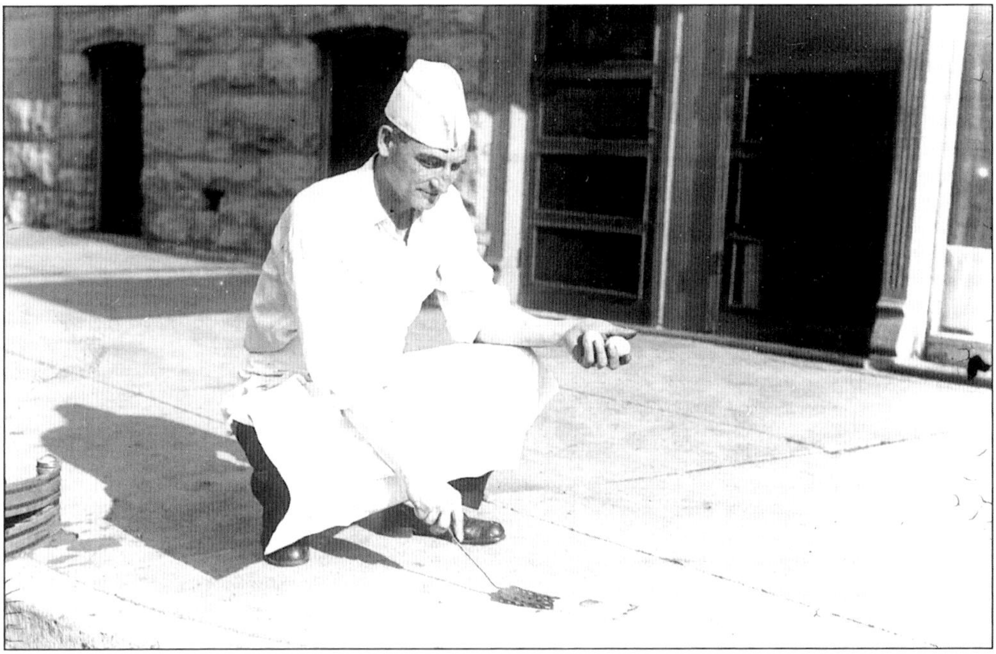

With temperatures reaching a 102 degrees in 1930, T.M. Travis of Travis Cafeteria tried to fry an egg in front of his business at 624 East Capitol. The experiment failed because the temperature needed to fry an egg is 186 degrees. The sidewalk was only about 115.

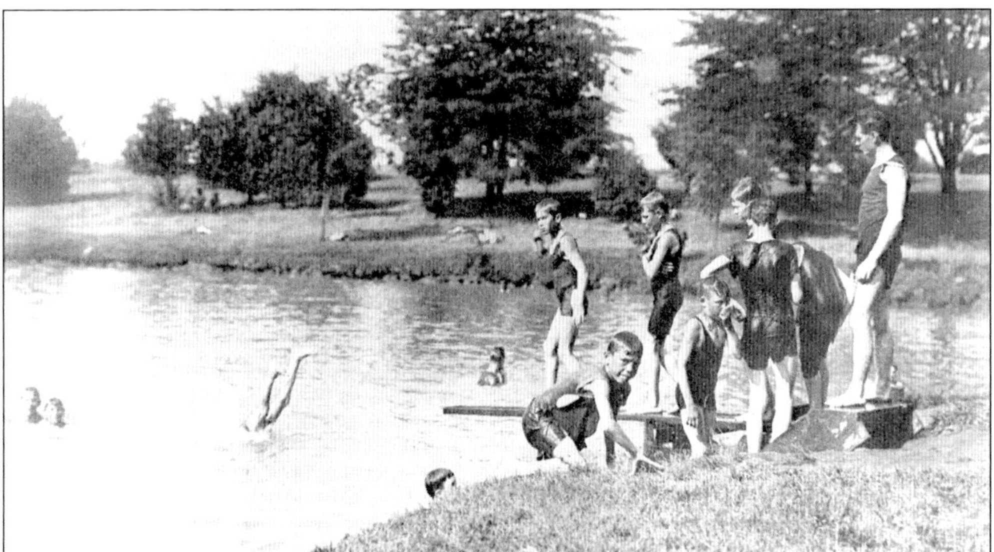

The old swimming hole has been a popular spot for boys since the early days of Springfield. These boys eagerly take turns diving into the swimming hole located in Lincoln Park in 1912.

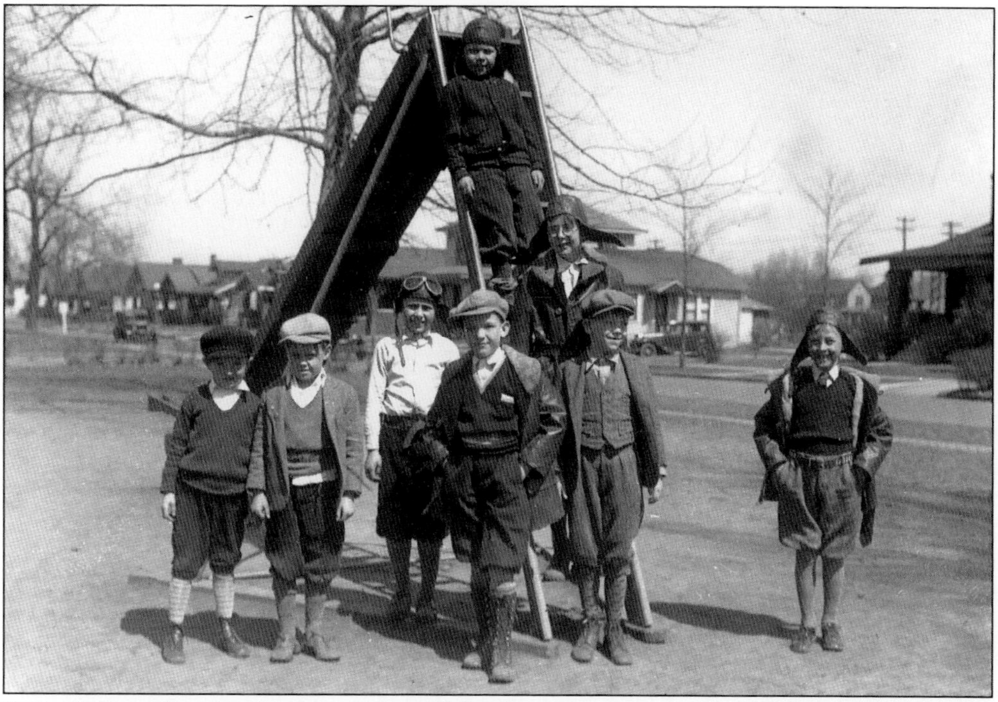

Springfield public schools were once noted for their spacious schoolyards where children could play like this one in the 1920s. These playgrounds, along with those at public parks, provided safe places to keep children off the streets.

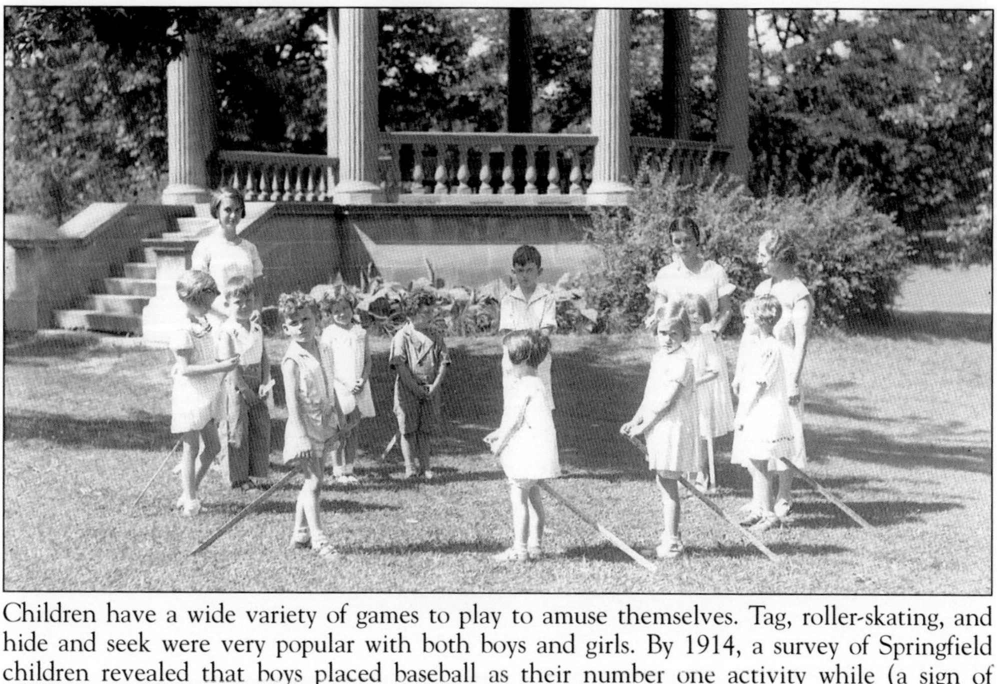

Children have a wide variety of games to play to amuse themselves. Tag, roller-skating, and hide and seek were very popular with both boys and girls. By 1914, a survey of Springfield children revealed that boys placed baseball as their number one activity while (a sign of changing times) girls enjoyed motion picture shows best. This group plays a game involving stick horses at Washington Park in the 1920s.

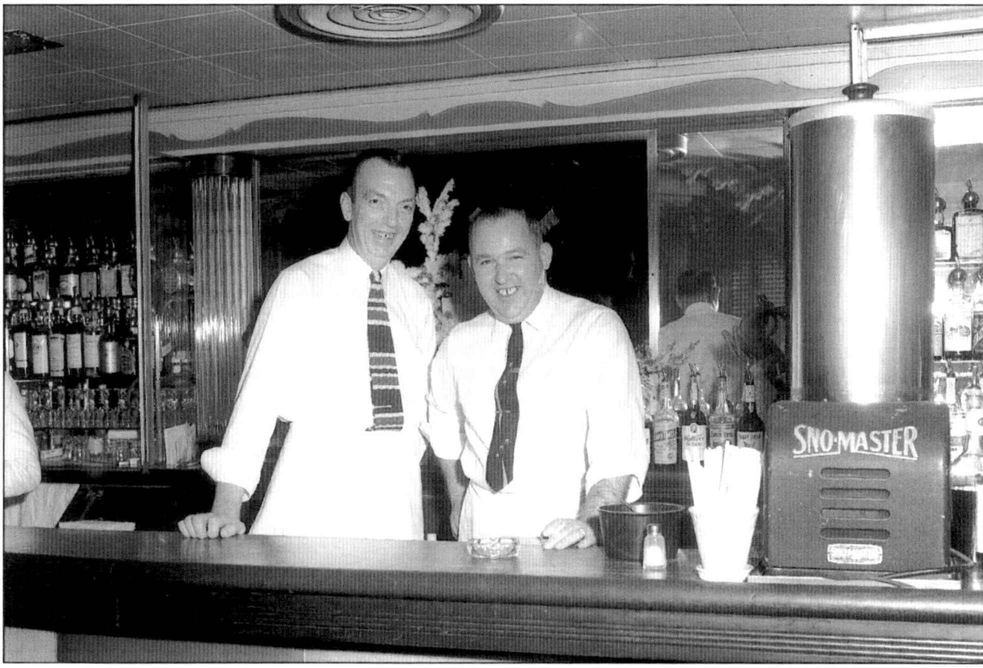

These two smiling gentlemen made sure the drinks were properly mixed at the Mill, a popular Springfield restaurant in 1957.

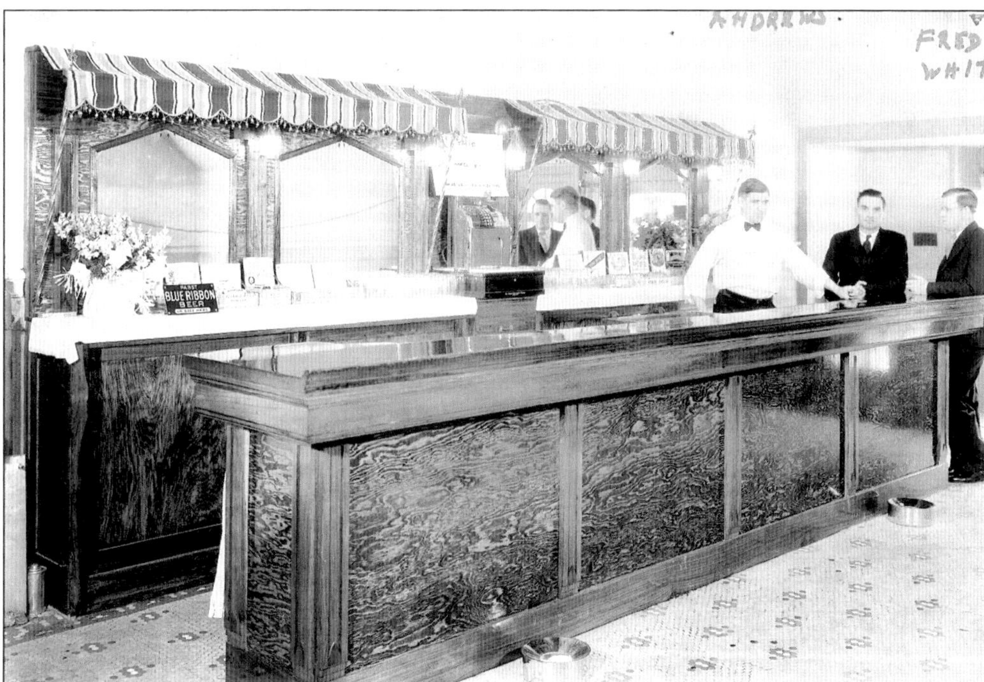

Among the items manufactured by the Fitzpatrick Mill in Springfield were bar fixtures. A showroom model of a complete bar setup is shown here, even outfitted with cuspidors on the floor, cigars on the back counter, back-bar mirrors, and awnings.

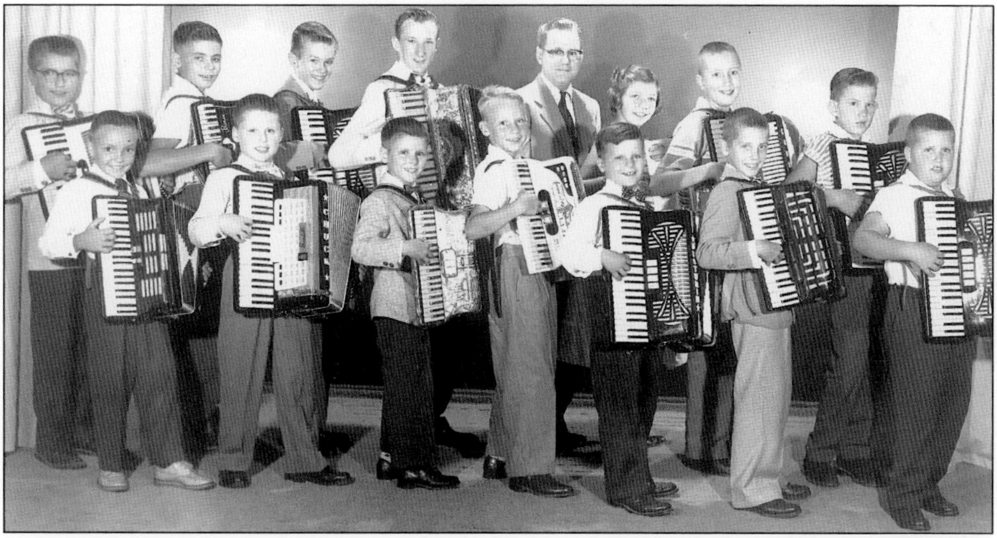

During the height of an accordion craze in the 1950s, instructor Roy Bertelli was giving lessons to over 100 students a week in his house. Bertelli is shown here with some of his students.

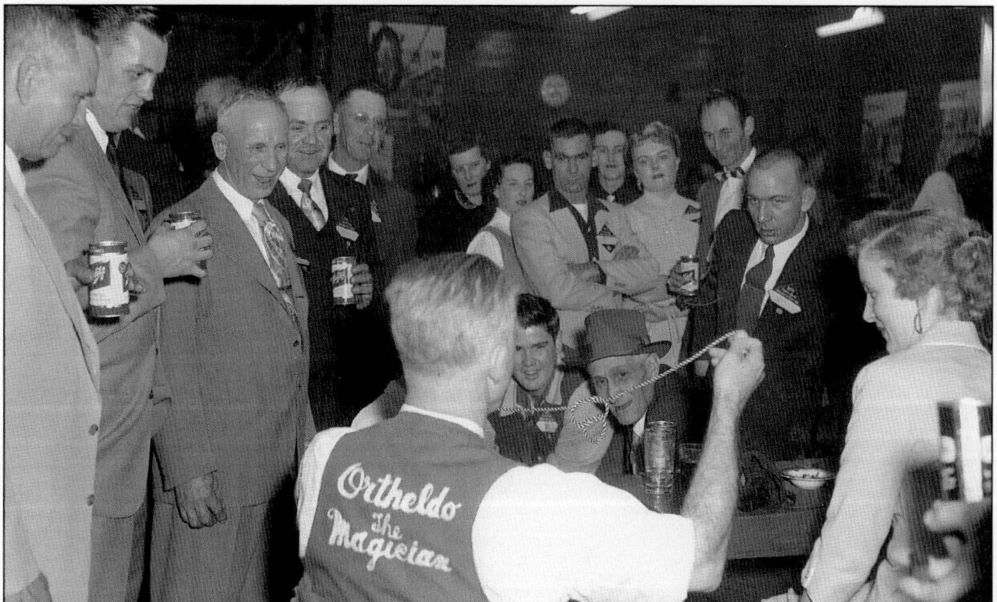

Magic! We are all part of the illusion because we want to believe. No one wants to see the hidden drawstring up the sleeve...the extra card. But the magic also depends on a performer who can keep the audience's eyes diverted—and that takes showmanship. The astounding escapes of Harry Houdini or the saw-the-girl-in-half dramatics of Harry Blackstone were as ritualized as any ballet; and how important are the props—tuxedo, tophat, and magic wand—that tell us some sorcery or other is imminent. Springfield's longest-running master of legerdemain was Ortheldo Smith, assisted by his wife, Dorothy. On stage, they became the mysterious "Ortheldo and Dorthe: Magician and Mentalist." But it was for local, intimate audiences that Ortheldo did his best magic. In this photo Springfield Auto Supply Company (SASCO) employees, cradling cans of Schlitz beer, crowd around at a company party in the 1950s.

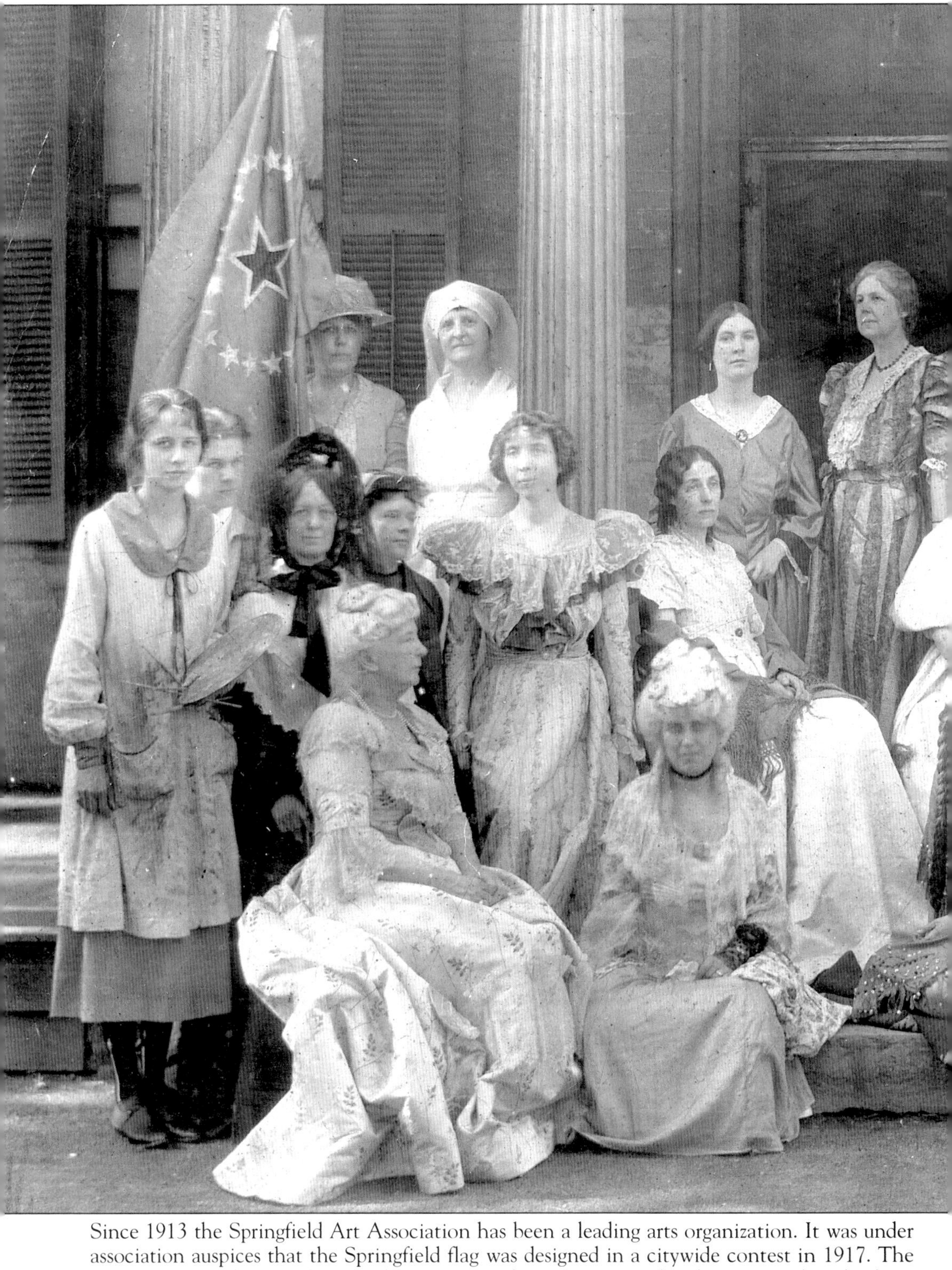

Since 1913 the Springfield Art Association has been a leading arts organization. It was under association auspices that the Springfield flag was designed in a citywide contest in 1917. The flag is displayed here, at far left, about 1920 at the Association's headquarters, Edwards Place.

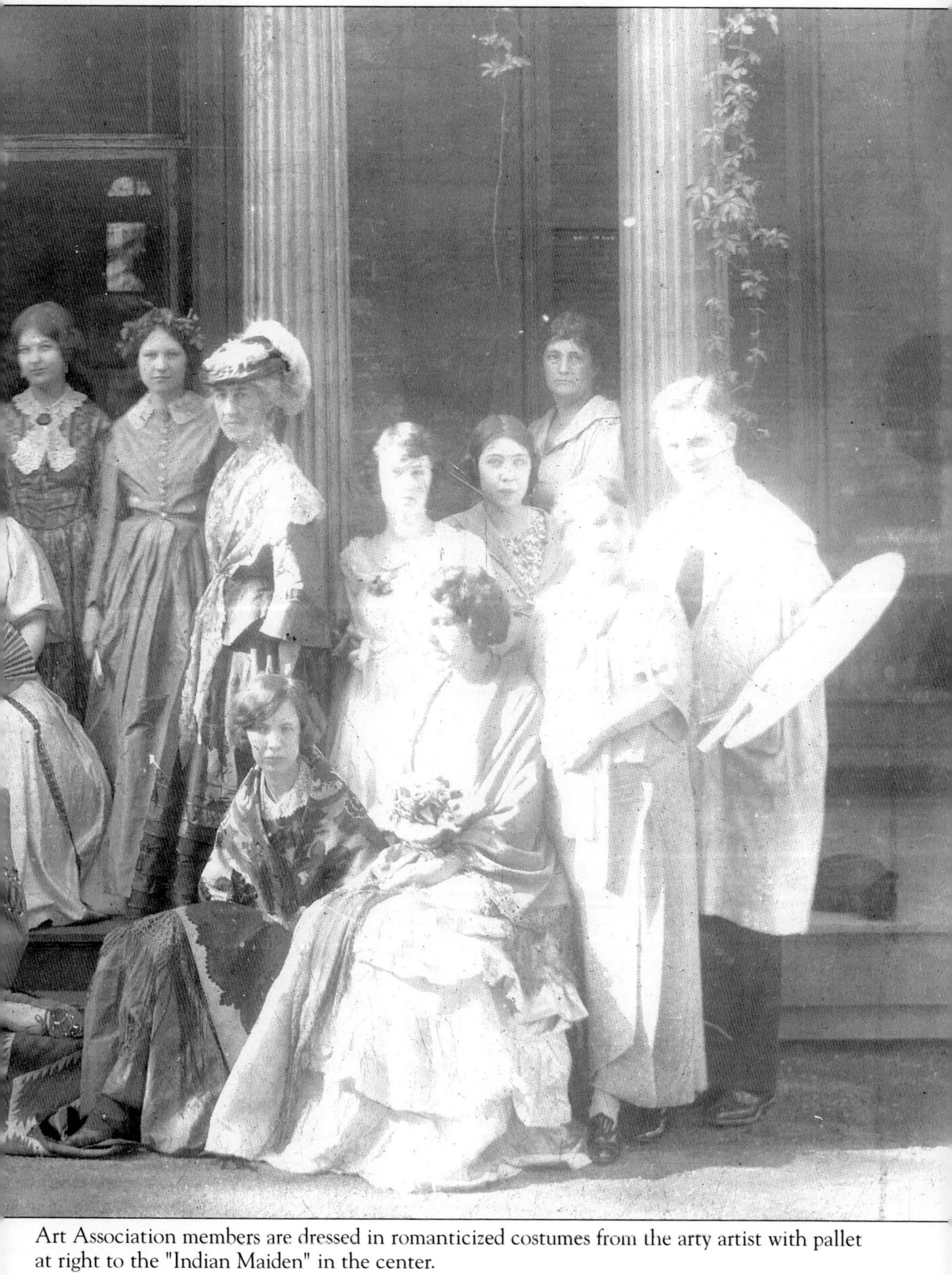

Art Association members are dressed in romanticized costumes from the arty artist with pallet at right to the "Indian Maiden" in the center.

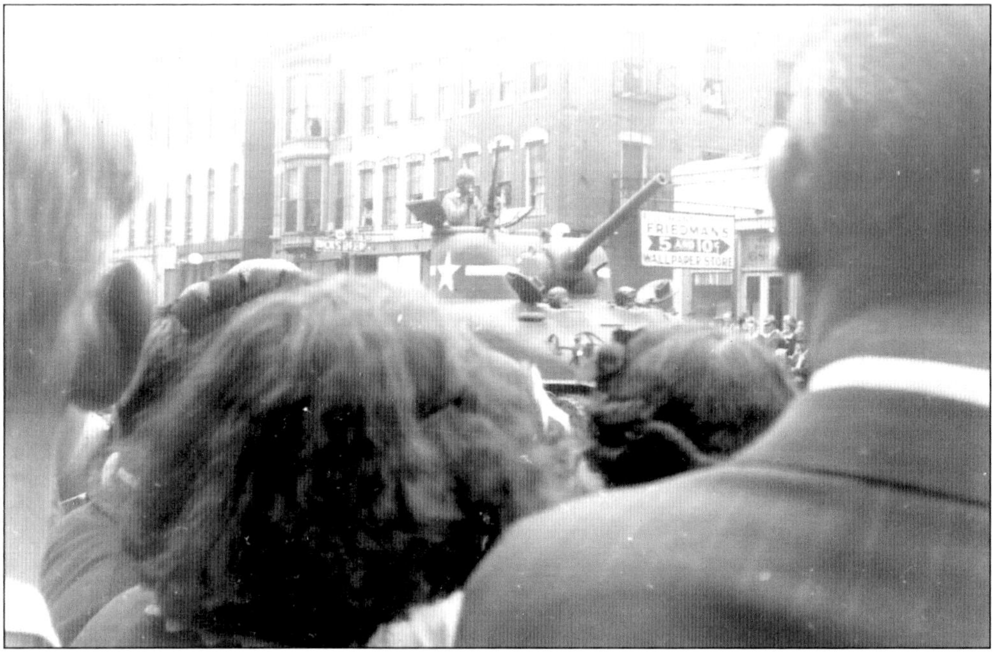

People crowd the sidewalks in the 100 block of North Sixth Street to watch military vehicles, including tanks, roll by in the this 1950s Armed Forces Day Parade. The Cold War era display of military might was assuring in that uneasy time.

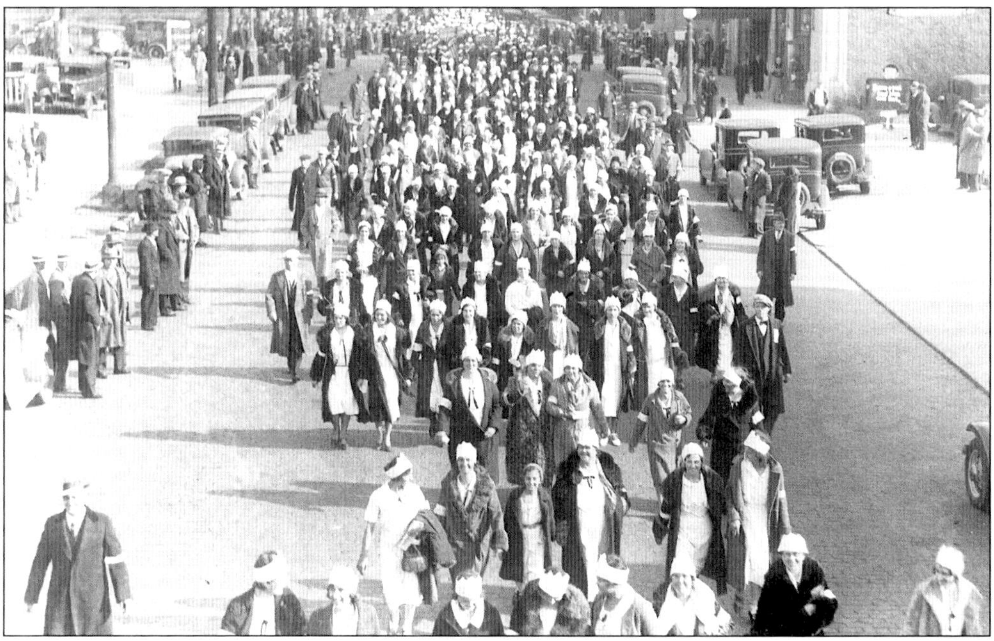

On January 27, 1933, five thousand members of the Progressive Miners of America Auxiliary marched in Springfield to present their program to Governor Henry Horner and the state legislature. Items in their agenda included unemployment insurance and civil liberties. These PMA women are shown marching down Capitol Avenue toward the statehouse, garbed in the white clothing of their order.

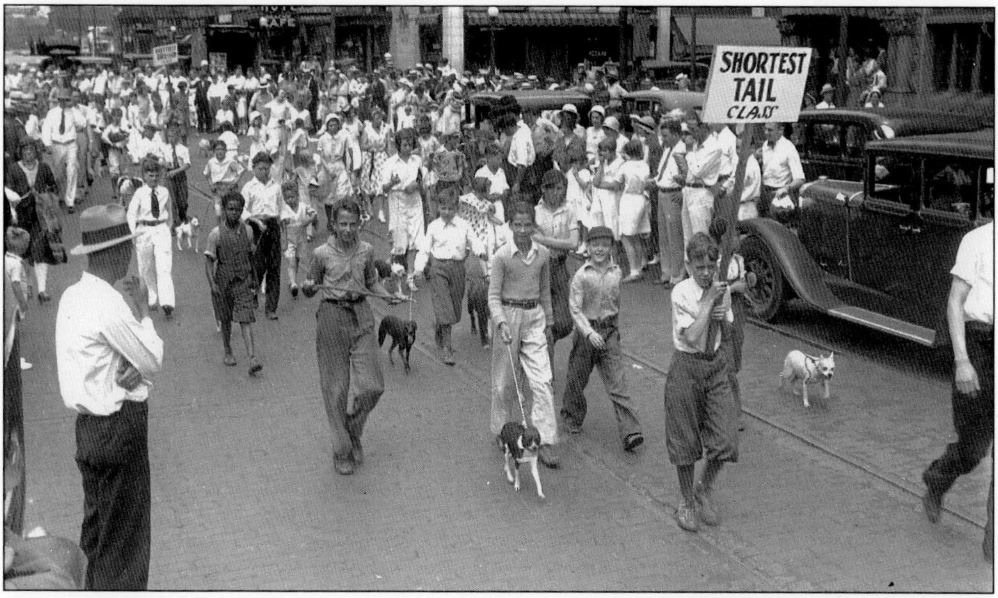

One of Springfield's more unique parades was the annual dog parade sponsored by the *Illinois State Journal* in the late 1920s. Hundreds of dogs were entered in 9 different categories. The dogs and their owners paraded through the downtown and were judged on the courthouse square. This group of dog owners representing the shortest tail class marches along Washington Street in 1929.

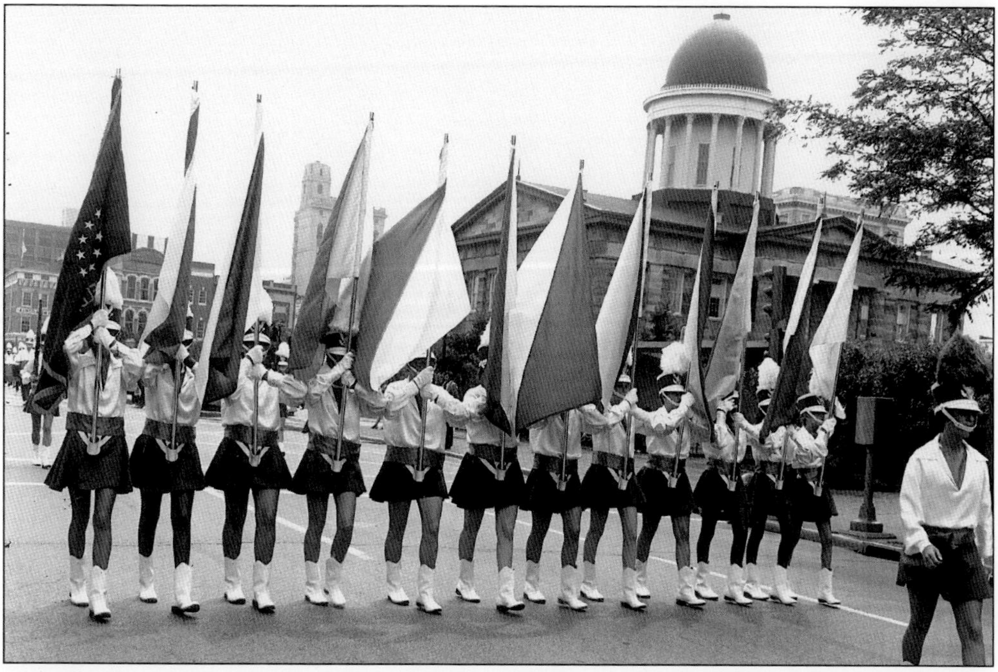

Springfield could once boast of two drum and bugle corps, the Falcons and the Capital Chargers. These groups merged in 1974 to create the Springfield Statesmen, which won numerous competitions. The corps fell on hard times in the early 1980s and disbanded. The flag detail leads the corps in a parade in downtown Springfield in the late 1970s.

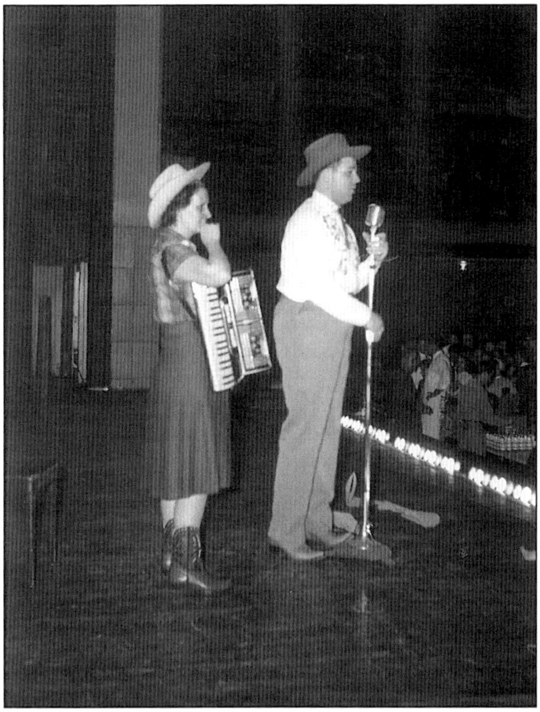

Bill Wingerter, also know as Wild Bill to young TV viewers of the Pegwill Pete Show, worked with his assistant, Marge, to emcee the local portion of a national telethon in the late 1950s.

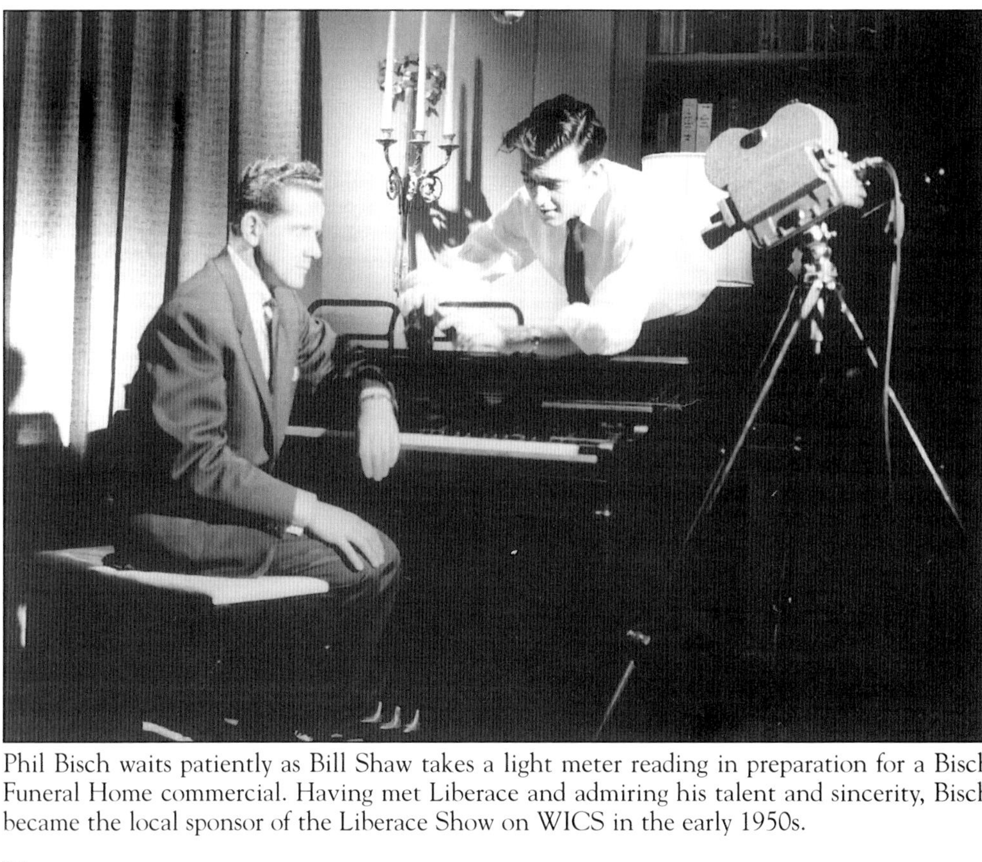

Phil Bisch waits patiently as Bill Shaw takes a light meter reading in preparation for a Bisch Funeral Home commercial. Having met Liberace and admiring his talent and sincerity, Bisch became the local sponsor of the Liberace Show on WICS in the early 1950s.

Popular children's movies of the late 1940s and 1950s such as Hop-a-long Cassidy often had western themes where the good guy always won. So, a western theme for local children's TV programs was a natural in the 1950s (right). But once the U.S./Russian space race dominated people's attention, children's programming changed with the times. The cardboard spaceship and astronaut in the photo below with their home-made appearance still manage an ominous look.

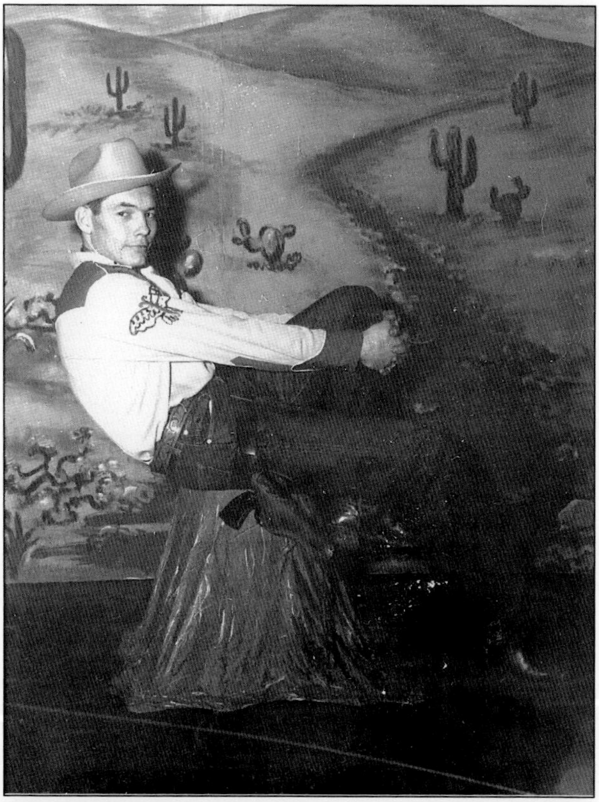

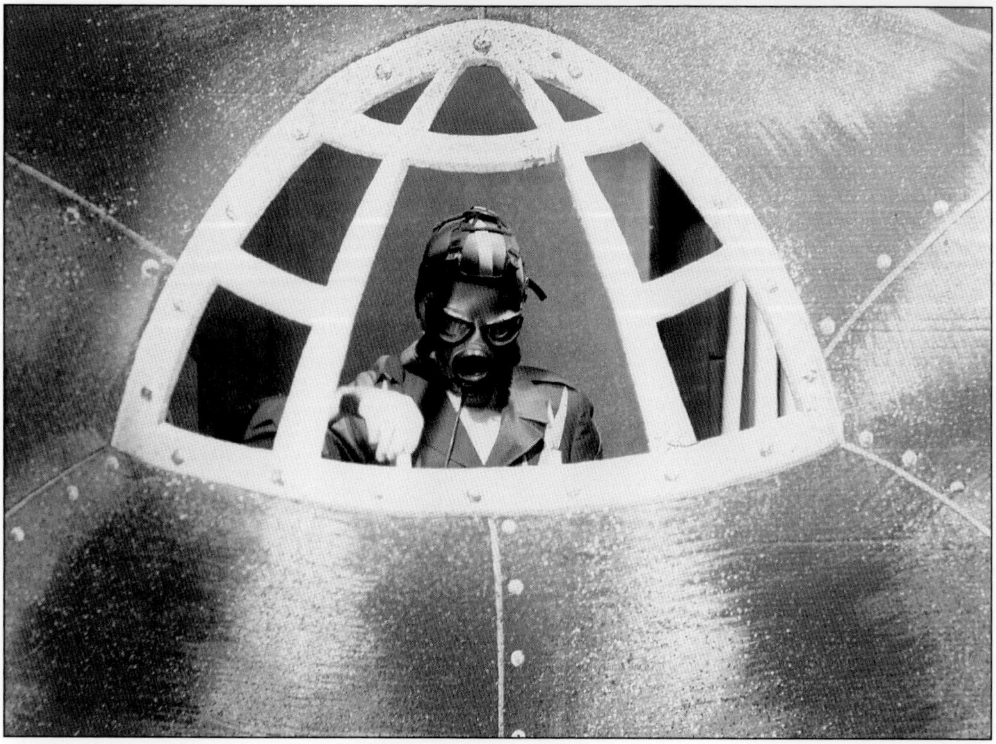

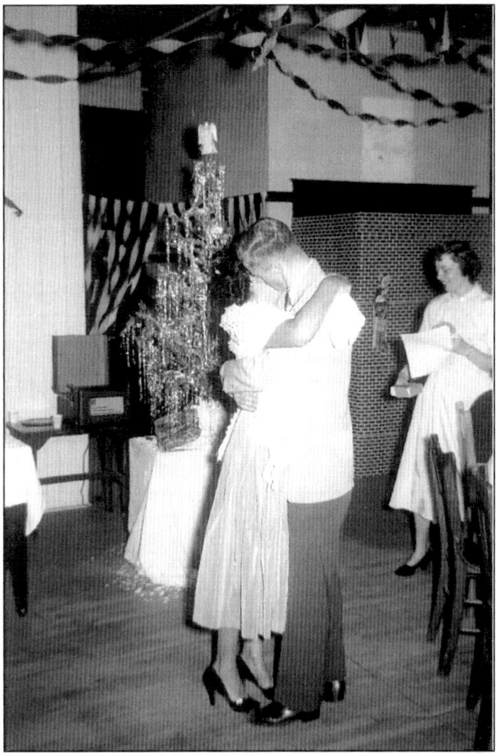

While getting a business education was a serious thing to students at Brown's Business College in the 1950s, life wasn't all work. This school Christmas party photo is tellingly titled "under the mistletoe?" Brown's closed in the 1990s.

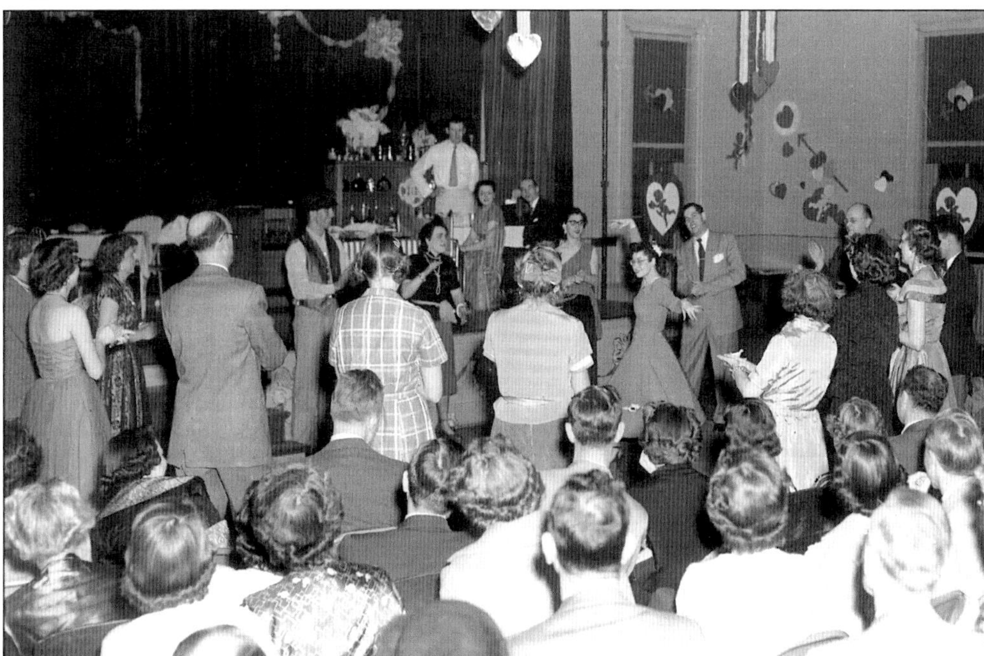

In school parties aren't all just for kids. This all-faculty Valentine's Party was held at Stuart School in February of 1953. The seated lady teachers have strikingly similar hairstyles seen from the back. Audiences watch an improvisational entertainer as she entertains with self-consciously artistic dance moves.

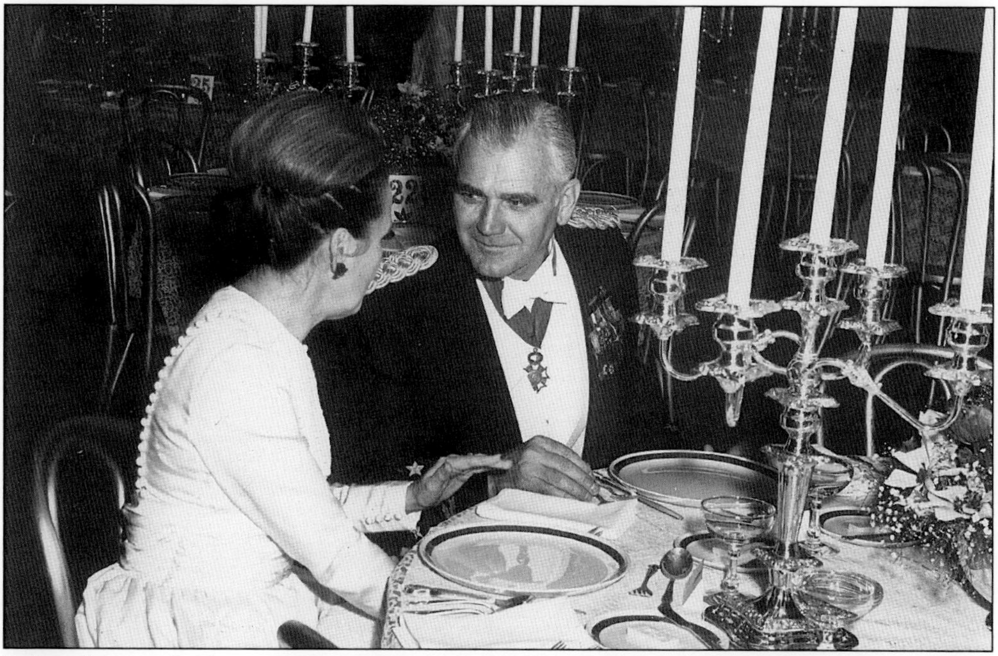

Political Springfield sometimes entertains lavishly. In 1970 General William Westmoreland was feted at the St. Nicholas Hotel for the Lincoln Academy Ball. Silver candelabra, gold chairs, linen tablecloths and an orchestra were part of the backdrop. But the real entertainment was the crowd of dignitaries. Mrs. Dorothy Ogilvie, wife of the Governor, makes polite dinner table conversation with the general.

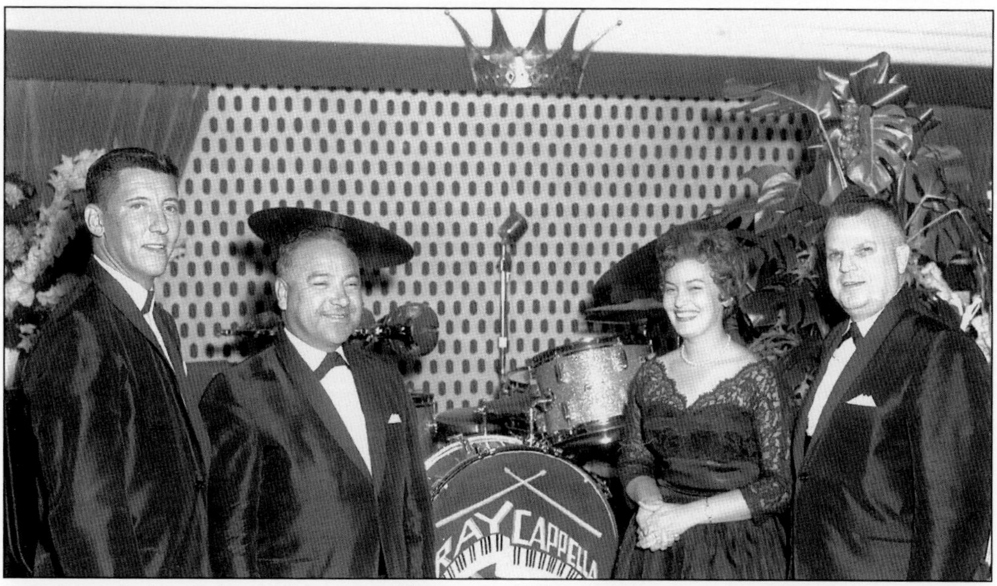

Ray Cappella headed one of Springfield's most well known bands in the 1940s and 50s. His was the house band at the locally famous Mill Restaurant for 31 years until it burned in 1972. Ray loved music so much he worked full time and played six nights a week. "I can feel pretty rough all day," he once said, "but 15 minutes after I start playing I feed good." Cappella (far right) and his band are shown in the 1950s.

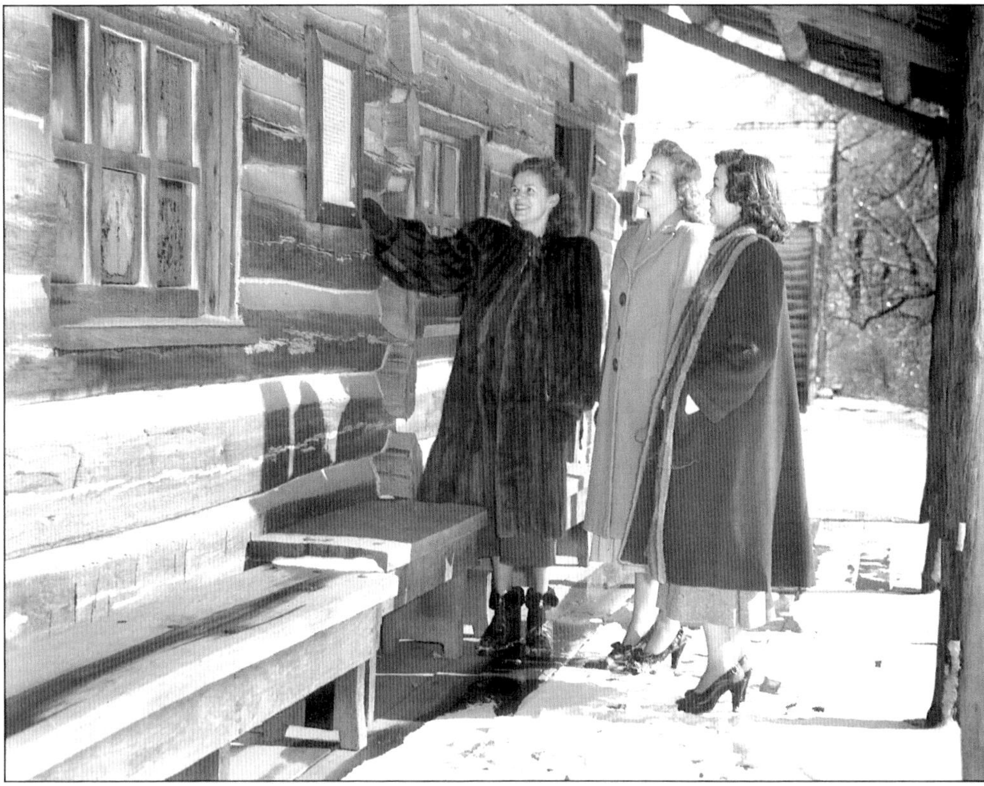

Ah, freshly fallen snow blanketing the cabins of New Salem. The aroma of woodsmoke acrid in the air and the woodsy smell of pine and moldering oak leaves. What could be more charming in a rustic way? And, what could be a greater study in contrast than these citified and daintily-shod ladies at the village's Hill-MacNamara store? They are all decked out in the Dior-inspired "new look" with its low hemlines. The two women at right have gracefully-cut cloth coats while their companion (no doubt smugly superior) wears a hefty fur, which today might be considered crass and vulgar at best and heartlessly cruel at worst.

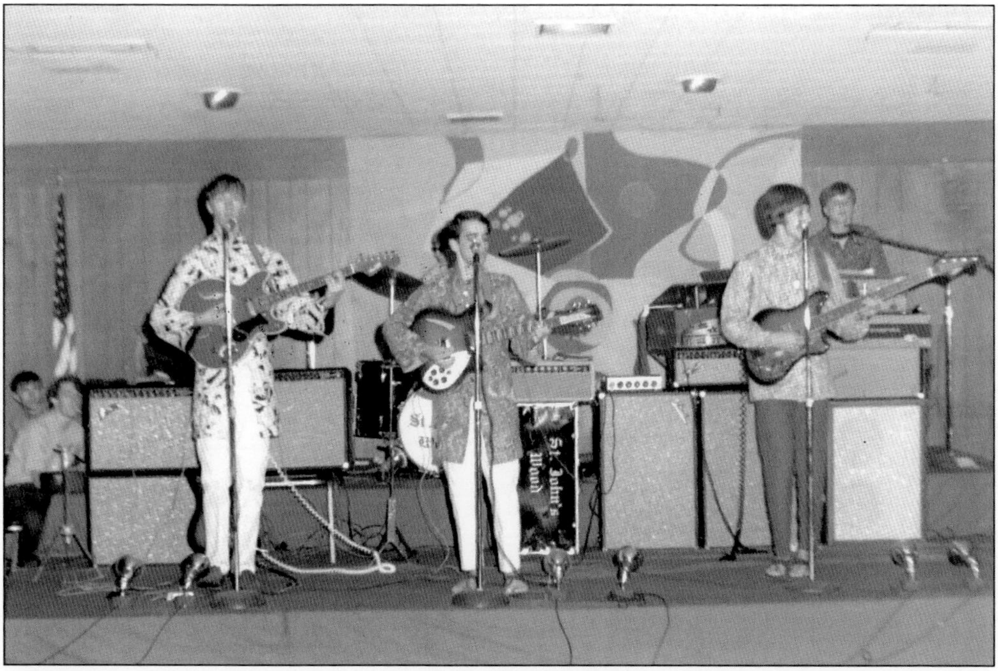

The band St. John's Wood performs at Springfield's old Myers Brothers Department Store in the 1960s. The members of the band are fashionably attired in the wildly-patterned, thigh length coats of the day. Myers owners continually promoted store events, from concerts to fashion shows, to boost sales.

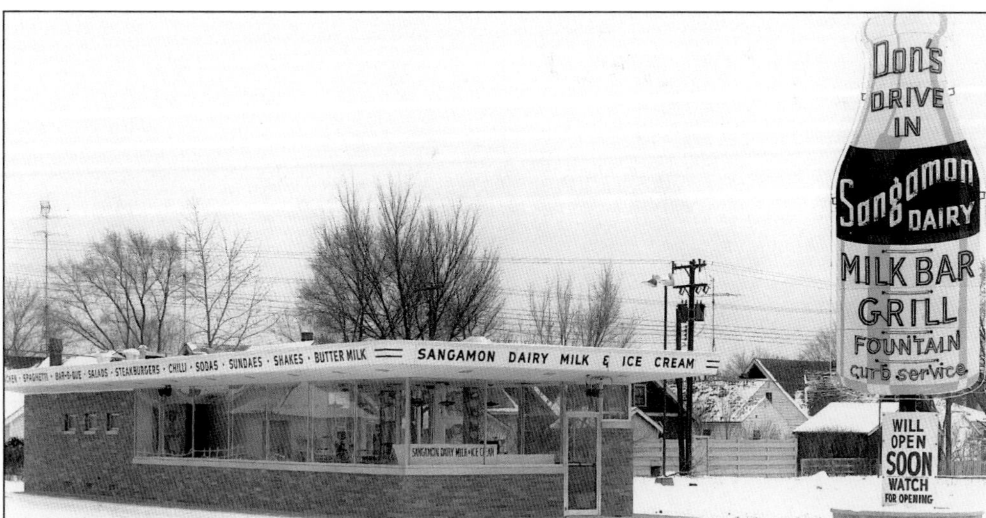

One of the popular eateries in Springfield during the late 1950s was Don's Drive In located at the corner of MacArthur Boulevard and Ash Street. The products of Springfield's Sangamon Dairy were a prominently featured part of the restaurant's menu.

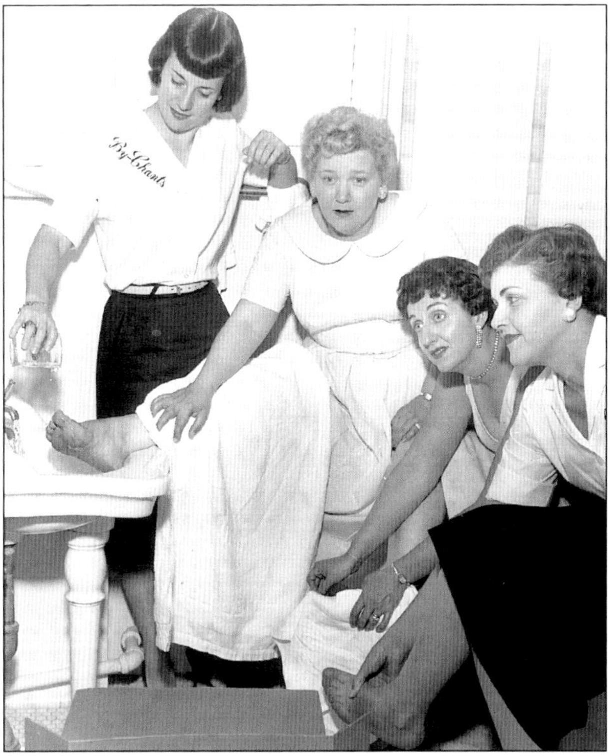

A regional championship for quartets and choruses that sang in four part harmony was held at Springfield's Leland hotel in the 1950s. This group of local hostesses playfully (and graphically) conveyed to a reporter tales of their fun filled but hectic day and aching feet.

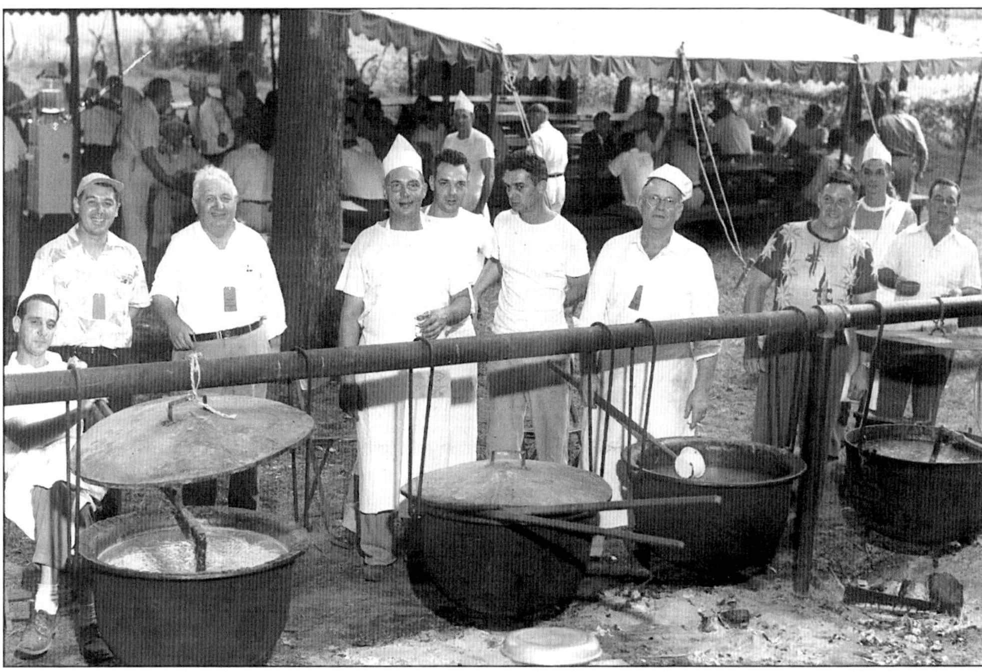

The Mozart Club, organized in 1906 by male choir members mostly from Saints Peter and Paul Church, held annual stag burgoos in the 1940s. For the uninitiated, burgoo is a mixture of beef, chicken, turtle or available meat and every conceivable vegetable around slowly simmered in large caldrons for several days.

Four

SPRINGFIELD PUBLIC LIFE

In 1948 Springfield was the subject of criticism in a derogatory article in the *Saturday Evening Post* publicly exposing our gambling, vice, and lack of community pride. After a generation of civic housecleaning, it was with a great sense of pride and accomplishment that Springfield basked in favorable light as one of *Look Magazine* and the National Municipal League's All American Cities in 1970. The award was for "citizen participation in the practice of democracy." With state initiatives through Governor Otto Kerner and the leadership of Mayor Nelson Howarth, the Springfield Jaycees submitted an application listing an impressive number of programs organized, rallied for and supported by volunteers, businesses, and organizations. The list included improved street lighting, public transportation, parks, low-cost housing programs, a Fair Housing Board, small business loans for minorities, downtown redevelopment, and donations to support the new Lincoln Land Community College, Sangamon State University, and a coming medical school.

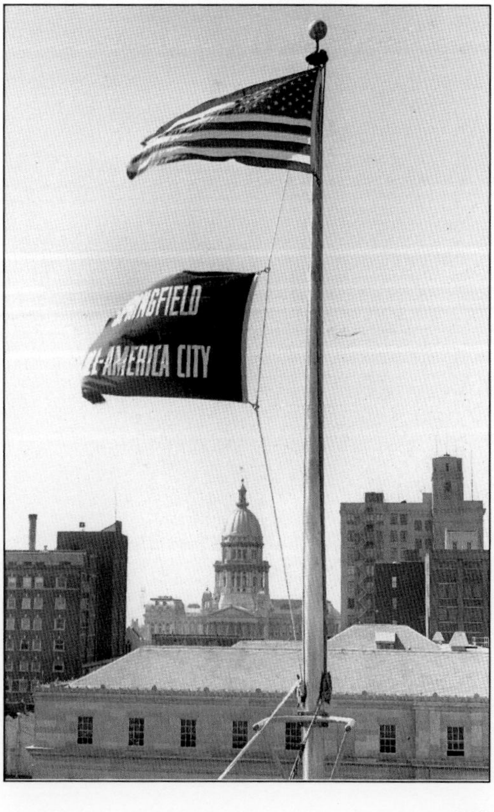

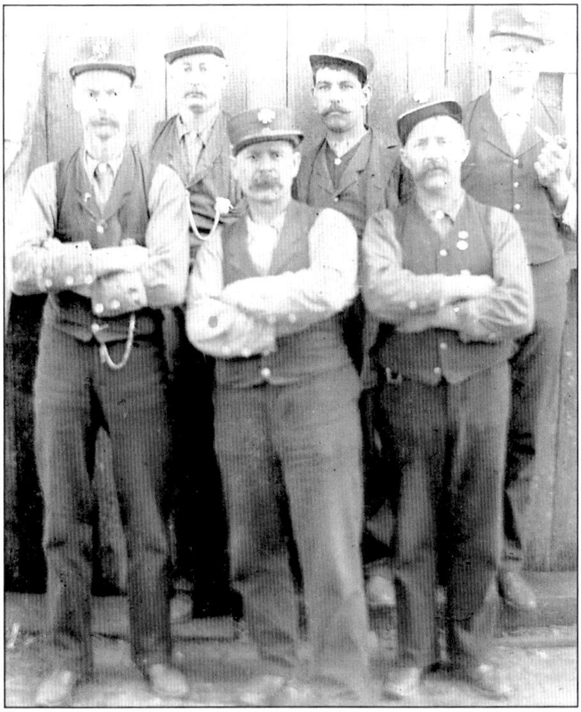

The Springfield Fire Department became a paid, city agency in 1869. Previously fire protection was by volunteer units with names like Red Rover Hook and Ladder and Young America Companies. Fireplugs too came in the 1860s, replacing the bucket brigades of earlier times. This crew, from the early 1900s, was still using horses to pull the engine; the first motorized vehicle did not come on the scene until 1914.

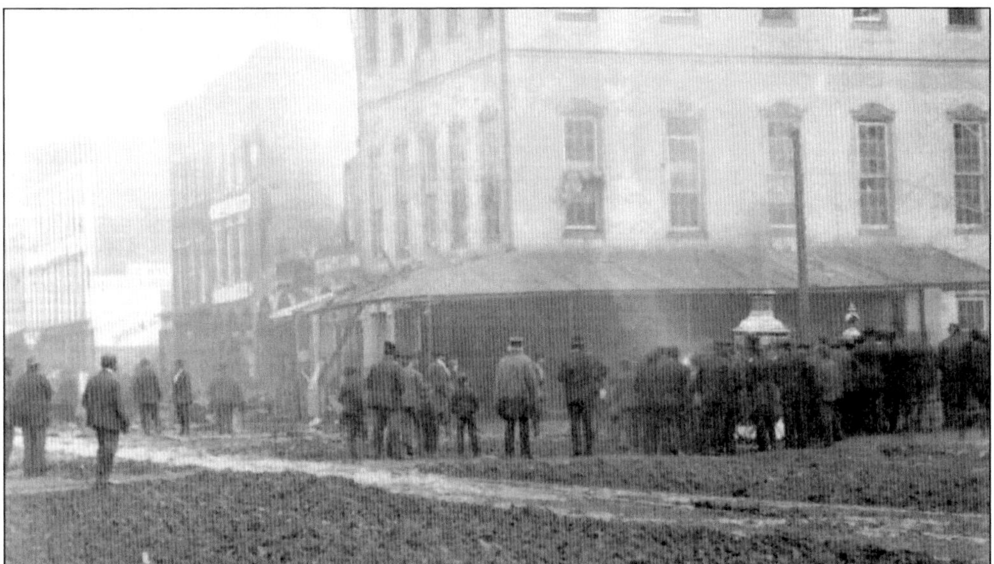

Fire has been an ever present danger to life and property. 19th century Springfield was devastated by two major blazes in the 1850s that nearly destroyed the east and west sides of the public square, interrupting business and commerce for several months. Springfield's hook and ladder companies took great pride, however, in being able to respond at a moment's notice. The old "pumper" is seen in action here in February 1871. The Masonic Hall, on the northeast corner of Fifth and Monroe streets, was extensively damaged from the blaze in the building to the north. The hall was rebuilt with a fashionable Mansard roof to match new buildings adjoining it. Ironically those were lost in another February fire—this one in 1980.

As automobiles became common in the early 1900s a new concern came to the city police force—traffic control. Brave officers stood guard in the center of traffic in downtown streets. Even after streetlights were installed by the 1920s, watchful policemen guided traffic as smoothly as orchestra conductors. This scene, from about 1960, recalls the end of an era. Regular traffic police patrols ended in that decade.

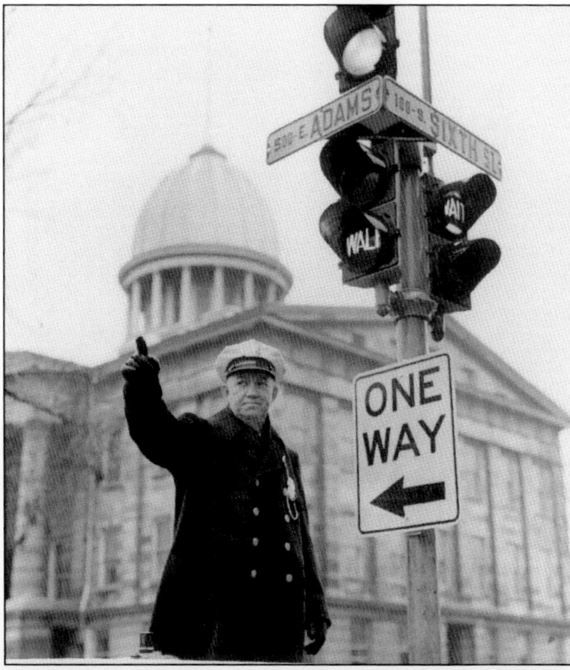

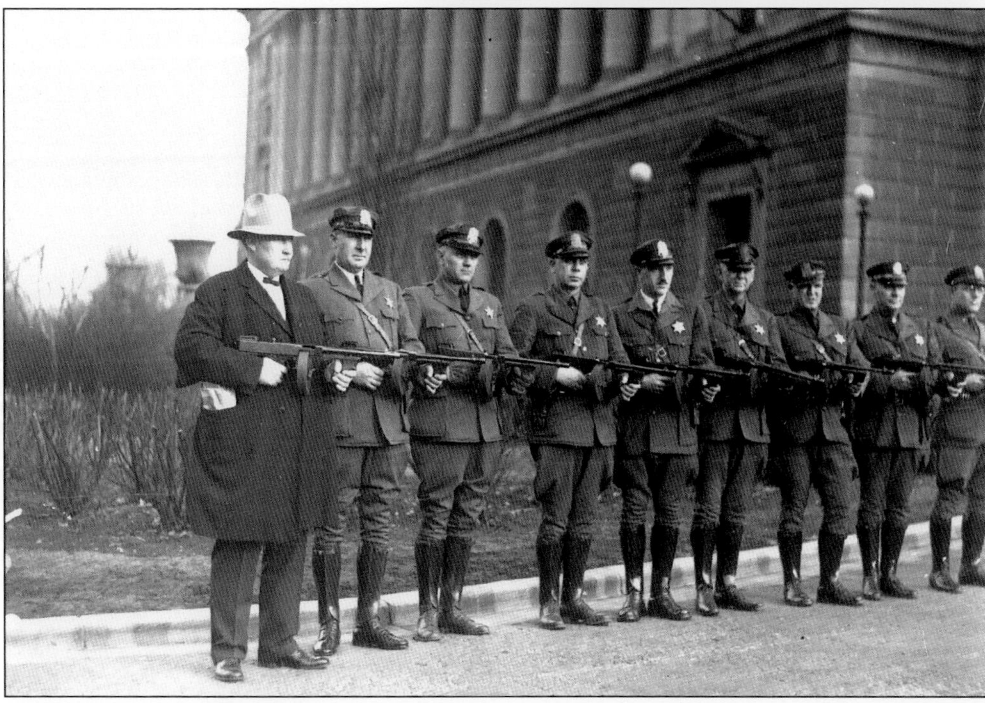

During the early 1930s, when the country was in the depths of an economic catastrophe, and there was great worry about the stability of our government, rampant boot legging and bank robbery epitomized by Bonnie Parker and Clyde Barrow underscored the lawlessness of the era. Government security forces, like the Illinois State Police shown here on the capitol grounds, made a great show of military style security precautions. This row of police, weapons at ready, were a reassuring sign to an uncertain community in those dark days.

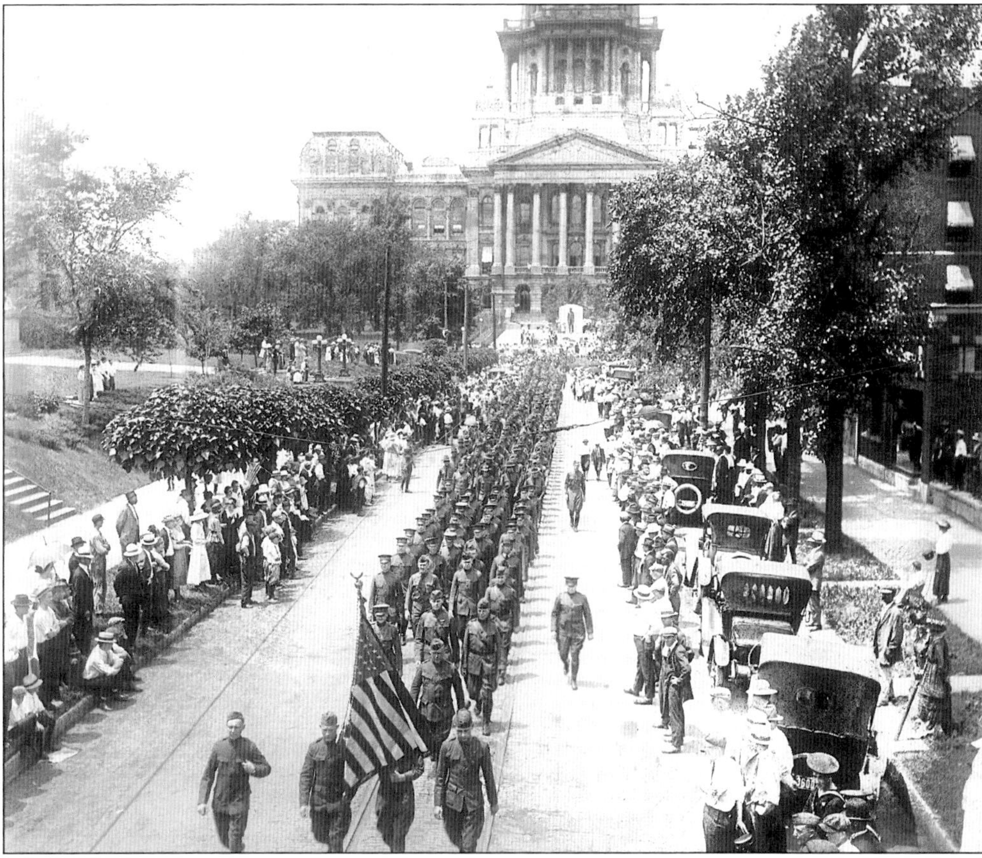

Over 4,500 Sangamon County men and women served in the First World War. After their return, a mammoth welcome home parade was held for them in 1919. An honor guard leads troops marching down Capitol Avenue in front of the Statehouse.

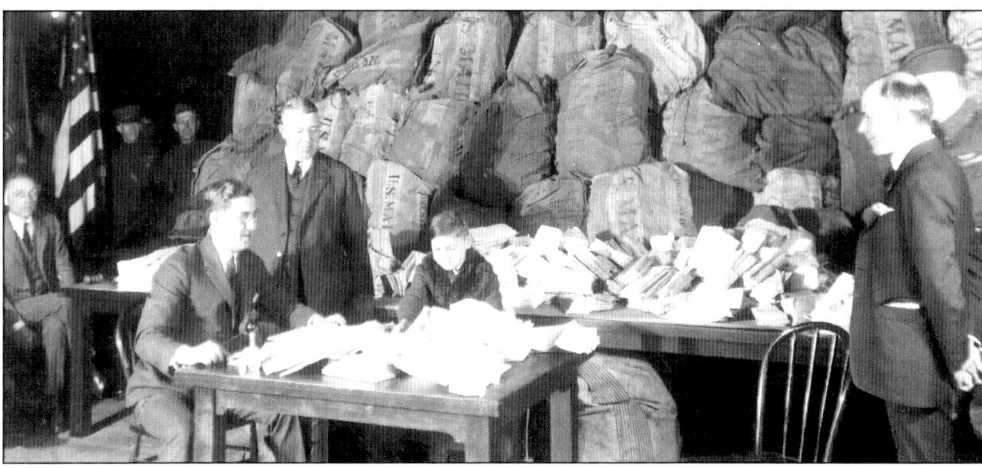

A big ceremony was held on January 24, 1923, for the initial drawing of applications for bonus claims of Illinois World War I veterans. Donald Heter, the son of Sergeant William Heter, was selected to draw out the tenth and last application during the ceremony. William Heter had recently been slain during a streetcar holdup.

With over 50 women from Sangamon County serving as nurses and Red Cross workers in World War I, little Clarissa Milligan had several examples to emulate. Clarissa is shown here dressed as a Red Cross nurse while her cousin wears a miniature army uniform.

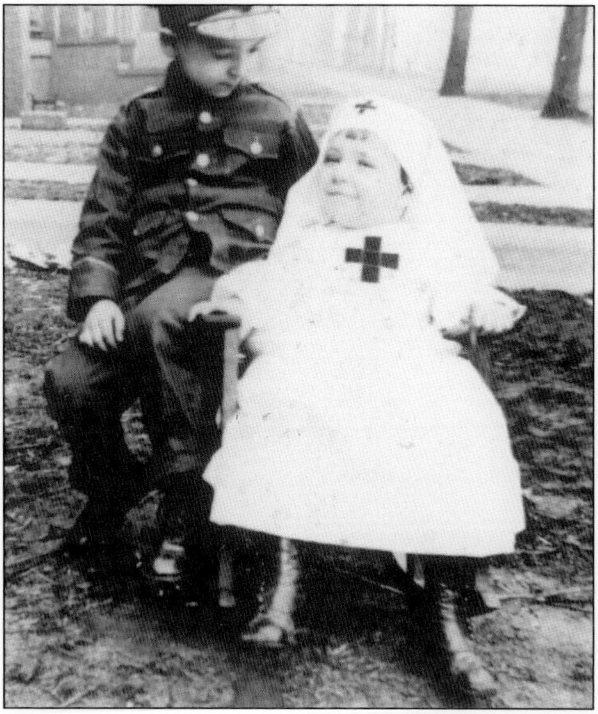

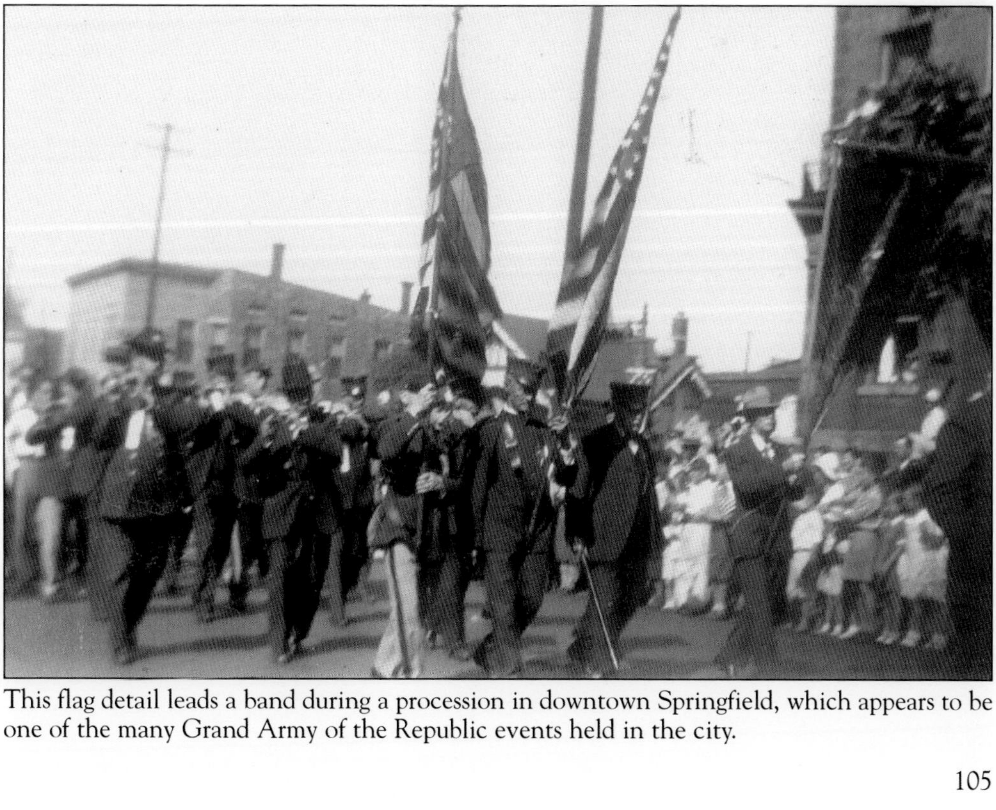

This flag detail leads a band during a procession in downtown Springfield, which appears to be one of the many Grand Army of the Republic events held in the city.

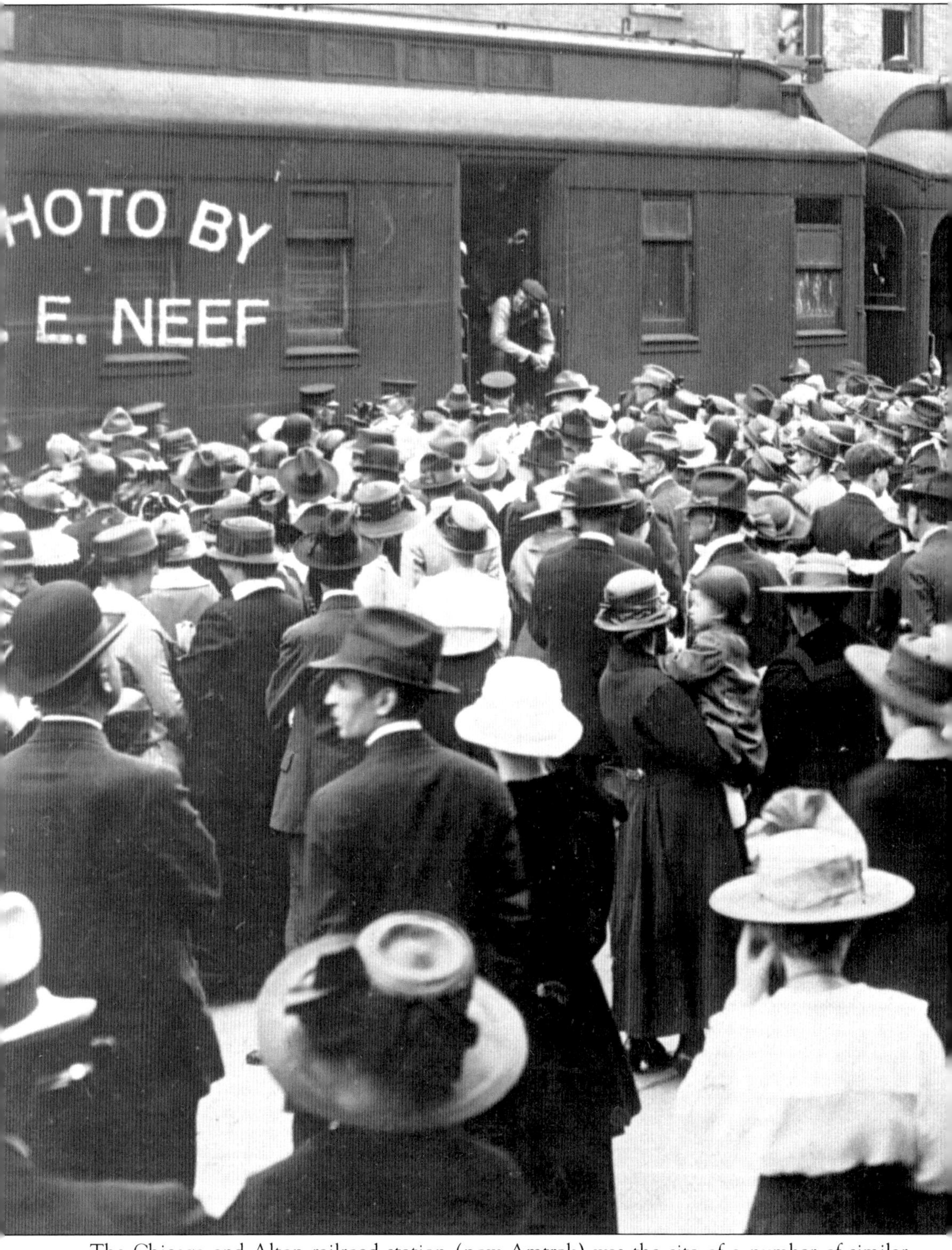

The Chicago and Alton railroad station (now Amtrak) was the site of a number of similar, emotional scenes as young men left to become soldiers and sailors in World War I. This farewell

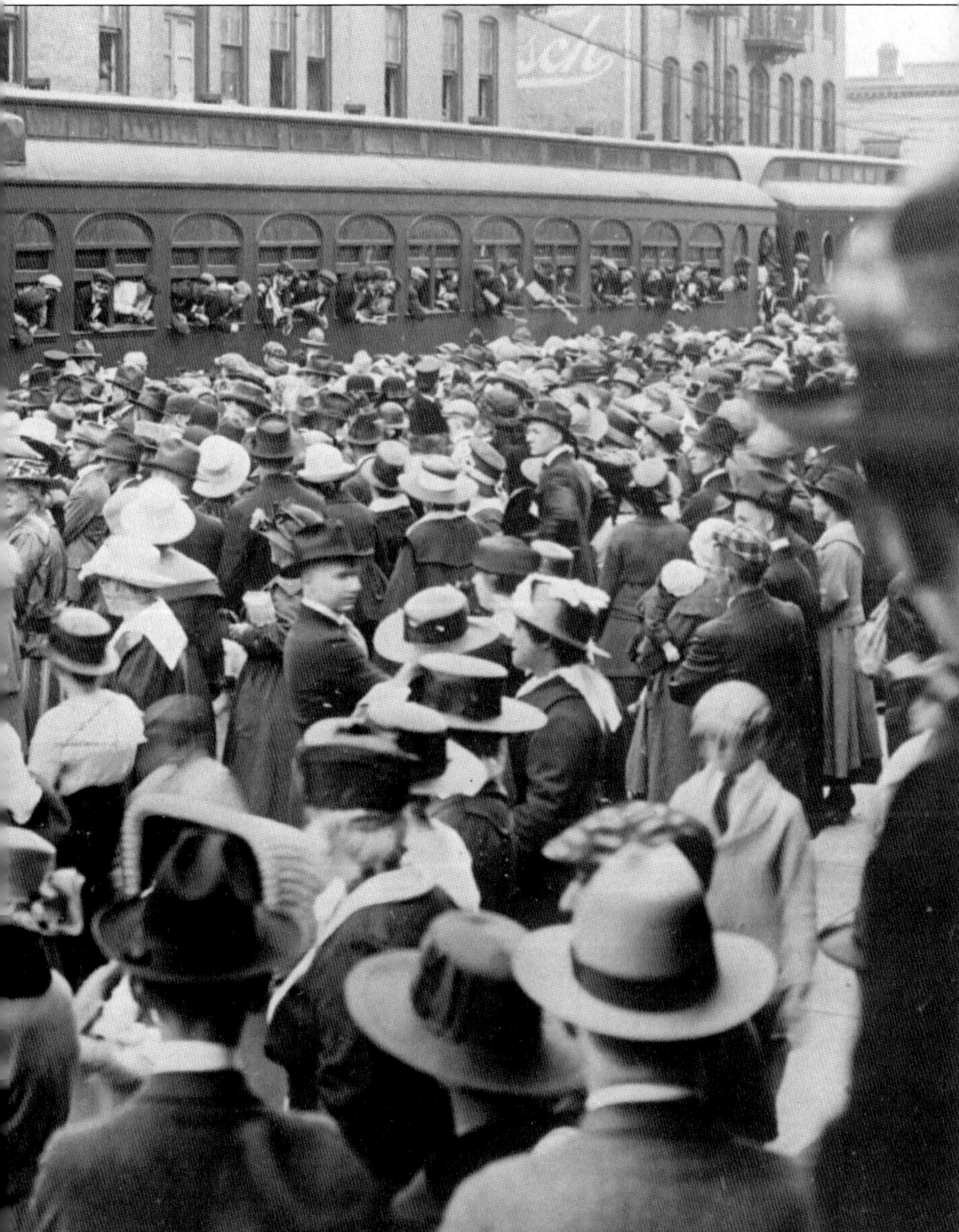

came near the end of the war on June 19, 1918. Inductees lean out railroad car windows for a last glimpse of loved ones.

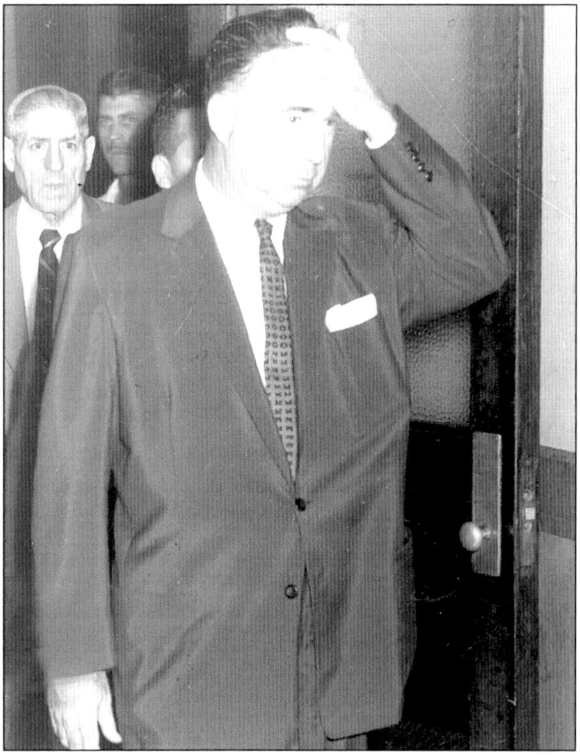

Public office holders sometimes betray our trust. One famous Springfield example was Orville Hodge. The Republican senator from southern Illinois became state auditor in 1953. He resigned abruptly three years later and was convicted of tapping the state treasury for more than a million dollars. He spent six years in prison but managed to regain a respectful place in his southern Illinois hometown during his last years. A distressed Hodge leaves the courtroom during his 1956 trial, the biggest news in Springfield that summer.

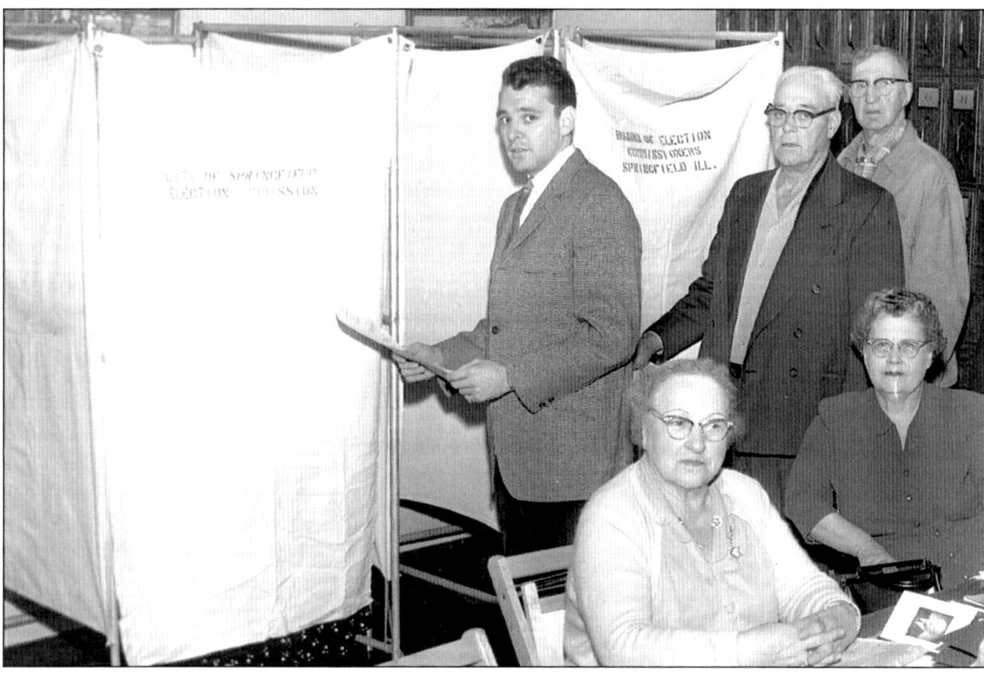

Voting in a political town like Springfield is not only a duty but also an important community event. Candidates for office—state, county and municipal—are often well-known members of the community, and often partisan feeling runs high. This scene from the 1960s shows election judges and voters at a local polling place.

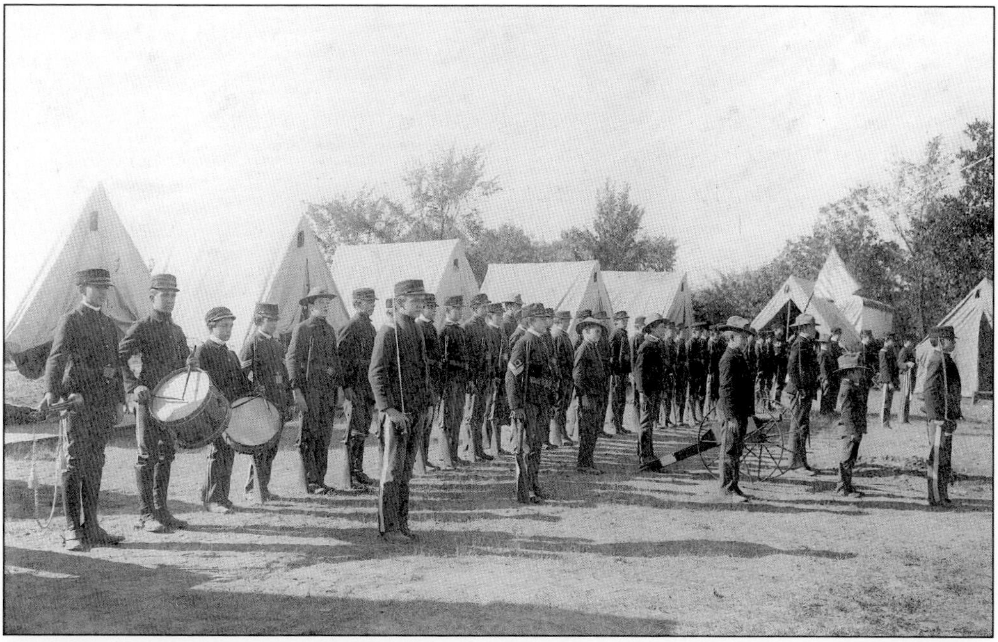

The Yates Cadets formed in 1900 and lasted about four years. They had no official military standing but were given old guns for drills by Illinois Governor Richard Yates—hence their name. About 85 elementary and high school boys belonged during that time. A nostalgic reunion was held in 1935 at the home of one former member, Springfield Mayor John "Buddy" Kapp. The 1901 photo shows a typical encampment.

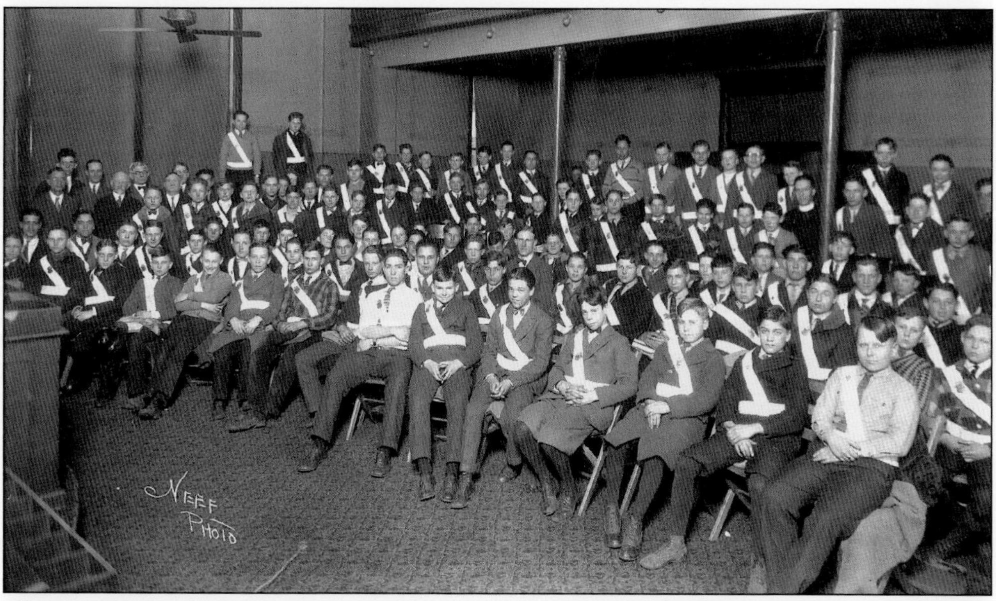

Chicago Motor Club President Charles M. Hayes originated the idea of patrol boys after witnessing a particularly terrible accident where children were struck by an automobile. His idea caught the public's imagination and within a few years almost every public and parochial school in the Illinois-Indiana area had adopted the idea. Springfield's first "class" of patrol boys is shown in this 1927 photo taken at city hall.

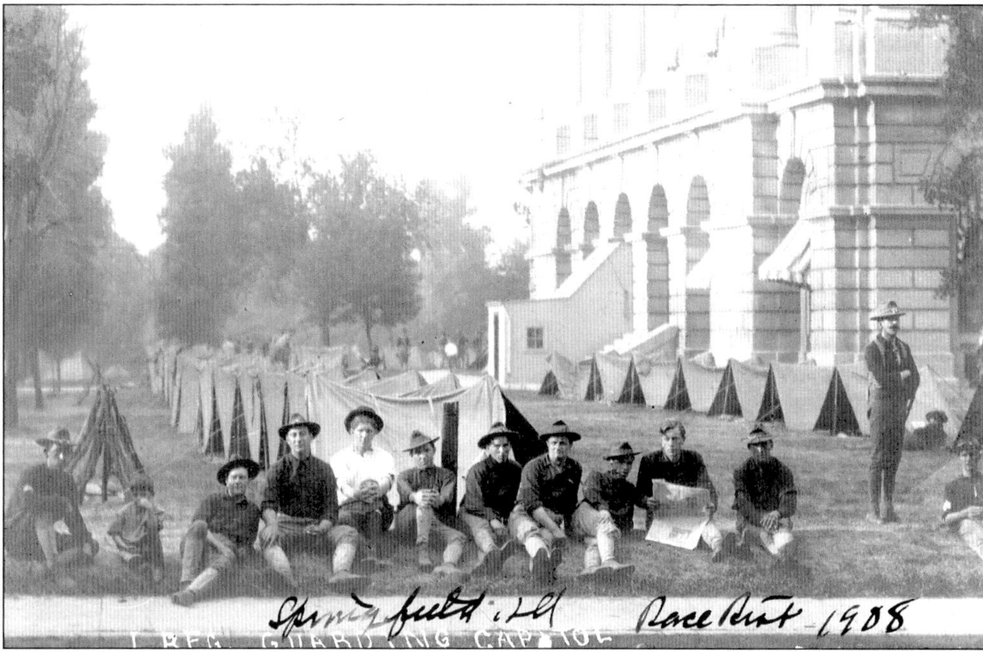

Over three thousand members of the Illinois National Guard were called up to patrol Springfield and quell mobs during the race riots of August 14 and 15 in 1908. Troops were stationed at strategic points throughout the city. These men were encamped on the lawn of the state capitol.

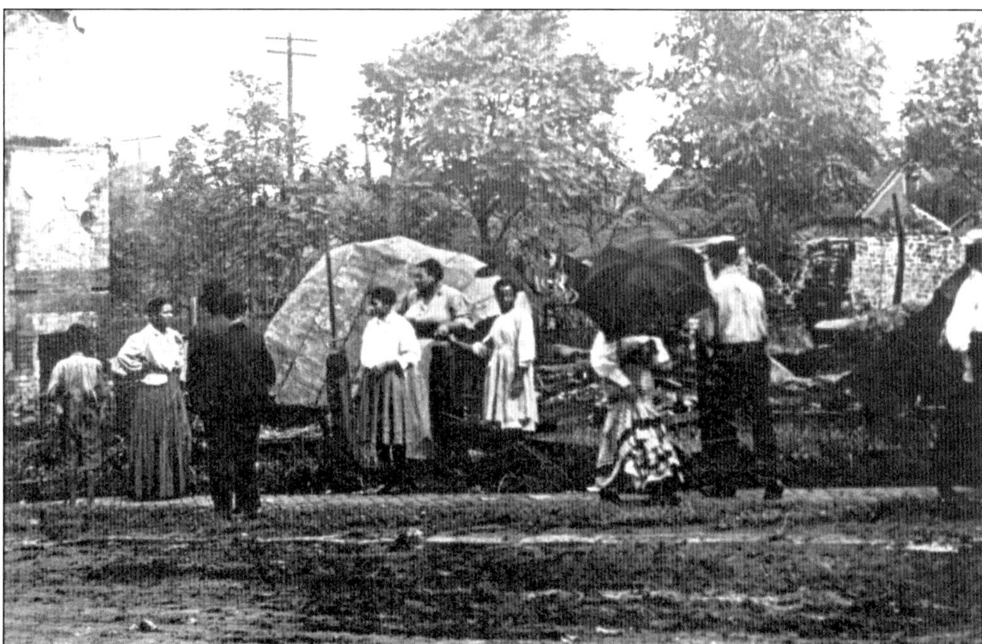

The black community in Springfield paid a heavy price during the race riots of 1908. Two men lost their lives and several others were wounded. Over forty families like the one pictured here lost their homes to arson.

During World War II, the Illinois State Fairgrounds served as a supply depot for the army air force. The fairgrounds also housed a number of Chinese troops, like this man pictured here, who were brought in for training purposes.

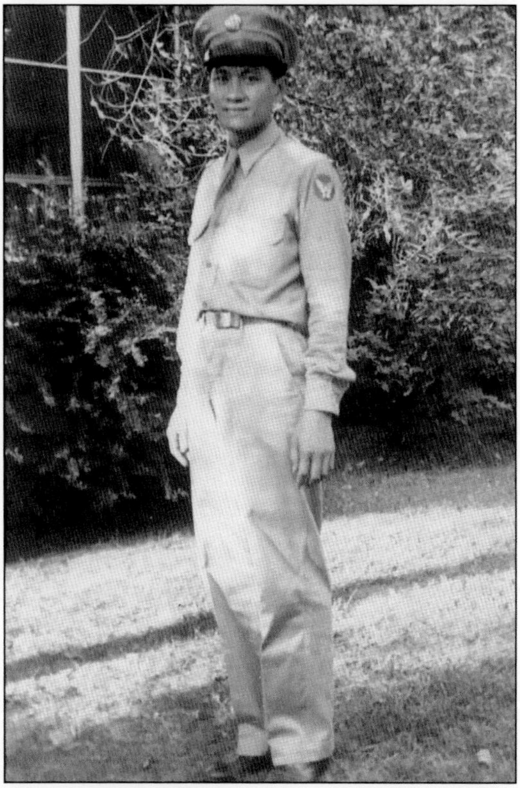

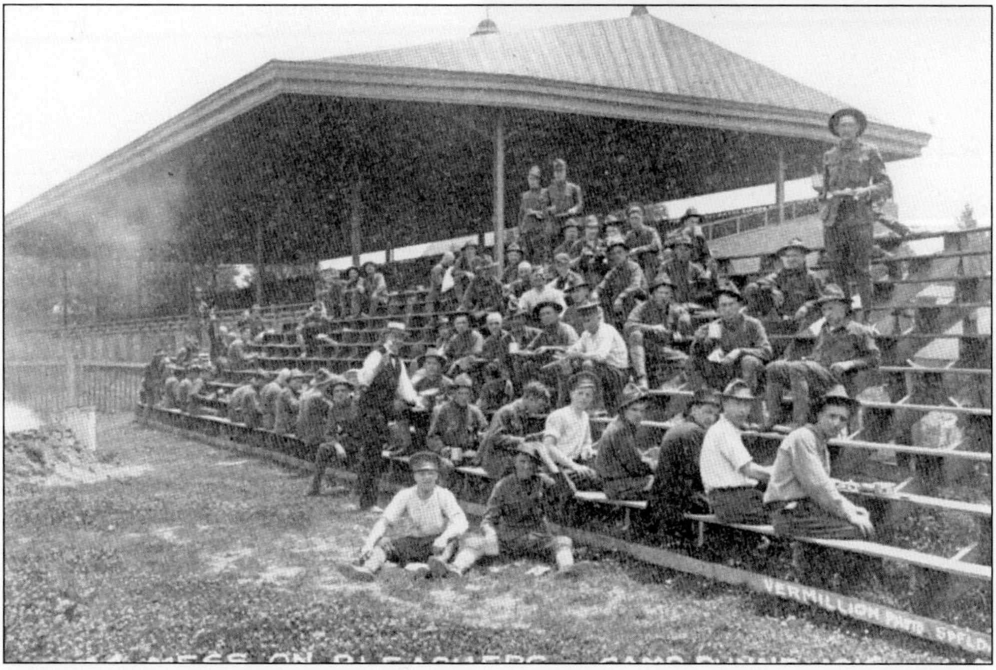

The bleachers at the Illinois State Fairgrounds served as mess tables and seats for Illinois National guardsmen in this 1916 postcard. The fairgrounds were named Camp Dunne in honor of Governor Edward Dunne during World War I.

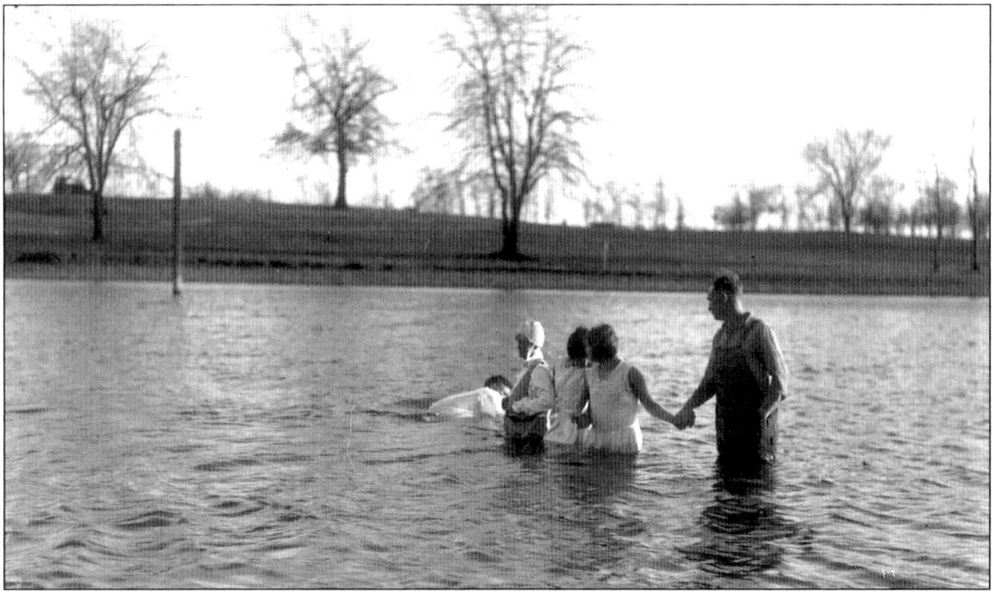

The evangelist Roy "Frosty" Foster baptized seven converts during a Full Gospel Assembly revival. Five women and two men braved a cold west wind along with Foster for the baptism in Bunn Park Lake on November 24, 1930.

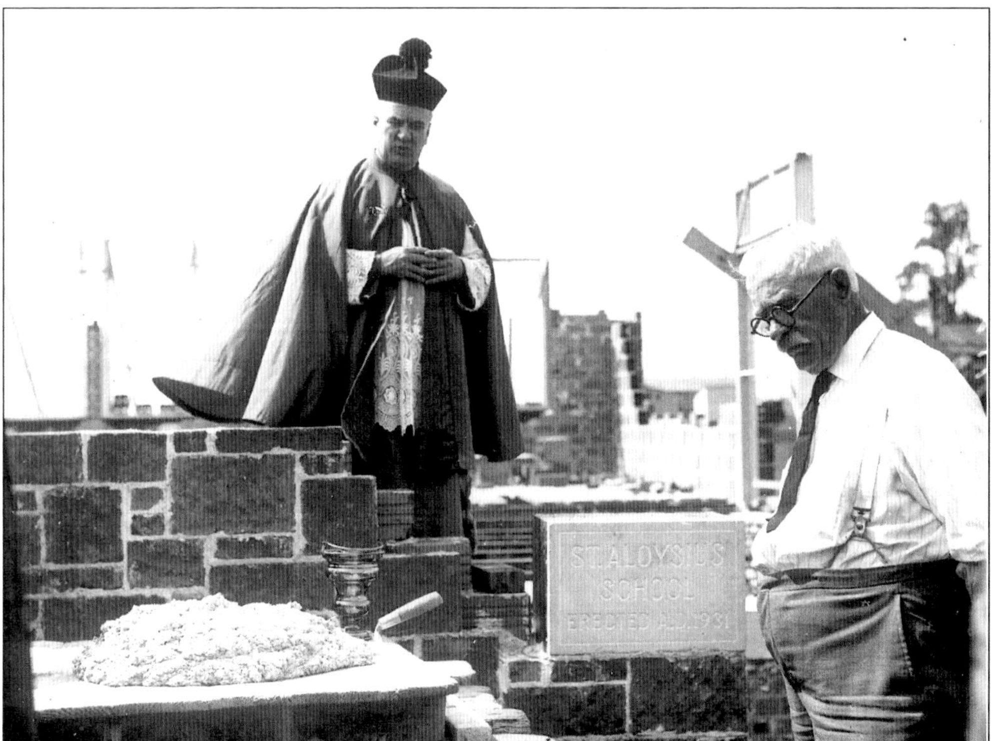

Monsignor Michael Tarrent gave the blessing at the laying of the cornerstone for Saint Aloysius combined church/school building on June 5, 1931. The building then being constructed is still in use as the parish school and a new church was built in 1955.

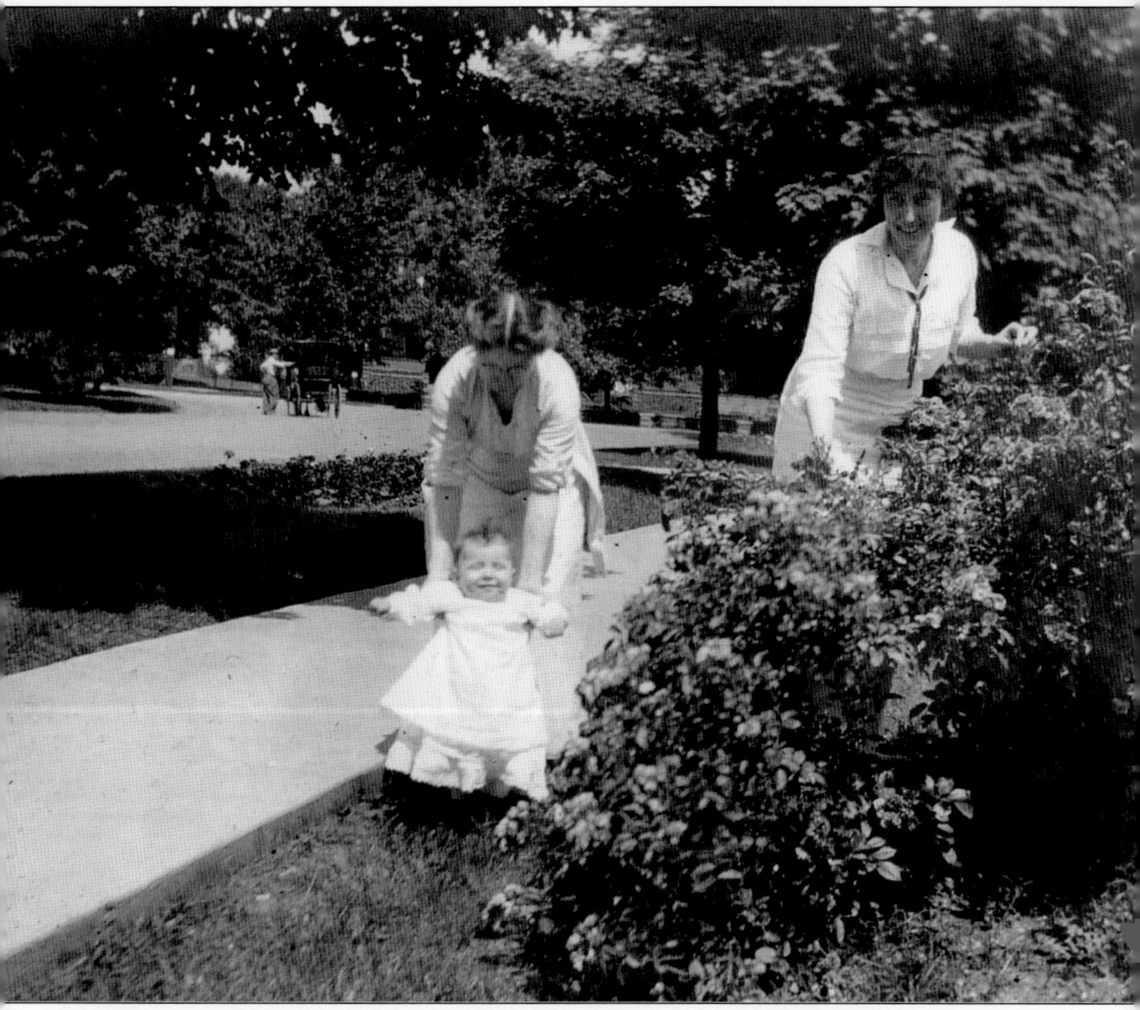

Two smiling women and an infant are embowered in summer's green leafiness in front of the Dr. Clarence Milligan House in the 1400 block of Holmes Avenue about 1918. Note the horse and carriage in the background.

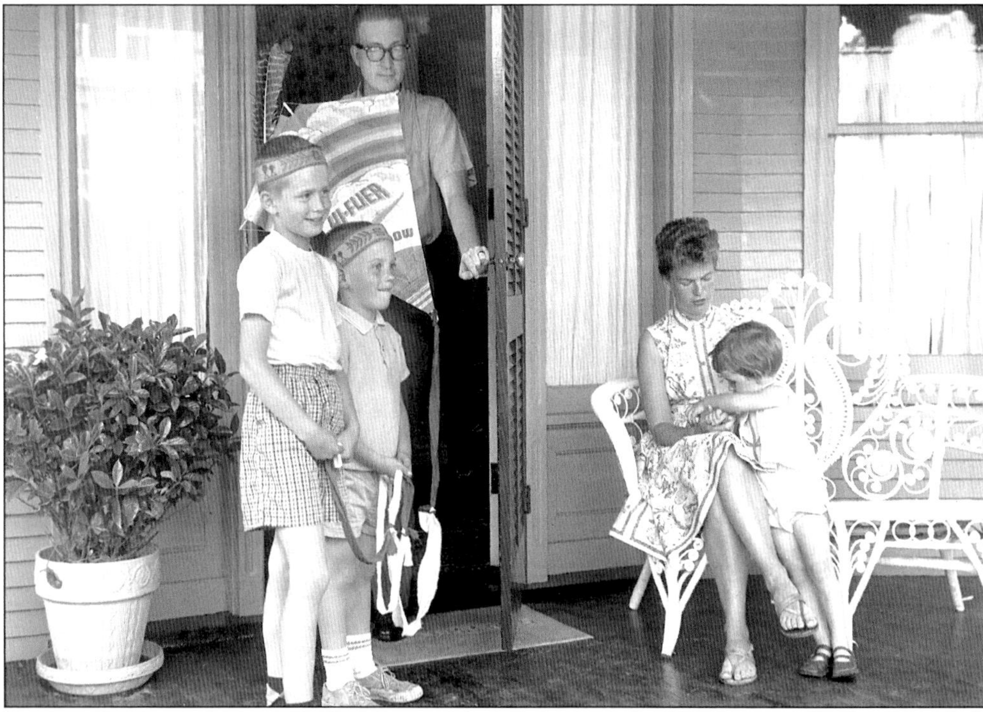

Springfield families have spent time together in many ways. Kite flying (above) is not as common a family activity as once it was. Still, windy, spring days bring out some families like this one seen above from the 1960s, ready for their flight. Another form of family togetherness could be in the family business. J.R. Fitzpatrick (center, left) with his daughter and son-in-law, Betsy and Tom Burton, and three of their children, are shown in the 1950s. The Fitzpatrick family operated a lumberyard, contracting business, and newspaper for 50 years.

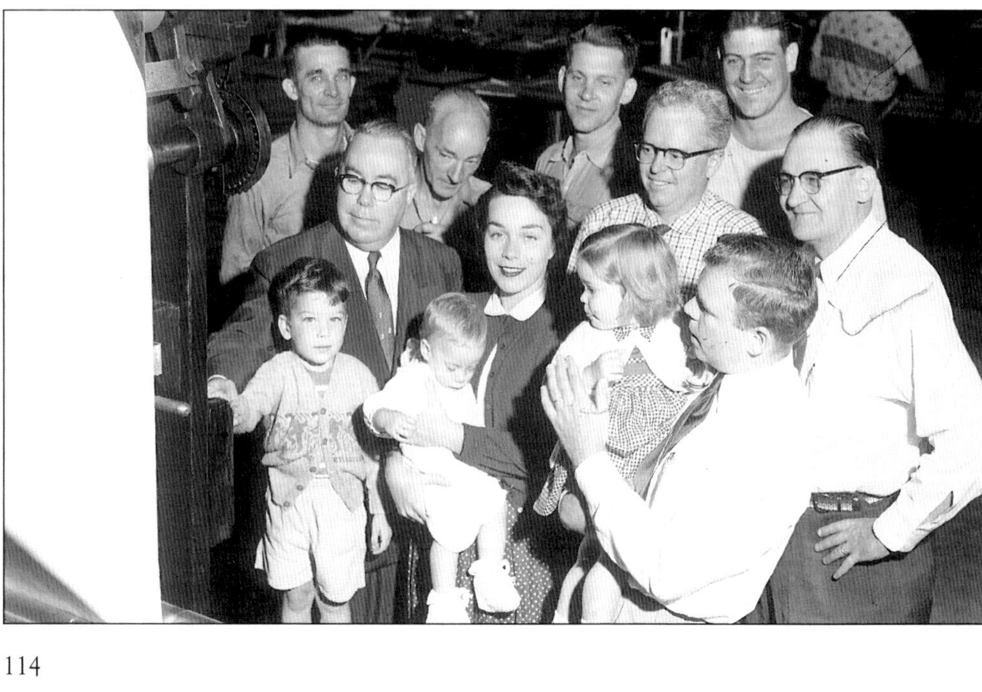

The teenager, that most maligned and misunderstood family member, came into their own in the 20th Century. Teens were first recognized as a distinct group beginning in the early 1900s. Since that time they have become the focus of surveys, opinion polls and advertising campaigns. During the baby-boom generation they seemed to be at the center of our universe. Two favorite teen pastimes, talking on the phone and learning to drive featured Springfield teens in these publicity shots from the 1960s. Below, Springfield High School driving instructor Roger Kendall shows a willing female student that tire-changing and vehicle maintenance are all part of the driving experience.

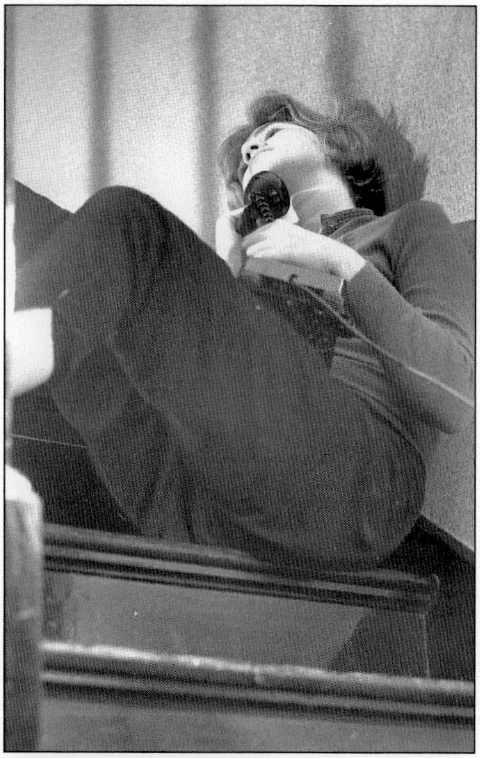

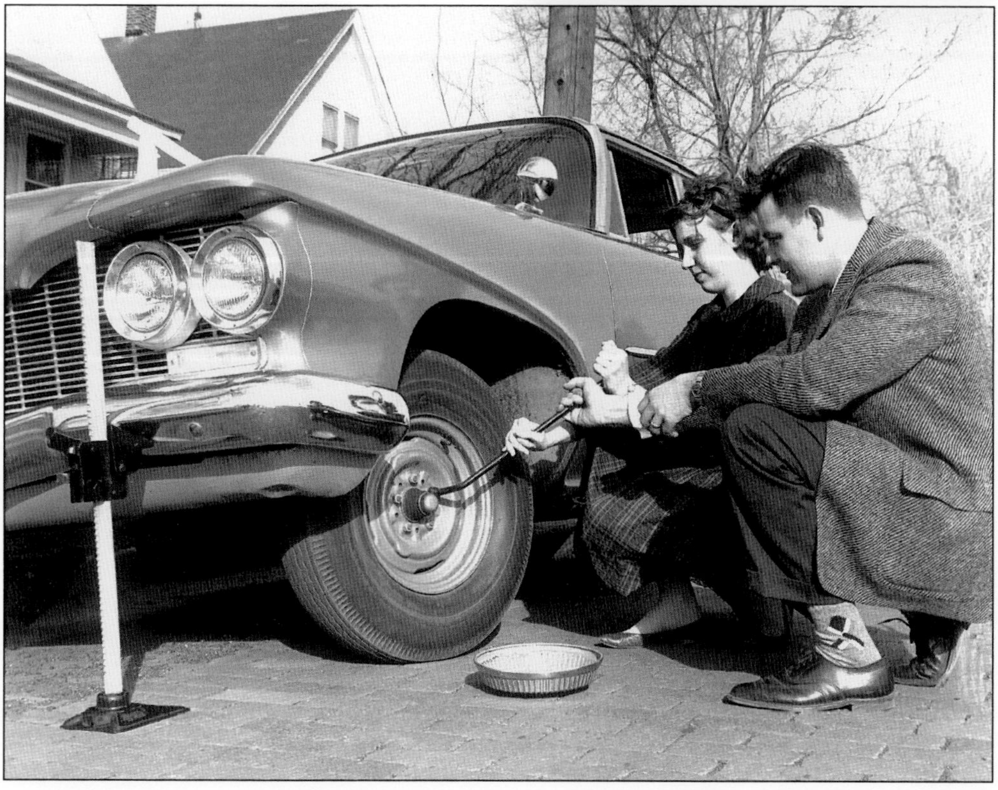

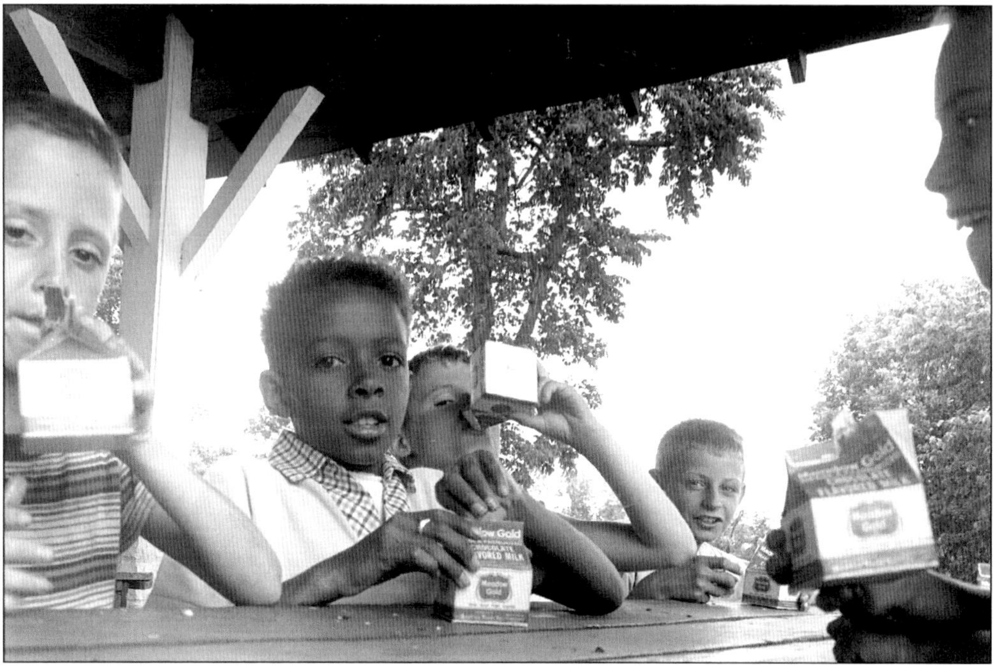

The Springfield Boy's Club was created in 1956 as a local solution to a perceived delinquency problem. The Club, now the Boys and Girls Club, provides a place for recreational and educational activities for local children. This group of young boys enjoy cartons of milk during an activities break in 1961.

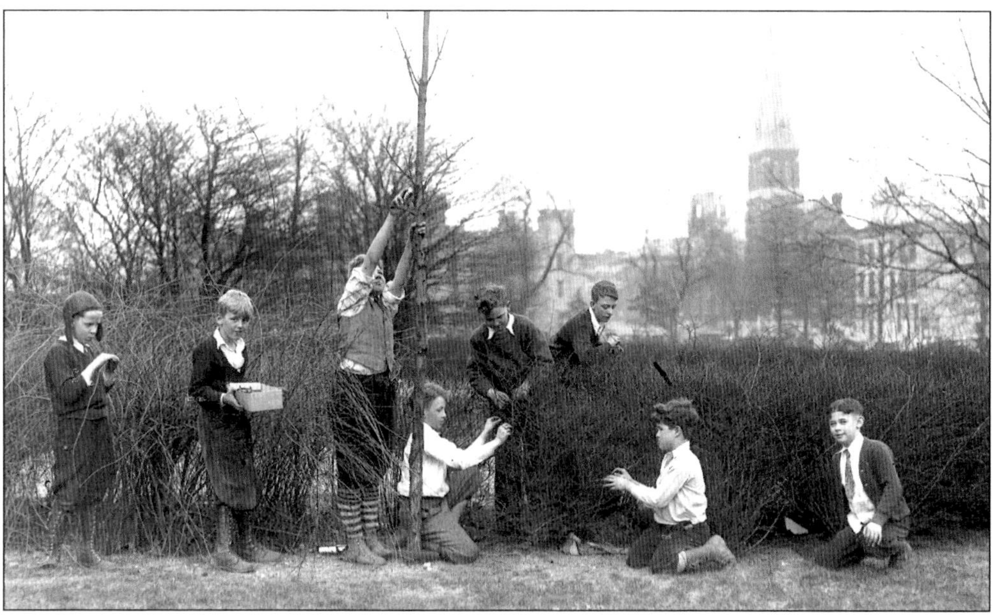

As a service project in 1932, Members of the A.R. Crook Collector's club in Springfield gather the cocoons of bag worms from the shrubbery of the state capitol grounds. The worms, which hatch in the spring, can be very destructive to trees and plants, stripping away much of the foliage.

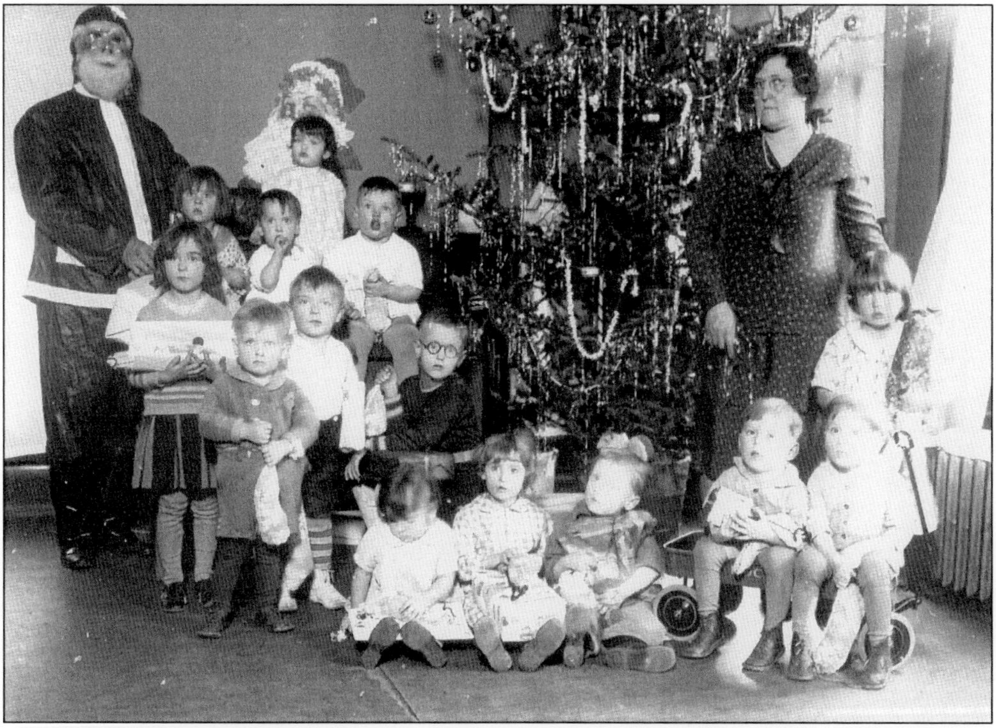

The Lioness Club of Springfield gave a Christmas party to the children of this Springfield day nursery in 1930. Gathered around the Christmas tree with Santa Claus, they soon left to go home and await more presents the following day.

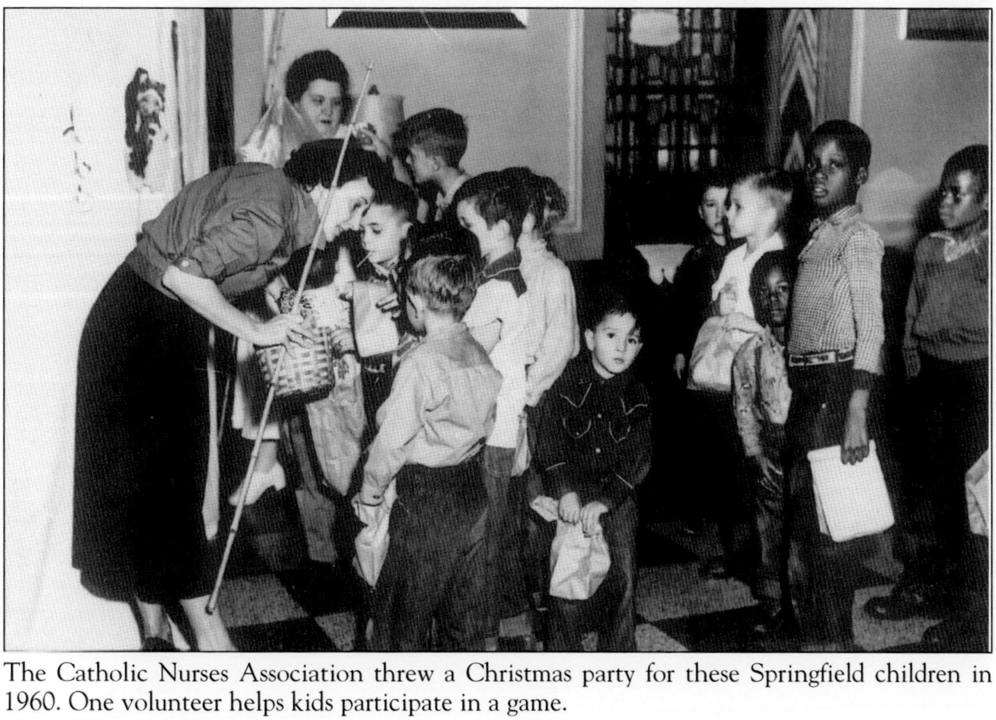

The Catholic Nurses Association threw a Christmas party for these Springfield children in 1960. One volunteer helps kids participate in a game.

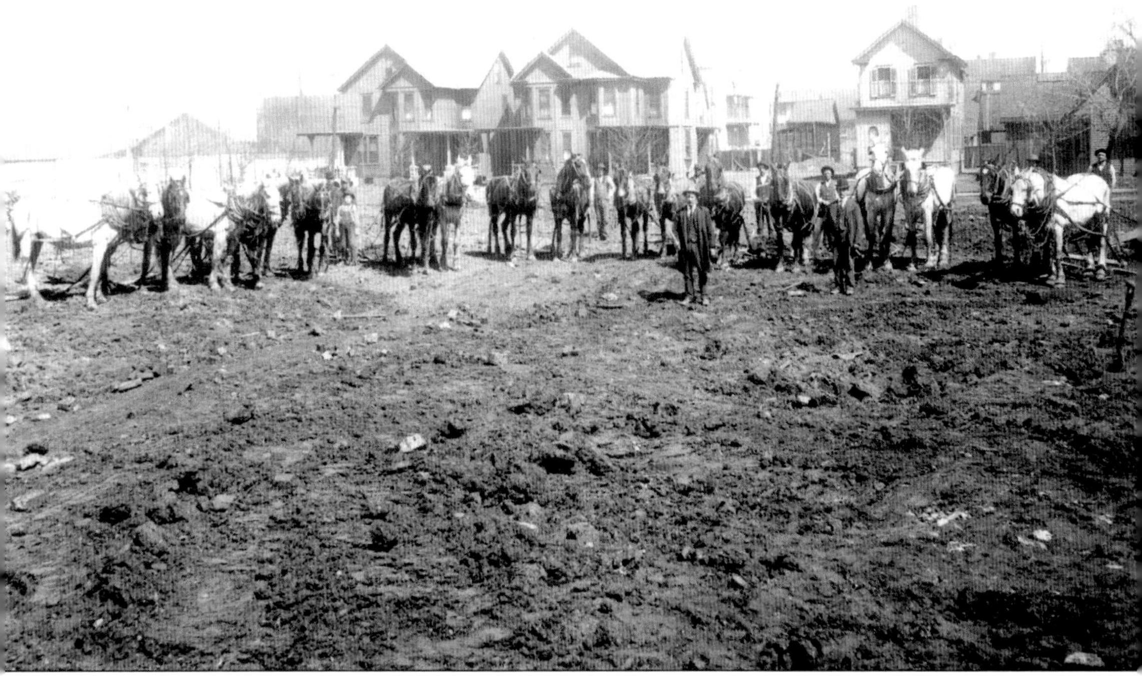

Horse drawn equipment and workman pose for the camera at the beginning of excavation for the new arsenal building in 1903. Today's construction work still calls for lots of manual labor, but the amount of work for man and beast prior to heavy mechanized machines seems incredible to us. Not many today remember the stone castle-like arsenal, destroyed in 1934 by a fire set by a 10-year-old boy who liked to see fire engines, flames, and smoke. The conflagration caused the loss of numerous state military records and supplies, but fortunately there was no loss of life. The present Armory was built in 1937 at Second and Monroe streets to replace the old structure. In the view shown here, the camera looks north towards a residential area in the 100 block of East Adams Street.

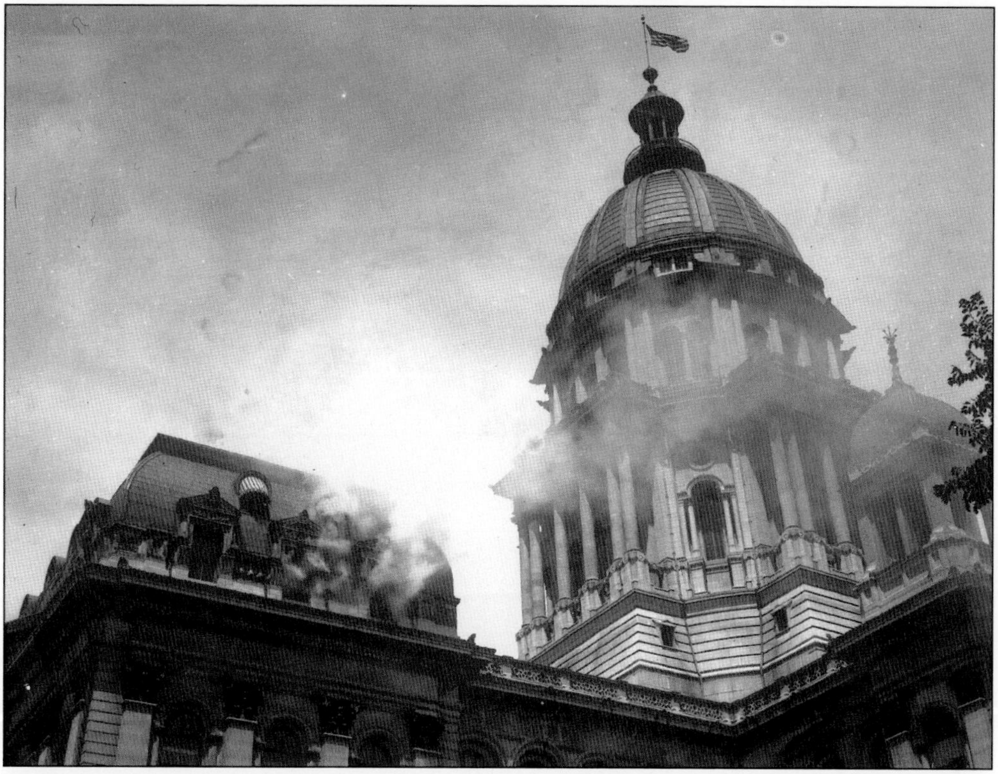

The fire that burned for three hours on an afternoon in July of 1933 in the south wing of the State Capitol was of unknown origin. The severest damage was confined to fifth and sixth floor offices. However, water damage reached even the House of Representatives and elevator shafts became water drainage pipes as firemen worked feverishly to control the blaze.

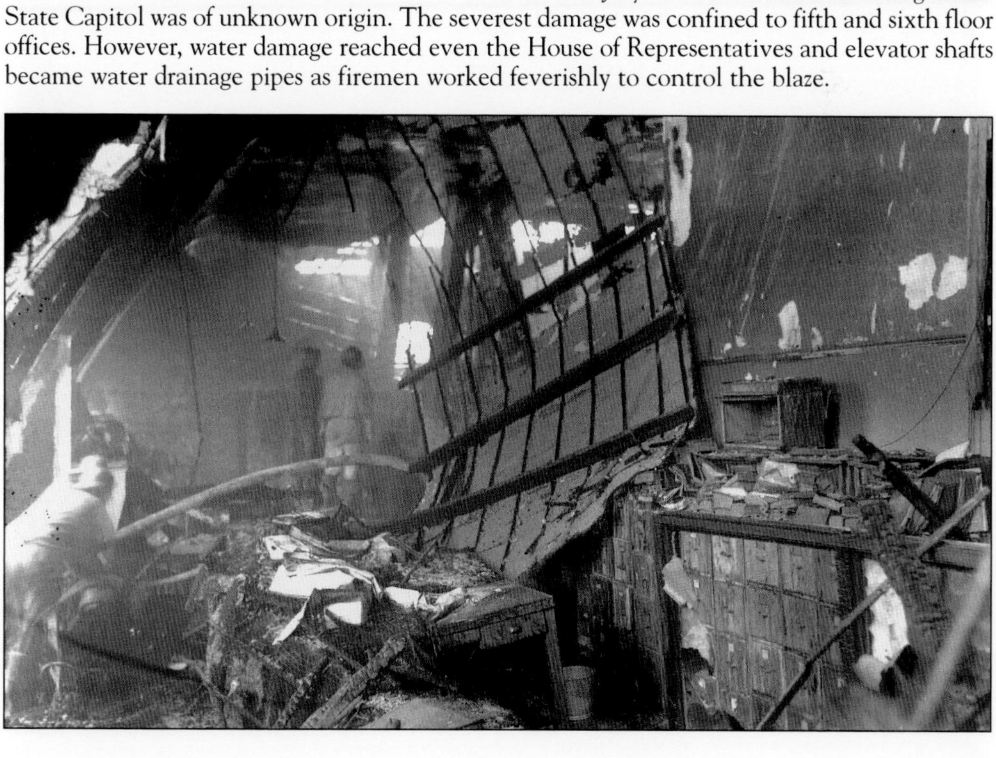

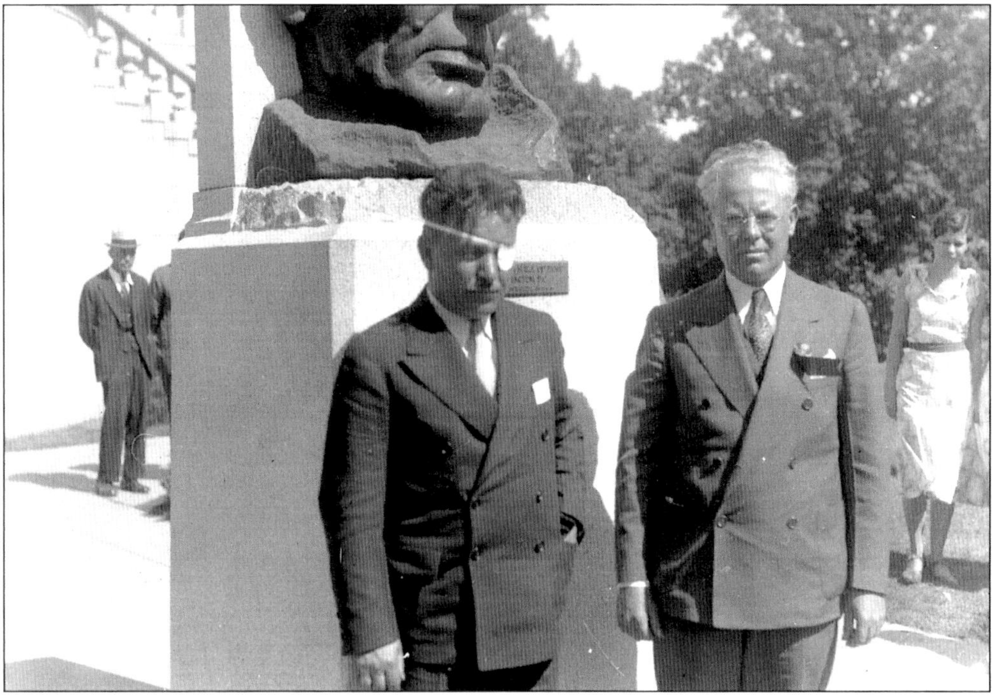

A visit to the Lincoln Tomb is obligatory for Springfield visitors, whether famous or obscure. In September 1933 famed aviator Wiley Post stopped in the city on his national tour shortly after setting a new record for an around-the-world flight. Post, at left, is shown with Springfield Mayor John W. "Buddy" Kapp.

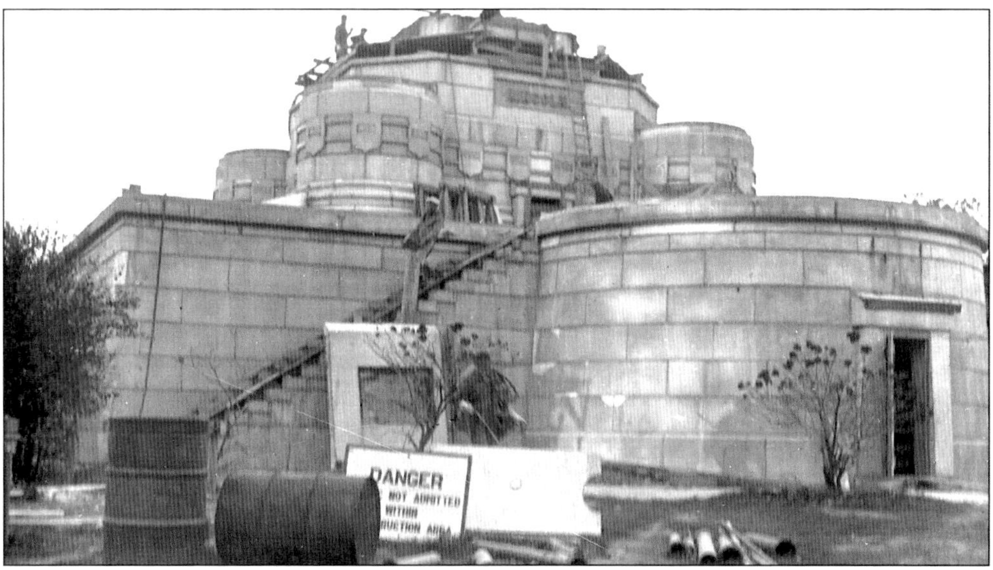

The Lincoln Tomb, completed in the 1870s, has been rebuilt twice, in 1899-1900 and in the early 1930s. This scene, from that second reconstruction, shows the monument after the familiar obelisk has been taken down to the base. At the rededication in June 1931, President Herbert Hoover spoke to a crowd of several thousand who filled the open lawns nearby. Guests of honor included many who had known Lincoln from his days in Springfield.

The Illinois Governor's Mansion is shown in the 1960s, a few years before a major renovation of the structure. Engineers reported that the mansion was in need of urgent repairs—"acute in some places." Their report further recommended "that no dancing be done on the first or second floors. . . ." The old house, now in its second century of existence, has been stunningly restored and again serves as home for Illinois governors and their families.

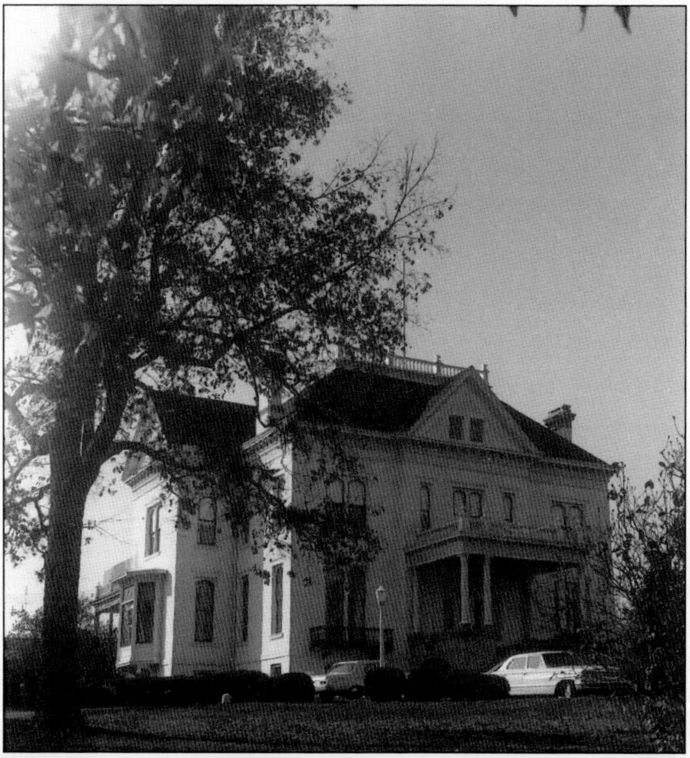

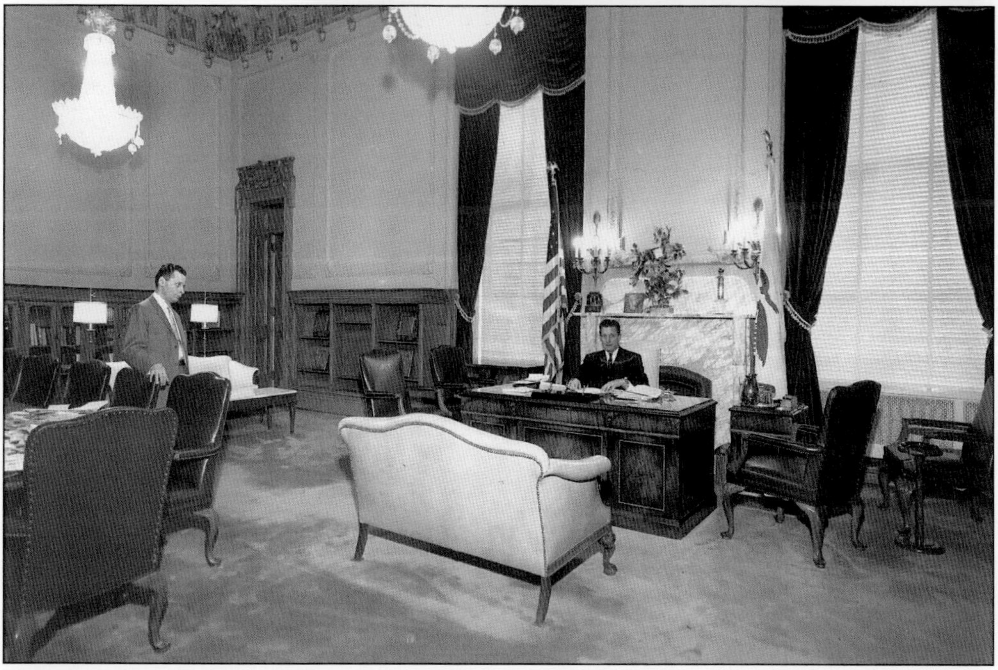

Governor Otto Kerner, remembered for his charm and urbanity, is shown in his office in the Capitol in 1961. The over-sized room with high ceilings, chandelier, mirrors, and swagged drapery, was geared to impress visitors. It's heroic size also tended to dwarf human-sized occupants, including the governor and staff.

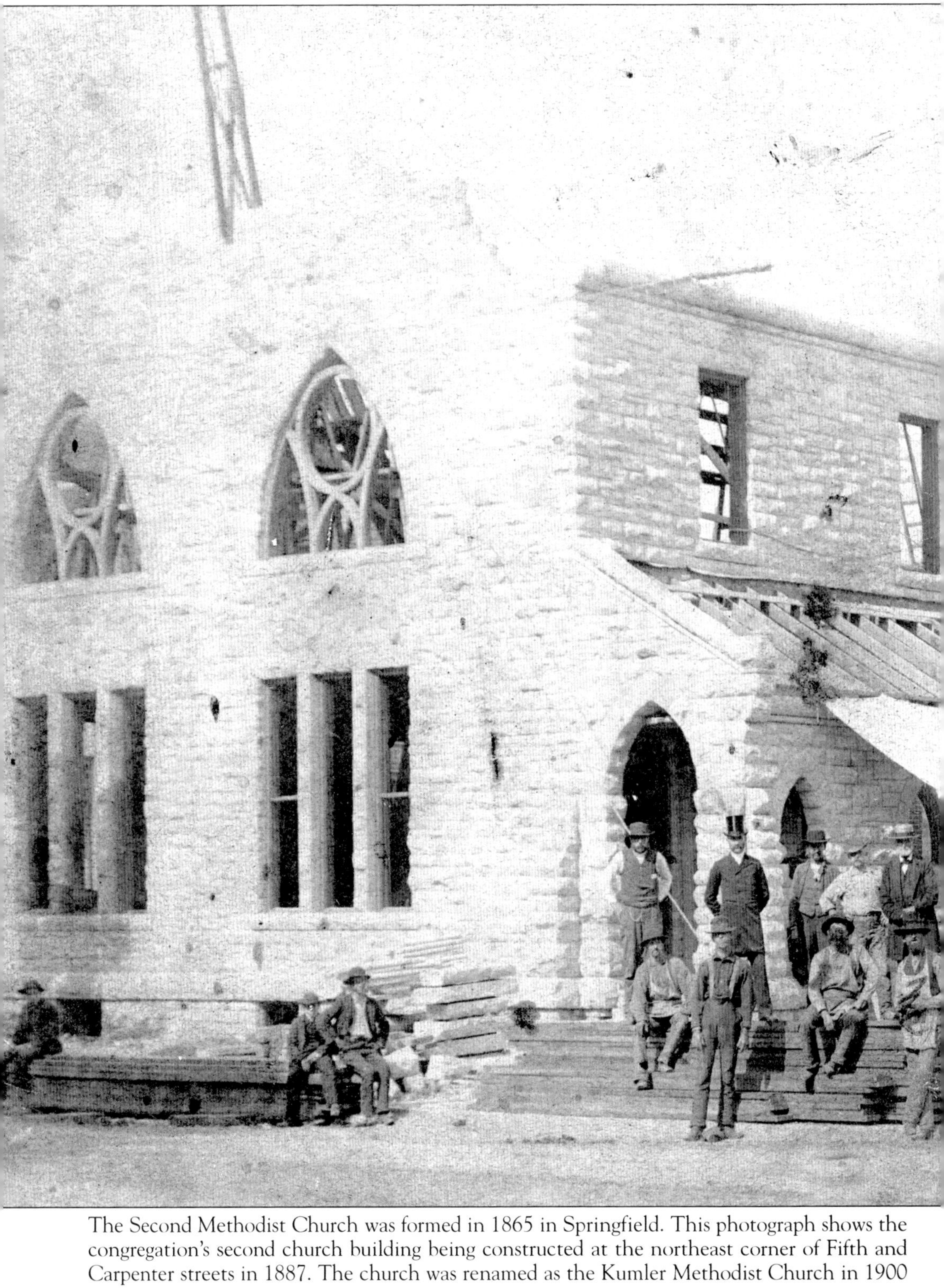

The Second Methodist Church was formed in 1865 in Springfield. This photograph shows the congregation's second church building being constructed at the northeast corner of Fifth and Carpenter streets in 1887. The church was renamed as the Kumler Methodist Church in 1900

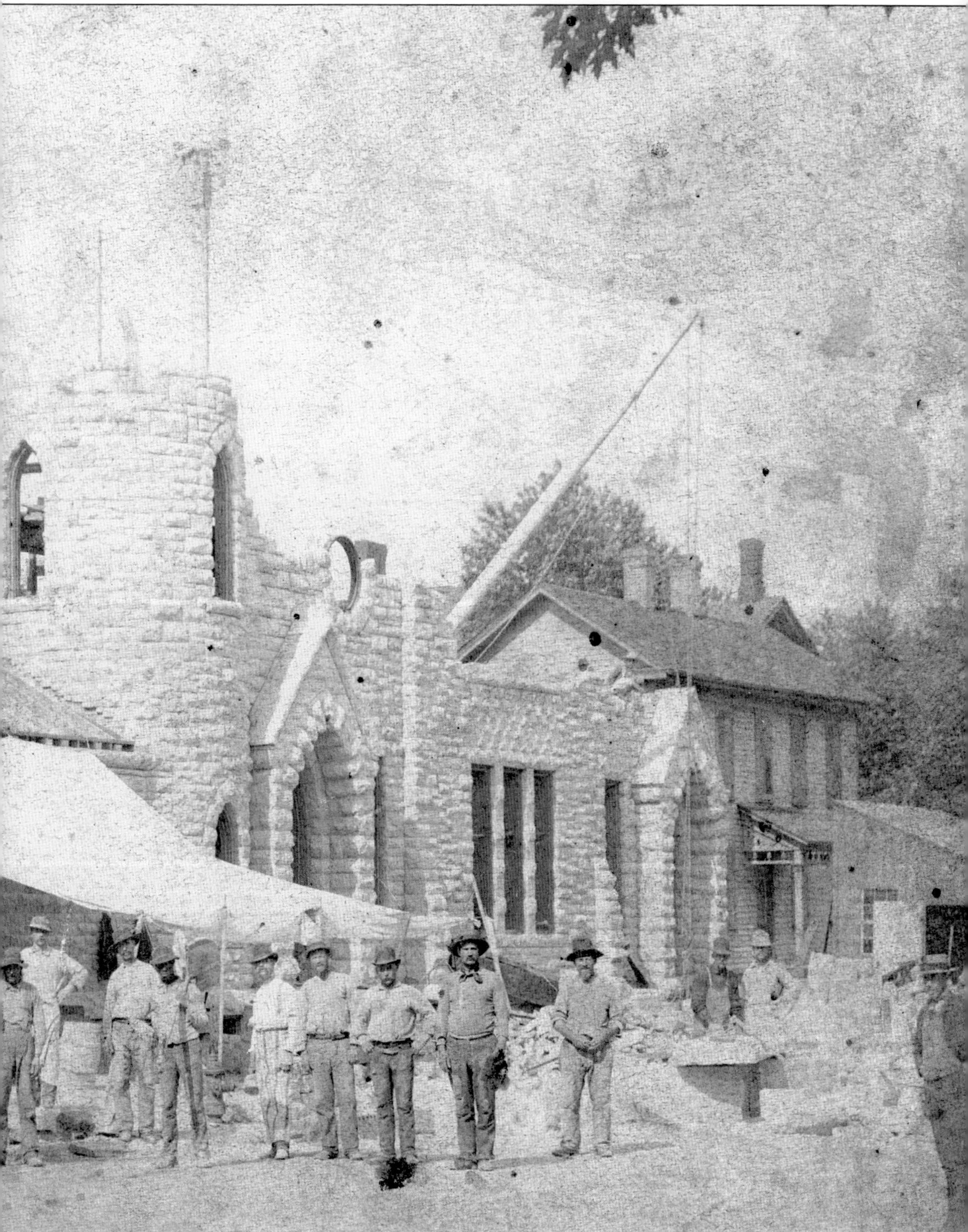

in honor of Reverend J.A. Kumler. The man wearing the tall silk hat in the back row at left is Reverend R.G. Hobbs.

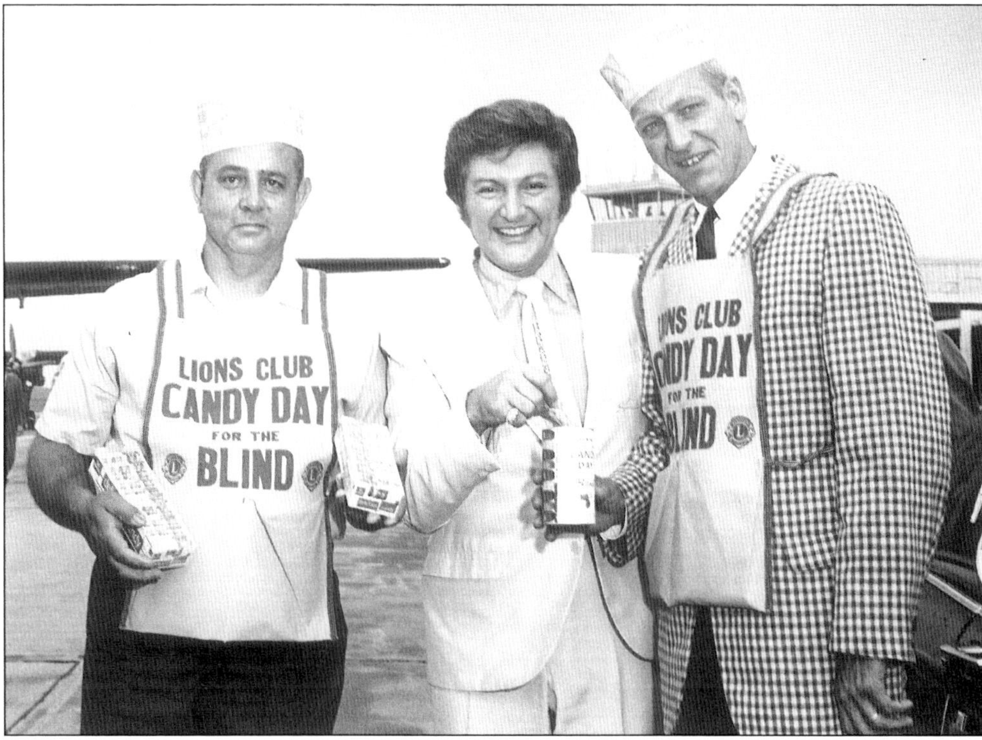

Liberace, awash in rhinestones and a caricature of "elegance" during his stage shows, looks almost subdued in this 1969 photo. "Mr. Showmanship," here for a State Fair grandstand performance, took a moment for a publicity shot promoting the local Lion's Club's fund raiser that year.

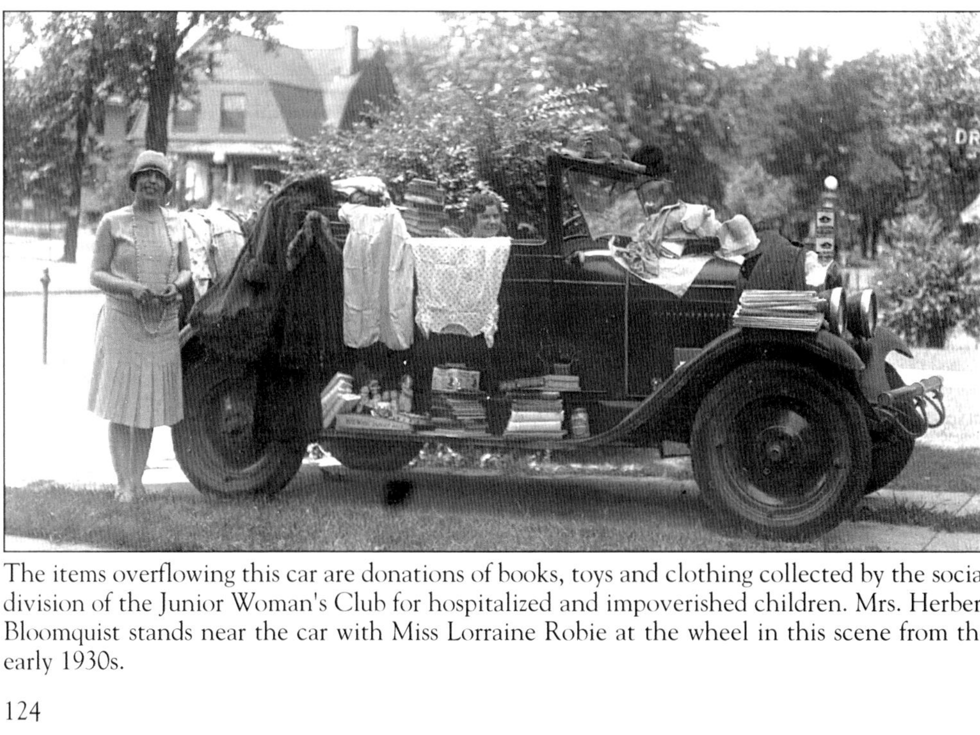

The items overflowing this car are donations of books, toys and clothing collected by the social division of the Junior Woman's Club for hospitalized and impoverished children. Mrs. Herbert Bloomquist stands near the car with Miss Lorraine Robie at the wheel in this scene from the early 1930s.

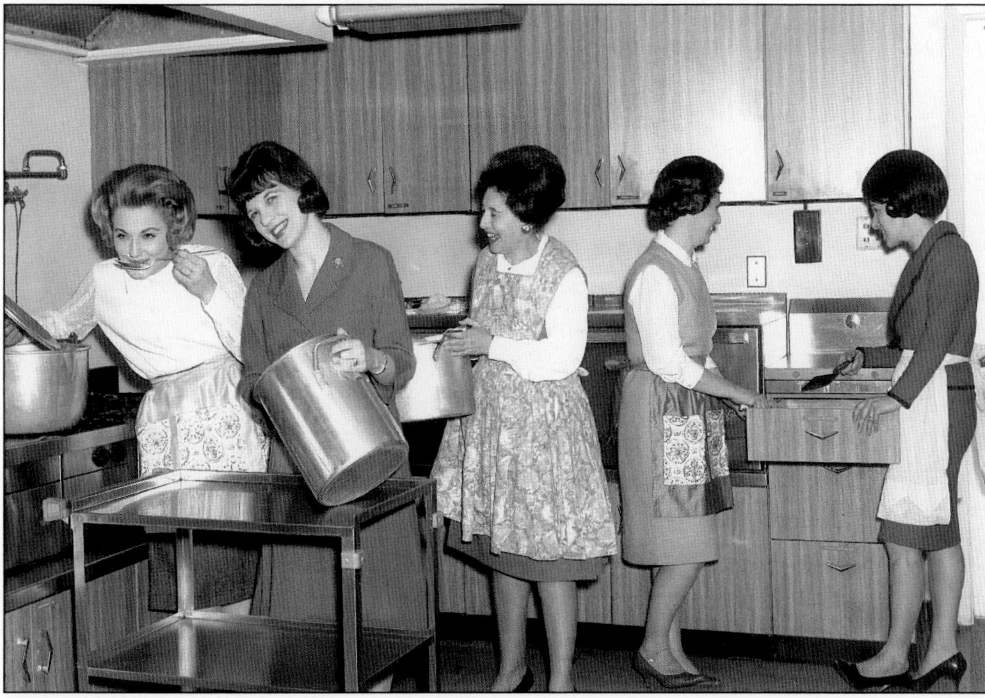

The B'rith Sholom Sisterhood, founded as a charitable group, try out various recipes for their annual Community Dinner. While traditional Jewish foods are on the menu, part of the fun was comparing family recipes that varied for the same dish. The event died out as traditional homemakers gradually became working women with less time for community service.

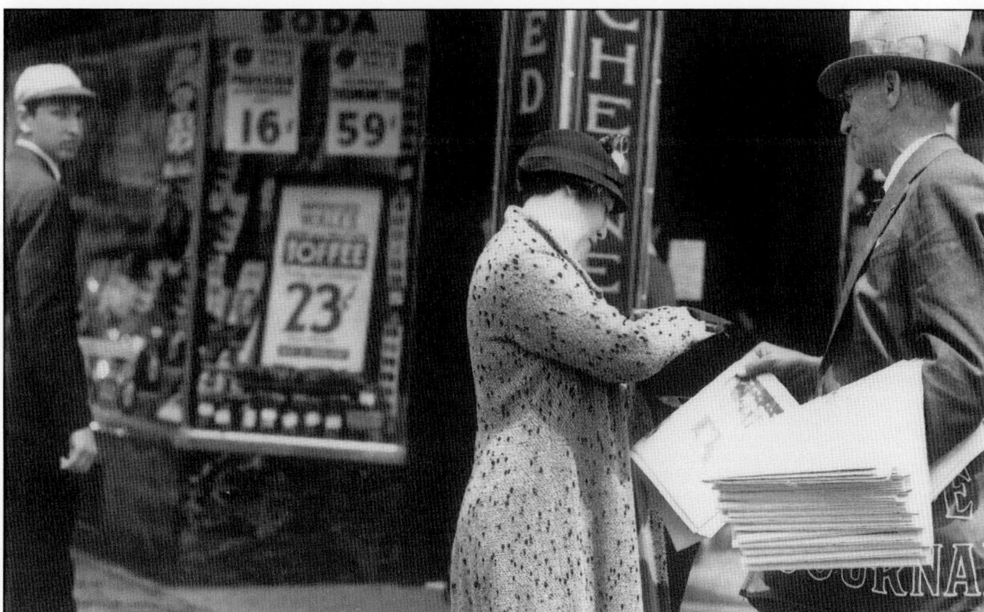

Preparing for hot summer days, Kiwanians do their part in 1935 to raise money for the Ice Fund by selling a special edition of the *Illinois State Journal*. In the days before refrigerators were common, the poor often had problems purchasing ice to keep milk fresh for their babies.

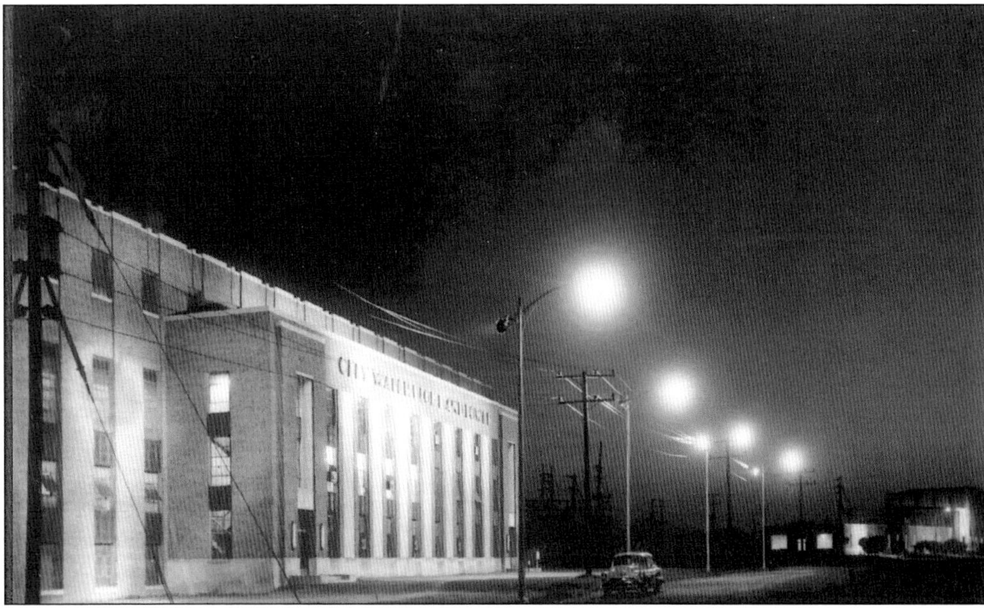

Springfield's first public water supply—four hand pumps on the public square installed in 1845—grew to our large model municipal utility City Water, Light and Power Department a century later. Much credit goes to Willis Spaulding, city commissioner, and "Father of Lake Springfield." A dramatically lighted lakeside power plant is shown in the 1950s.

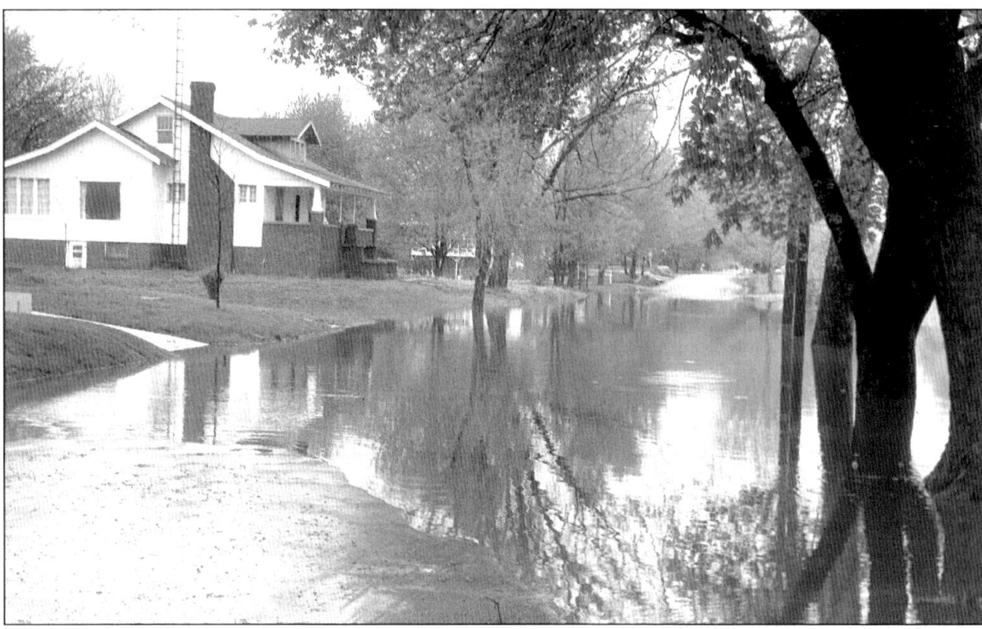

Springfield officials have long had to be concerned not only with paving city streets, but also dealing with their flooding during periodic heavy rains. A series of major storm sewer reconstructions was finally required to alleviate the worst problems. This 1950s scene of South Eleventh Street documents what was once a recurrent problem. Zimri Enos, one of our early engineers, claimed the flooding problem originated when natural drainage was blocked by our incessant street building improvements.

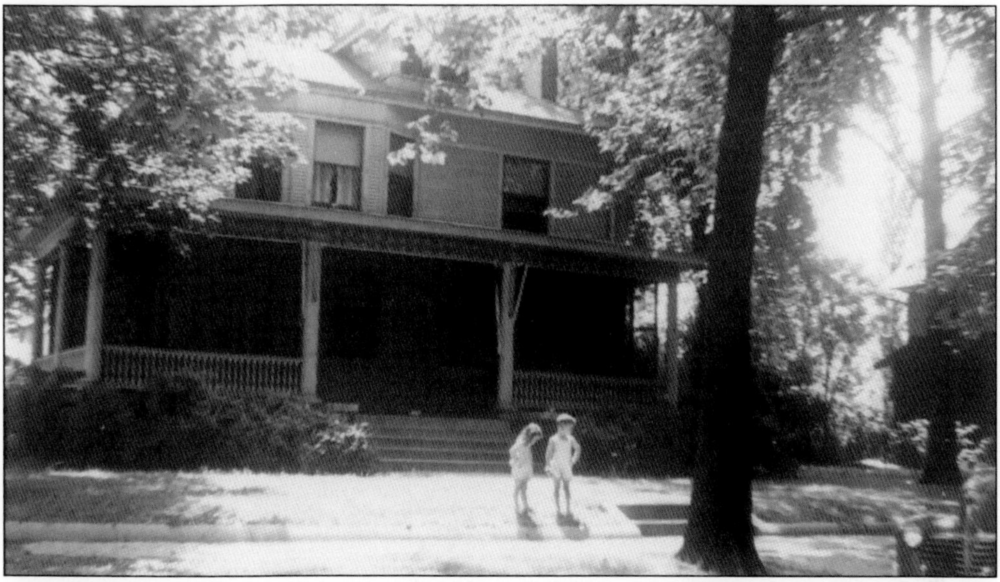

A special survey of Springfield of 1914 found that "in every part of Springfield, the single family house with a good sized yard or lawn is the rule. . .the great advantage that Springfield has over many other cities of its size and larger." Even today that characteristic is evident in the city. This 1940s view of a house on tree-shaded Whittier Avenue conjures up the nostalgic image of the neighborhood of our childhood—whether fact or not.

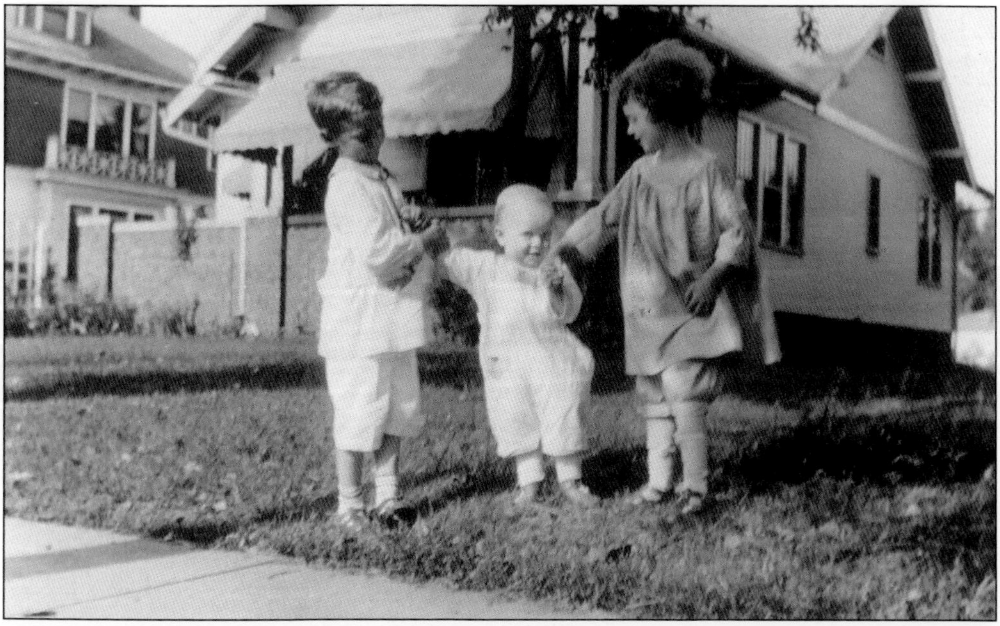

When Springfield's historic Hawthorne Place neighborhood opened a century ago, its location at Lowell and South Grand was considered way out in the country. The stylish new development appealed to members of the business, commercial and merchant class looking to escape the noise, dust and congestion of central Springfield. Housing filled the lots including, by the 1920s, that darling of the middle classes, the Bungalow. This typical one on Lowell Avenue was built for Charles Virden and his wife, Minnie, in the early 1920s.

Index